ECOTHEOLOGY
VOICES FROM SOUTH AND NORTH

ECOTHEOLOGY
VOICES FROM SOUTH AND NORTH

Edited by
DAVID G.
HALLMAN

WCC PUBLICATIONS
1211 Geneva 2, Switzerland

ORBIS BOOKS
Maryknoll, New York 10545

Second Printing, February 1995

© 1994 WCC Publications, World Council of Churches,
150 route de Ferney, 1211 Geneva 2, Switzerland

First published jointly 1994 by WCC Publications, Geneva, Switzerland, and
Orbis Books, Maryknoll, New York 10545, USA

Printed in the USA

The Catholic Foreign Mission Society of America (Maryknoll) recruits and trains
people for overseas missionary service. Through Orbis Books, Maryknoll aims to
foster the international dialogue that is essential to mission. The books published,
however, reflect the opinions of their authors and are not meant to represent the
official position of the society.

Library of Congress Cataloging-in-Publication Data

Ecotheology: Voices from South and North / edited
    by David G. Hallman
      p.   cm
    ISBN 0-88344-993-5 (pbk.)
  1. Human ecology – Religious aspects – Christianity.
  2. Environmental protection – Moral and ethical aspects.
  3. Environmental protection – Developing countries.
  4. Indigenous peoples – Attitudes.   5. Ecofeminism.
  I. Hallman, David G.
  BT695.5.E33   1994
  261'.8362-dc20   94-12140
                                                        CIP

Cover design: Rob Lucas

ISBN WCC 2-8254-1131-0
ISBN Orbis 0-88344-993-5

Contents

Acknowledgments and Sources

First and foremost I express my appreciation to the authors who responded promptly and enthusiastically to the invitation to contribute to this book. Some of these chapters have been published elsewhere in a somewhat different form, and I am grateful to publishers who have granted permission to reprint them.

— Pepz Cunanan, whose article first appeared in *Tugon — An Ecumenical Journal of Discussion and Opinion*, Vol. XII, no. 2, 1992, published by the National Council of Churches in the Philippines;
— Margot Kässmann, whose Bible studies were prepared for the 1993 Gurukul Summer Institute on Ecological Theology, Bangalore, India;
— Renthy Keitzar, whose Bible studies were presented at the same event;
— K.C. Abraham;
— Tony Brun, whose article is based on his 1993 course on ecological theology at the Seminario Bíblico Latinoamericano, San José, Costa Rica;
— Milton Efthimiou, whose article was first presented at the WCC ecumenical gathering during the Earth Summit in Rio in June 1992;
— Wesley Granberg-Michaelson;
— Kwok Pui-lan, whose article is reprinted with permission from *The Ecumenical Review*, Vol. XLIV, no. 3, July 1992;
— Larry Rasmussen, whose paper was prepared for the October 1993 meeting of the commission for the WCC Programme Unit on Justice, Peace and Creation;
— Samuel Rayan, whose article is reprinted with permission from the *Vidayjyoti Journal of Theological Reflection*, Vol. LIV, no. 3, March 1990;
— M. Adebisi Sowunmi, who first presented her paper at the WCC's seventh assembly (Canberra 1991);

— Tsehai Berhane-Selassie;
— Chung Hyun Kyung, whose article is a summary of discussions at a June 1992 consultation on African and Asian spirituality in Colombo, Sri Lanka;
— Aruna Gnanadason, whose paper was presented to the 1993 Gurukul Summer Institute;
— Anne Primavesi, whose article appears in a different version in *Theology and Ecofeminism*, 1994 yearbook of the European Society of Women in Theological Research, eds. Mary Grey and Elizabeth Green, published by Grünewald in Mainz and Kok Pharos in Kampen;
— Rosemary Radford Ruether, whose paper was presented at the 1993 ecotheology course at the Seminario Bíblico Latinoamericano;
— Rob Cooper;
— Stan McKay;
— George Tinker, whose article first appeared in *Sojourners*, October 1992;
— Edward Antonio;
— Leonardo Boff;
— M.L. Daneel;
— Dieter Hessel, whose article is based on a paper prepared for a conference at the Hastings Center, Briarcliff, NY, in October 1992 and published in *Theology and Public Policy*, Vol. V, no. 1, summer 1993;
— Catherine Keller, whose paper was first presented to the 1993 Whistler (Canada) Summer Institute on Environment and Population and is included here with the permission of SUNY Press, publisher of the papers from the institute.

My own article is based on a presentation at the 1993 Gurukul Summer Institute. I am grateful to J. Russell Chandran for having invited me to participate, as well as to the faculty and students of the 1993 courses on ecotheology at the institute and of the Seminario Bíblico Latinoamericano, out of which the concept for this book grew.

Laurice Mahli, my assistant at the United Church of Canada, efficiently expedited the considerable correspondence involved in preparing this book. Elizabeth Cook of the Seminario Bíblico Latinoamericano translated a number of articles that were received in Spanish or Portuguese. Irene Ty, a colleague in Toronto, inputted some of the papers which were not available to me on computer diskette. Richard Lawrence helped me to locate a contribution to the book from a Maori perspective, and my colleague Glenys Huws first brought George Tinker's article to my attention.

My initial contacts about the publication of this book were with Wesley Granberg-Michaelson, then a member of the World Council of Churches staff; subsequently, the WCC Office of Communication has worked closely with me on it. They were enthusiastic about this project from the beginning, which was encouraging for me.

Finally, to my life-partner William Conklin, I am as always deeply indebted. Without his support and understanding, the book could not have been completed, at least not in this century.

1.

Introduction

Beyond "North/South Dialogue"

David G. Hallman

The idea for this book surfaced in a quiet park in San José, Costa Rica, in February 1993. I was working on a series of lectures on ecological theology and ethics at the Seminario Bíblico Latinoamericano. That morning, my office in Toronto had relayed an invitation to participate in a similar course at the Gurukul Summer Institute in Bangalore, India, in May. I had received both invitations because these theological colleges were interested in input from someone active on environmental issues within a church in an industrialized country who could also reflect on global issues in the aftermath of the UN Conference on Environment and Development (UNCED), the Earth Summit in Rio de Janeiro in June 1992.

Obviously, these courses were not the first occasions for Christians from the North and the South to discuss issues of ecological theology and ethics. In addition to various regional events, the World Council of Churches had provided such frameworks and forums going back to the programme on just, participatory and sustainable society in the early 1970s. More recently and more explicitly, the inter-relationships of environment and development became a focus of attention after the 1983 Vancouver assembly with the call to a conciliar process on justice, peace and integrity of creation (JPIC). The discussions gained momentum with the world convocation on JPIC (Seoul 1990), the WCC's seventh assembly (Canberra 1991) and the ecumenical gathering in Rio at the time of UNCED.

Yet, I sensed something new about this moment. Both the Seminario Bíblico Latinoamericano and the Gurukul Summer Institute cited UNCED and the profile it gave to the interconnections of environment and development as part of the rationale for their organizing, for the first time, a course on ecological theology and ethics. I recognized in the invitations from these two Southern theological colleges an intention not only to explore God's will for the totality of creation but also to extend their reflections more broadly by involving sisters and brothers from the North. As I sat in the park, I experienced a growing sense of excitement at being able to participate in these programmes but was somewhat frustrated that the exchanges would be limited to those involved in the courses. How might the dialogue extend more widely?

The WCC responded enthusiastically to the idea of a book bringing together articles of the most current thinking on ecological theology and ethics from Southern and Northern perspectives. We decided not to limit contributions to those two courses but to broaden the input thematically and geographically. The result is a collection of articles from people around the world who are on the cutting edge of work on ecological theology and ethics in their societies.

Environment and development

A central issue in South-North discussions about ecology is how concern for protection of the natural world relates to meeting the basic needs of the world's poor. Harsh judgments have been directed back and forth between people involved in environmental issues and others active in development concerns, including those in the churches.

Development workers in both South and North have looked with suspicion as environmental concerns rose on the agenda of Northern countries, non-governmental organizations (NGOs), churches and international bodies. They saw the North having achieved a materially rich standard of living at the expense of the environment in Northern countries and in many Southern ones which they had colonized, not to mention the damage to the global atmosphere. Now those industrialized nations wanted to impose restrictions on development so as to protect their own life-styles. There was also a sense that Northerners were attracted to the environment as *the* new issue of the day. Further, people in the development community feared that attention to ecological concerns would divert scarce human and financial resources from the more immediate justice issues of poverty and hunger.

For their part, those in environmental networks perceived people working in development as operating out of anthropocentric frameworks similar to the exploitative economic models which have caused so much environmental damage, seeing the natural world as having only instrumental value — a resource to meet human needs.

An exciting aspect of UNCED and the NGO Global Forum was the converging analyses of the linkages between environment and development. Despite its shortcomings, UNCED and the extensive preparatory process leading up to it opened some new doors. Conceptually, the argument was won that environment and development are inextricably linked. Credit is due in part to UNCED but at least as much to NGOs for their critique of UNCED's inability really to manifest that interconnection. In some ways, the churches had been ahead of secular society by their focus on the relationships of justice, peace and integrity of creation. UNCED provided the churches an opportunity to critique the common threats that undermine ecological sustainability and social justice, as well as to articulate a vision of shalom, a way of living together within the human family and with the totality of creation as "one earth community".

The articles in this book attest to that inter-relatedness of the environment and development agendas. Moreover, they demonstrate how the ecotheology discussion within the global ecumenical community cuts across the traditional socio-political and geographical divisions between North and South. In reading these contributions, one hears passionate arguments from both South and North about the need to address ecological destruction *and* economic injustice. There are distinctions in the analyses about the interconnections, which arise out of the differences in the contexts of the writers, but the commonalities of perspective far outweigh the differences and move us a long way from the polarizations of even a few years ago.

An evolving theological agenda

While celebrating this common commitment, I would contend that significant differences remain, not so much in analyses of the past as in agenda for the future. The struggle towards "one earth community" characterized by ecological sustainability and socio-economic justice would be greatly advanced by focused reflection and action on some specific themes within the North and within the South.

I believe that churches in the North have not yet come to grips with the degree to which Christian theology and tradition are implicated in the Western capitalist development model that has dominated our countries since the industrial revolution, many other countries through the colonial periods and more recently every part of the world that is touched by the new "global economy". This goes well beyond the famous critique of Lynn White Jr and the theological responses to it. It has to do with economics, cultural values, worldviews and even understandings of faith. A sign of our lack of progress here is our limited impact on the materialism and consumption which pervade

North America and Europe and are the source of many of our ecological problems including toxic wastes, exorbitant energy consumption and greenhouse gas emissions.

There is homework that Southern theologians could do which would significantly advance the theological basis for "one earth community". The liberation theologies from the South revolutionized approaches to biblical interpretation, critiqued social, economic and political systems and connected faith to practice in their own contexts. They have had a profound influence in other regions of the world as well. Liberation theology is grounded in real life experience and in a recognition of God's preferential option for the poor. In our growing understanding of environmental threats, we see many of the same destructive forces at work as those which oppress the world's poor. By focusing the insights, analyses and processes of liberation thought on the needs of our non-human as well as human sisters and brothers in creation, Southern theologians are perhaps better placed than Northerners to articulate a theory and praxis for the liberation of the natural order from the bondage to which human principalities and powers have subjected it. Such insights could help us all better to understand what it would mean, in word and action, to value the intrinsic worth of all creation.

We are in the early stages of a profound conceptual shift in theology that will move us far beyond stewardship theology as a response to human exploitation of God's creation. Most theological thinking on the ecological crisis has been from the perspective of human supremacy among the species. Even if we now talk more in terms of responsibility than domination, our approach is still a management model in which we humans think we know best. By breaking open that conceptual prison, feminist theology and insights from the traditions of indigenous peoples are both critically important groundings for the emerging ecotheology, as the articles in those chapters demonstrate.

How ecotheology can help us rediscover scripture is apparent in the contributions on the biblical witness. Some people involved in ecological concerns are convinced that the Bible is so culturally bound that its only contribution is a destructive one which sanctions human exploitation of creation. But listening to the word of God with ears sensitive to the ecological crisis is exhilarating. God has not abandoned us. God is speaking powerfully and poignantly through scripture if we are prepared to hear the messages. Preaching on ecotheology using the regular lectionary readings has been a consistent source of new insights for me.

Ethical implications

The ecological crisis presents the church with an evangelical opportunity. After UNCED, a group of Canadians who had been involved in Rio organized a small think tank which has come to be called "The Commons Group", a word play on the global commons and the fact that we were meeting in facilities of the Canadian House of Commons. The Commons Group involves politicians, government bureaucrats, members of NGOs, scientists, ethicists, theologians and representatives of international agencies. Our meetings explore the ethical value dimensions of sustainable development. The non-church participants have repeatedly expressed appreciation to the church for providing this forum in which they can discuss fundamental questions of values, ethics and spirituality, without which human societies will make little progress in addressing the inter-related crises of ecological destruction and economic injustice.

That experience is being repeated frequently. The secular community is looking not only to the Christian church but to all living faiths to contribute from their traditions, insights and visions. The evangelical opportunity is to respond creatively to this appeal and legitimize the role of values and ethics in the struggle towards sustainable development. The secular community senses a need for those foundational values and so is opening the door to church participation. Our challenge is to put substance on the bare bones of that invitation.

Ethics is the meeting ground. We should not expect those engaged in concerns of environment and development necessarily to subscribe to our theology. Through actively participating in the public dialogue, our role as church is to discern from our theology ethical implications for the many complex and contentious issues and contribute them to the broader debate. We must do so with humility. We stand rightly accused of having allowed our scripture and tradition to be co-opted through several centuries of exploitation of members of the human family and the wider creation. Furthermore, we are relatively late arrivals to an awareness of the seriousness of the ecological crisis. But now that we are here and are being looked to for assistance in addressing the ethical complexities facing the global community, let us be active participants. Ethical issues related to sustainable development discussed in this book include the injustice of current international economic systems, the relationship of environment and democracy, the accountability of transnational corporations, the relative roles of North and South in addressing climate change, the biotechnology revolution and population pressures.

From whence cometh our hope?

A striking impression one gains from the articles in *Ecotheology: Voices from South and North* is the persistence of hope. The problems of ecological destruction and global poverty are certainly of a magnitude and intractability to elicit unmitigated despair. And yet, what emerges from the contributions here is not resignation but conviction, vision, celebration and humour. In a word, hope.

Just as there is a danger of proclaiming cheap grace, so is there easy hope. An international WCC consultation in 1993 developed a study document for churches on climate change. The participants debated using the Isaiah imagery of God's creating "new heavens and a new earth" (Isa. 65:17a). We eventually decided to avoid it for fear of feeding a fatalism already too present in our societies which suggests that God will look after it all, so that humans need not worry about an issue such as climate change, much less radically alter their life-styles and societies to reduce the emission of greenhouse gases.

What passes here for hope in God's omnipotence is little more than an insidious negation of human responsibility. Hope does not rest in a quick fix from an ecological *deus ex machina*. Nevertheless, the foundation of our hope does lie in the God who loved this creation into being, who bestowed the human with the capacity to choose between life and destruction and who became incarnate to save us from our sinfulness and bring life in all its abundance. God will not abandon us. God is ready to open our eyes to a more loving relationship between humanity and all creation — when we are ready to have them opened. God will provide the spiritual nourishment that we need to sustain us for the long journey ahead. The vision of the shalom kingdom, the "one earth community" of all God's creatures living in harmony and justice, is grounded in God's unfailing love.

Hope is important not only for sustaining our spirits but also for practical pedagogical reasons. In the late 1980s, I wrote a book, *Caring for Creation*, which described the major environmental issues and the role that Christians could play in addressing them. Many readers told me how overwhelmed they felt on reading of the magnitude of the ecological crisis. Was there no hope? I concluded that educators and activists need to do much more to articulate a vision of how things could be different, of how we could live in ways that did not create these problems in the first place. *A Place in Creation — Ecological Visions in Science, Religion and Economics* was the result: an attempt to discern the elements of a new vision for the relationship of humans to the rest of creation.

What I found most hopeful in writing this second book were the commonalities that emerged across the disciplines. Learnings from the conceptual revolution in physics in this century and the insights of biology, astronomy and chaos theory had their parallels in the blossoming ecotheology pursuits of the past few decades. Around the edges in economics, there were also thinkers and practitioners exploring more sustainable and just approaches to organizing the economic life of societies. The hopefulness here is the presence of God's Spirit throughout different realms of human endeavour, illuminating common themes of the inter-relatedness of all creation. People need to experience that hopefulness and vision of how things could be different if they are to be empowered to respond to the ecological crisis. It can come not just from religious frameworks but from secular contexts as well.

This points to a further source of hope. We are created into community — that of our immediate families, our faith grouping, our local community, our country, the global relationship of the human family and indeed the totality of creation. In the struggle to bring about the shalom kingdom, we do not function as individuals but as members of sustaining and energizing communities. We need to identify allies from whom we can learn and in conjunction with whom our efforts are more effective. Over the past few years leading up to and subsequent to UNCED, churches have formed important relationships with non-governmental organizations, international agencies, women's groups, indigenous peoples and other faiths. Through such working together, the goals of ecological sustainability and economic justice are more realizable.

Ecotheology: Voices from South and North is intended as a modest contribution to realizing those goals. It is published in the hope that it will animate more reflection within Christian communities and stimulate more engagement on our part in the broader community.

2.

The Biblical Witness

The Prophet of
Environment and Development

Jose Pepz M. Cunanan

At the beginning of the 1990s the Philippines was shaken to its roots by natural and human-caused disasters:

• On 16 July 1990 a killer earthquake (7.8 on the Richter scale) rocked the island of Luzon, leaving innumerable scars on the landscape and infrastructure and terrifying the people with death and displacement.

• On 12 June 1991 the eruption of Mount Pinatubo literally baptized the Philippines with fire and brimstone. Ashfall covered large areas of central Luzon, and a typhoon, with wind and rain, mixed the ash and boulders to form the rolling and rushing *lahar* which buried villages and farmlands, roads, schools, homes, churches and factories. The populace in the rural and urban areas and the indigenous communities on the mountainsides had to be evacuated. Casualties rose in the aftermath of the eruption. Satellite photos revealed the global impact of the volcanic eruption. Worldwide the skies and the climate were affected in varying degrees.

• On 5 November 1991, a deluge in Ormoc City, in the island of Leyte, joined this list of calamities. The combination of rains and strong winds from Typhoon Uring with the erosion resulting from the denudation of the mountain forests of Ormoc proved to be a deadly formula. Flash floods brought down rotting logs, mud and other debris that destroyed everything in the path of the Ormoc River towards the sea and along its banks. The natural forces together with human-made environmental destruction resulted in the death of at least 8000 persons. Thousands more were unaccounted for.

The weak and slumbering ecological consciousness of the Filipino people was rudely awakened by these nightmarish first-hand experiences, which have left indelible marks on the lives and livelihood of people.

Although these phenomena have natural causes, their association with human-caused destruction has also raised awareness of the inter-relatedness and interdependency of ecological systems. These cause-and-effect relationships have exposed the devastation of the forests by loggers, both licensed and illegal. And the destruction of the forest ecosystem has further deteriorated into soil erosion, lack of water and drought and alterations in climatic conditions.

Another realization is that environment and ecology are not merely natural concerns that can be left to physical scientists, bureaucrats, business people and politicians alone. The use, abuse and misuse of the environment affect everyone: the old, the young, even the unborn. Chemical pollution and radioactivity are no respecters of age, race, sex, creed or status in life. Yet it is often those who benefit the least from industrial and chemical concerns and military installations who are the ones whose lives are the worst affected by the detrimental waste products from them.

As the environmental factor has become increasingly crucial for our lives as people and communities locally, nationally and globally, there is a growing consciousness that we are all aboard a spaceship called "Earth". Recent international ecumenical gatherings have underscored the importance of creation in the biblical heritage and in the struggle for justice and peace. Reflection on environmental and ecological phenomena calls us to take stock of our own roles and tasks in the protection and care of the earth, God's creation.

In the midst of natural disasters and environmental calamities, many people respond in panic and confusion. People seem always to find themselves surprised in the face of such destruction. Although typhoons and summer drought spells are part of our annual rhythm, we are still unprepared for these natural phenomena each time they take place. With uncertainty and chaos all around, scientific and rational explanations give way to the voices of prophets of gloom and doom and manipulators of panic and hysteria. In their anxiety people are easily swayed by such predictions and prognostications. Amidst disaster and danger they are alert to any report or analysis on the radio or television, in the newspaper, even by word of mouth. Those who need comfort and consolation await with eagerness the messages of religious leaders. For when one's physical and spiritual foundations are shaken, it is important to be able to hold onto the resources of faith, hope and life.

I would like to share some insights which I have found helpful in dealing with environmental events and issues. These I have learned from someone I would call the "prophet of ecology and development", the Old Testament prophet Joel.

The book of Joel in the Old Testament is a very short document — three chapters, 73 verses. Consequently, it is included among the "minor prophets". But the brevity of Joel's book does not diminish the importance and impact of his message. Joel provides a concise but comprehensive and holistic approach to ecology and environment which offers a basic framework for dealing with natural and human-caused environmental disasters. I would encourage readers unfamiliar with Joel to take time to read through the 73 verses he wrote. When it comes to environment and development, Joel is exciting and stimulating, even intriguing, though some may find it controversial and unsettling.

In summary, Joel has outlined a seven-point programme of environmental-developmental awareness and action:
1) awareness of the ecological situation;
2) call to mourning, lamentation, repentance (change in values and lifestyles);
3) organizing people along environmental and spiritual concerns;
4) warning of impending judgment and destruction;
5) restoration and renewal of environment and society;
6) people's participation and roles in the transformation of society;
7) political, economic and social components of the ecological and development agenda.

Awareness of a situation of crisis and calamity

We noted above that a natural reaction in times of crisis and calamity is that of alarm. Rumours of impending crisis give way to panic buying among those who can afford it; others must simply settle for panic without buying. Prophets of doom sprout like mushrooms after a thunderstorm.

Joel may sound like a contemporary environmentalist, but he has some distinct characteristics from which present-day ecological advocates could learn. Joel displays the true character of a prophet. In the midst of a crisis, he was a rational, clear-thinking fellow, who looked at the situation and made a very detailed and objective description of it. His language and style — even his use of poetry to provide an accurate analysis of the extent of the environmental damage and its impact on the people — contributed to a fuller understanding of the situation. In a way, he was in control of the situation rather than letting the occasion take control of him.

Instead of losing his senses, Joel used them to gain confidence and mastery of the situation. Looking events straight in the eye, he did not lose sight of the causes of the disaster and was able to stay on top of the situation in terms of how God works on people and creation to bring about renewal and transformation beyond destruction and desperation.

A scientist colleague in the environmental movement has cautioned that when we talk about the environment, we should not sound like alarmists. Environmental advocates who appear hysterical in their desire to forewarn others about the critical state of the environment tend to call more attention to their own personalities and behaviours than to the message and issue at hand.

We are often reminded to be *calm* in the event of earthquakes and similar dangers. A crisis demands sober, clear thinking, analysis, reflection and action. To lose one's senses is to lose control of the situation, thus wasting valuable time and opportunities to respond to it.

It is useful at this point to hear first hand Joel's vivid call for environmental awareness (Joel 1:2-4,6-7,9-12,17-20; 2:2-10):

Hear this, O elders,
   give ear, all inhabitants of the land!
Has such a thing happened in your days,
   or in the days of your ancestors?
Tell your children of it,
   and let your children tell their children
   and their children another generation.

What the cutting locust left,
   the swarming locust has eaten.
What the swarming locust left,
   the hopping locust has eaten,
and what the hopping locust left,
   the destroying locust has eaten...

For a nation has invaded my land,
   powerful and innumerable;
its teeth are lions' teeth,
   and it has the fangs of a lioness.
It has laid waste my vines,
   and splintered my fig trees;
It has stripped off their bark and thrown it down;
   their branches have turned white...

The grain offering and the drink offering are cut off
   from the house of the Lord.
The priests mourn,
   the ministers of the Lord.

The fields are devastated,
   the ground mourns;
for the grain is destroyed,
   the wine dries up,
   the oil fails.
Be dismayed, you farmers,
   wail, you vinedressers,
over the wheat and the barley;
   for the crops of the field are ruined.
The vine withers,
   the fig tree droops.
Pomegranate, palm and apple —
   all the trees of the field are dried up...

The seed shrivels under the clods,
   the storehouses are desolate;
the granaries are ruined
   because the grain has failed.
How the animals groan!
   The herds of cattle wander about
because there is no pasture for them;
   even the flocks of sheep are dazed...
For fire has devoured
   the pastures of the wilderness,
and flames have burned
   all the trees of the field.
Even the wild animals cry to you
   because the watercourses are dried up...

Like blackness spread upon the mountains
   a great and powerful army comes;
their like has never been from of old,
   nor will be again after them
   in ages to come.

Fire devours in front of them
   and behind them a flame burns.
Before them the land is like the garden of Eden,
   but after them a desolate wilderness,
   and nothing escapes them.

They have the appearance of horses,
   and like war-horses they charge.
As with the rumbling of chariots,
   they leap on the tops of the mountains,

like the crackling of a flame of fire
   devouring the stubble,
like a powerful army
   drawn up for battle.
Before them peoples are in anguish,
   all faces grow pale.
Like warriors they charge,
   like soldiers they scale the wall.
Each keeps to its own course,
   they do not swerve from their paths.
They do not jostle one another,
   each keeps to its own track;
they burst through the weapons
   and are not halted.
They leap upon the city,
   they run upon the walls;
they climb up into the houses,
   they enter through the windows like a thief.

The earth quakes before them,
   the heavens tremble.
The sun and the moon are darkened,
   and the stars withdraw their shining.

Lamentation, repentance and change

When the people find themselves victims of natural and human-made environmental calamities, the prophet of environment must show sensitivity and identification with their sufferings, sharing in the sorrows of the victims (among whom the prophet is often included).

A prophet must learn to recognize this moment as an occasion for mourning and lamentation. There is a period of bereavement and the sense of loss must be acknowledged. This is a most difficult time. One is sometimes at a loss for words in the midst of grief, and tears are then the only means of expression.

After a calamity, the call is for people to change their values, their ways and life-styles. To return to old ways and to resume the very activities that led to the disaster would be an invitation for another calamity. But people often forget even the most recent crisis and difficulties. It is so easy to go back to the disastrous practices that destroy our forests, erode our soil, poison and pollute our earth, air, water and food.

We are called upon to change our ways and go by other alternatives. We are called to be creative, to explore new methods that will sustain our lives and livelihood. We should aim to rebuild rather than return to our destructive and risky ways.

Mourning and lamentation echo through chapter 1 of Joel as the prophet describes the effect on the people of the devastation wrought by the swarms of locusts: "wake up, you drunkards, and *weep*" (v.5) for the grapes for wine-making have been destroyed; "*lament* like a virgin dressed in sackloth" (v.8) because her betrothed has died; "the priests *mourn*" because they have no offerings for the Lord (vv.9,13); "*be dismayed*, you farmers, *wail*, you vinedressers" at the ruined and withered crops (vv.11-12).

> ...surely, joy withers away
>   among the people...
> Is not the food cut off
>   before our eyes,
> joy and gladness
>   from the house of our God? (vv.12,16)

In chapter 2, then, we hear the call to repentance and to change of life (vv.12f.,17):

> Yet even now, says the Lord,
>   return to me with all your heart,
> with fasting, with weeping and with mourning;
>   rend your hearts and not your clothing.
> Return to the Lord, your God...
>
> Between the vestibule and the altar
>   let the priests, the ministers of the Lord, weep.
> Let them say, "Spare your people, O Lord,
>   and do not make your heritage a mockery,
>   a byword among the nations.
> Why should it be said among the peoples,
>   'Where is their God?'"

Organizing people around ecological and religious concerns

A disaster, natural or human-made, usually results in confusion and often in the breakdown of social, economic and political systems. There are disruptions of basic services and displacements of persons, families, even communities. Moreover, one crisis can lead to another. Calamity does not come alone, but is usually accompanied by homelessness, hunger, disease, interruption of livelihood, drought. Ecological disasters occur in cycles, and with the breakdown of one system the others are likewise affected.

The survival instinct leads each person to go it alone under such circumstances. Social organization suffers as people fend for themselves. What is the response of a prophet of environment if the people are in a chaotic state and in dispersion? Again, we discover a lead from the prophet Joel. In a situation of crisis, recognizing the immensity of the problem, Joel called on the people to stay together, to unite, to organize. Alone, one's chances are slim, but together the prospects may be better.

Joel saw the need for the dispersed victims to be organized for sharing their experiences and resources. Being alone and separated could make the victims weaker and more vulnerable; in unity they discover strength and solidarity. A common experience of calamity can be a unifying element. Even with limited resources, people can begin to rebuild their lives, families and communities.

Joel tried to bring people back to their senses and to their resources of faith in order to deal with the disaster that had struck them:

Sanctify a fast,
    call a solemn assembly,
Gather the elders
    and all the inhabitants of the land
to the house of the Lord your God,
    and cry out to the Lord...

Blow the trumpet in Zion;
    Sanctify a fast;
call a solemn assembly;
    gather the people.
Sanctify the congregation;
    assemble the aged;
gather the children,
    even infants at the breast.
Let the bridegroom leave his room,
    and the bride her canopy (1:14; 2:15-16).

Warnings of impending judgment and destruction

Before a disaster there are often signs of approaching destruction. Many of these are readily observable: perceptible tremors, gathering clouds, suffocating air, dying rivers, eroded hills and denuded mountains, destructive practices in production, the use of pollutant chemicals, radioactivity due to nuclear tests and bombings, affluent and wasteful life-styles, excessive and abusive use of non-renewable resources.

There are also the unexpected natural phenomena over which we do not have control. For these we can only hope that effective disaster-preparedness makes decisive and efficient responses possible when they occur.

Joel warned the people and nation regarding the impending judgment and destruction, as well as pointing to ways and means to prevent these (1:15; 2:1f.,11,30f.; 3:2-8):

Alas for the day!
For the day of the Lord is near,
    and as destruction from the Almighty it comes...

Blow the trumpet in Zion;
    sound the alarm on my holy mountain!
Let all the inhabitants of the land tremble,
    for the day of the Lord is coming, it is near —
a day of darkness and gloom,
    a day of clouds and thick darkness!...

The Lord utters his voice
    at the head of his army;
how vast is his host!
    Numberless are those who obey his command.
Truly the day of the Lord is great;
    terrible indeed — who can endure it?...

I will show portents in the heavens and on the earth, blood and fire and columns of smoke. The sun shall be turned to darkness, and the moon to blood, before the great and terrible day of the Lord comes...

I will gather all the nations and bring them down to the valley of Jehoshaphat, and I will enter into judgment with them there, on account of my people and my heritage Israel, because they have scattered them among the nations. They have divided my land, and cast lots for my people, and traded boys for prostitutes, and sold girls for wine, and drunk it down.

What are you to me, O Tyre and Sidon, and all the regions of Philistia? Are you paying me back for something? If you are paying me back, I will turn your deeds back upon your own heads swiftly and speedily. For you have taken my silver and my gold, and have carried my rich treasures into your temples. You have sold the people of Judah and Jerusalem to the Greeks, removing them far from their own border. But now I will rouse them to leave the places to which you have sold them, and I will turn your deeds back upon your own heads. I will sell your sons and your daughters into the hand of the people of Judah, and they will sell them to the Sabeans, to a nation far away; for the Lord has spoken.

Environmental degradation and ecological destruction are not disasters simply on their own. They are part of the whole matrix of life which includes the social, the economic and the political. Environmental calamities also affect the lives and relationships of persons, families, communities, nations. The exploitation of resources has human as well as economic components.

Restoration and renewal of the environment and society

There is in the message of Joel an element of hope. Degradation and destruction are recognized as parts of the lives and experiences of people and nation. They are not, however, the final scenario. God, in his creation and design, has better plans; and the prophet of environment articulates this vision of restoration and renewal (2:13f.,18-27; 3:16-18):

Return to the Lord, your God,
    for he is gracious and merciful,
slow to anger, and abounding in steadfast love,
    and relents from punishing.
Who knows whether he will not turn and relent,
    and leave a blessing behind him,
a grain offering and a drink offering
    for the Lord, your God?...

Then the Lord became jealous for his land,
    and had pity on his people.
In response to his people the Lord said:
I am sending you
    grain, wine, and oil,
    and you will be satisfied;
and I will no more make you
    a mockery among the nations.

I will remove the northern army far from you,
    and drive it into a parched and desolate land,
its front into the eastern sea,
    and its rear into the western sea;
its stench and foul smell will rise up.
Surely he has done great things!

Do not fear, O soil;
    be glad and rejoice,
    for the Lord has done great things!

Do not fear, you animals of the field,
  for the pastures of the wilderness are green;
the tree bears its fruit,
  the fig tree and vine give their full yield.

O children of Zion, be glad
  and rejoice in the Lord your God;
for he has given the early rain for your vindication,
  he has poured down for you abundant rain,
  the early and the later rain, as before.

The threshing floors shall be full of grain,
  the vats shall overflow with wine and oil.
I will repay you for the years
  that the swarming locust has eaten,
the hopper, the destroyer, and the cutter,
  my great army, which I sent against you.

You shall eat in plenty and be satisfied,
  and praise the name of the Lord your God,
  who has dealt wondrously with you.
And my people shall never again be put to shame.
You shall know that I am in the midst of Israel,
  and that I, the Lord, am your God and there is no other.
And my people shall never again
  be put to shame...

The Lord roars from Zion,
  and utters his voice from Jerusalem,
  and the heavens and the earth shake.
But the Lord is a refuge for his people,
  a stronghold for the people of Israel.

So you shall know that I, the Lord your God,
  dwell in Zion, my holy mountain.
And Jerusalem shall be holy,
  and strangers shall never again pass through it.

In that day
the mountains shall drip sweet wine,
  the hills shall flow with milk,
and all the stream beds of Judah
  shall flow with water;
a fountain shall come forth from the house of the Lord
  and water the Wadi Shit'tim.

People's participation in transforming society

People are not passive spectators and recipients of the transformation of society. People are active participants, who have roles to play and tasks to perform in bringing about the vision and hope of the reign of God.

The leadership of the powerful few is valuable in the governance of peoples and nations, but the broad participation of the people is a decisive element in the transformation of society and humanity. The traditional indicators of wealth, social status and education are no longer the sole determinants in society. These have to be transcended in order to bring about the renewal and regeneration that God uses in the coming of his kingdom.

Everyone, including the weak and powerless, young and marginalized, has something to do. Each will be empowered accordingly in order to contribute creatively and dynamically to the processes of change and transformation of creation and society. This inclusiveness is evident in many verses from Joel: "Gather the *elders* and *all the inhabitants* of the land to the house of the Lord your God" (1:14); "gather *the people*. Sanctify the *congregation*; assemble the *aged*; gather the *children*, even *infants* at the breast. Let the *bridegroom* leave his room, and the *bride* her canopy. Between the vestibule and the altar, let the *priests*, the ministers of the Lord weep" (2:16-17).

> Then afterward
>   I will pour out my spirit on *all flesh*;
> your *sons* and your *daughters* shall prophesy,
>   your *old men* shall dream dreams,
>   and your *young men* shall see visions.
> Even on the *male and female slaves*
>   in those days, I will pour out my spirit (2:28-29).

Politics, economics and ecology

Many people would like to set environmental and ecological issues apart from the political, economic, social and cultural dimensions of society. They assume that environmental concerns have nothing to do with the policy- and decision-making processes in politics and business.

They see it as quite all right to be involved in environmental campaigns for tree-planting and reforestation, clean water and air and organically produced vegetables and fruits. But one must not say anything about logging bans, boycotts of pesticides and industrial fertilizers, mono-culture crops, transnational agri-businesses, open-pit mining or chemical and radioactive pollution.

Everybody is concerned about air, water, soil. Health is every person's and every corporation's concern. From every point on the ideological spectrum, environment is part of the political programme. Even the military and those engaged in commercial logging recognize that it is in their own interest to be perceived as pro-environment.

The environmental element is integral to the development or underdevelopment of a people or a nation. The impoverishment of a people is closely related to how natural resources, technology and trade are distributed, processed and exploited.

This is the most controversial element of the environmental movement, and many would like to keep their distance from it. But Joel took exception to this stance. He advocated a most radical position, seeing this as the survival point. In many ways, environment and economics are the last lines of defence for the weak and powerless, the marginalized and impoverished. What is involved here is the *militancy* of the powerless and impoverished over against the *militarism* of the powerful and affluent.

An eminent Filipino economist once suggested in a discussion on sustainable development that economics and environment should not be seen as the neutral subjects of free enterprise: trade, market, competition. They are the subjects of fierce and combative control and monopoly — not only for crops and products but also for future markets. Among the final battles being fought by most Third World countries are debt and environment (natural resources). The prospects are not very promising.

Joel recognized how the tools of production for the sustenance of life (symbolized by plows and sickles) could also be used as tools of warfare, control and domination, even death and destruction: "Beat your plowshares into swords, and your pruning hooks into spears; let the weakling say, 'I am a warrior'" (3:10).

This is the most controversial section of the prophet's message. It is open to debate and disagreement from various points along the religious, political and economic spectra. This is an area in which continuous interaction among the various positions should take place and all options be explored.

Still, such an attitude of openness does not simply mean keeping quiet about the issues. The prophets of environment will have to position themselves in this controversy and articulate their convictions and commitments for the renewal and transformation of people and of society. What follows is my own interpretation of the present ecological and development dynamics in which we must be actively engaged.

The struggles of the Filipino people have had many shades and colours. Resistance was waged against foreign invaders through centuries of colonialism, taking up the causes of independence, liberation and self-determination through opposition to foreign rule and domination, rebellion and revolution, resistance to martial law, demands for land reform, food and job security and access to basic services in housing, education, health, water, energy and the like.

All these are basically struggles for the essentials of daily life and existence. There are political and ideological principles and ideals, but these are rooted in the prayer and search for "daily bread", sustenance, survival and humane development.

The prophet of environment fights for survival, not for conquest and domination but in defence and protection of basic human rights. The most debilitating force in our societies is impoverishment: unemployed and non-productive parents, underfed and undernourished children, unschooled and unskilled youth, mothers who lack the food to cook for their families, children living literally in the streets. This poverty is further aggravated by the debt burden, which drives up the price of essentials, thus limiting the access to them of the general population. All of this is in stark contradiction to the life of the rich in Philippine society and in the world. The control and monopoly of natural resources and technology are sharpened by the lack of access by the majority of people.

The present struggles are about survival. The causes go far beyond imperial conquests for "faith and king", for "sword and cross". The struggles go across race, religion, geography and even ideology. The focus has been sharpened on the struggle for the basic necessities of life. Food is at the very core.

Monopoly, domination and control are targeted on the production, processing and distribution of the basic necessities. The terms of supply are dictated not by those involved on the production line, but by those who control capital, technology and communication. This stranglehold has reached to the very source of life, the germ-plasm. Biogenetics is controlled not by the pursuit of scientific knowledge but by the desire to dominate the very genesis of life. Scientific and academic pursuits have become business enterprises that attempt to deprive people of their natural and normal access to sources of livelihood.

The very origins and forms of life have been systematically taken away from the peasants, the workers, the producers, those who labour and sweat for their livelihood. Everyone is simply turned into a user, a consumer, a dependent.

Figuratively and symbolically speaking, the last battlefields are drawn around the means of survival. Food is an instrument of the fight for survival. The one who controls food is the one who conquers, decisively and completely. Rice fields, plantations, farms and pasture lands, even the seedling nurseries and laboratories are included in the list of the final battle zones.

The ownership, control and use of natural resources are not the exclusive rights of business corporations and their agents. These are the common wealth of the people, which must be claimed and protected. These are their final lines of defence. If these are conquered, then the struggle in its various shades and colours, for whatever cause or ideology, is likewise lost.

Those who would venture into the field of environment and development should be forewarned that this is not a neutral and sanitized arena. This is no picnic area or holiday resort. Rather one must always expect the unexpected, for these are grounds full of traps and pitfalls, confrontations and conflicts. These are minefields filled with risks and dangers.

These are critical and decisive times in history, as the very existence of humanity and of the whole earth is threatened. Ecology is an animating and creative arena, in which the potential for liberation and holistic development of people are to be pursued and gained for the impoverished, deprived and marginalized of the earth. The last decade of the twentieth century and the ushering in of the twenty-first century are golden moments when the renewal and transformation of society, humanity and of the earth can take place. It may be our last chance, and so, by God's grace, we have to make the most of it.

Covenant, Praise and Justice in Creation

Five Bible Studies

Margot Kässmann

1. God's covenant to preserve creation
Genesis 8:18 — 9:7

Methodology: role play

One might expect a series of Bible studies on creation to start with Genesis 1-2. Beginning with the new covenant after the flood, however, underlines from the outset that in talking about creation, we are always speaking from the side of the *broken* creation. The judgment of the flood stands like a wall between our time and the first creation. A contemporary theology of creation must therefore start with the reality of violence against and destruction of creation.

God created and it was very good indeed (Gen. 1:31). We know how good creation is: water, clear and fresh, the source of life, fish and plants in an endless cycle providing food for humankind. Not only that, creation holds beauty: the colours of the sky at sunset, the sparkling of a waterfall and, perhaps the most beautiful play with colours, the rainbow. From the beginning, the only part of creation that threatened all this was the human being. From the beginning there was misunderstanding of what it means to be co-creators. Instead of care for God's creation, what was stressed was "fill the earth and subdue it" (Gen. 1:28); and this biblical quotation has been used time and again to legitimize abuse, misuse, rape of what God created.

The source which Old Testament scholars identify as P (the priestly text) sees the flood as a cosmic catastrophe. The oceans in the heaven fall down upon the earth and the water from below pushes up. Creation starts to sink back into chaos. Unlike the source known as J — the other theologian to report about the flood — P sees the threat not only to human beings and animals, but to the whole world. The life-threatening power of water is certainly well known — one need only to think of the floods in

Bangladesh in recent years or the potential consequences for low-lying islands and coastal areas of rising sea levels due to global warming.

The account of the flood proves God's power to destroy what God has created and demonstrates that every word of grace that will follow does not weaken God's wrath over sin. God's saving of creation comes from God's heart, as P expresses it very anthropomorphically: "God remembered Noah" (Gen. 8:1). Many centuries later, the letter of Peter draws a comparison with baptism: the water of the flood is a judging water, on the other side of which is life out of the grace of the living God (1 Pet. 3:20f.).

While J ends the story of the flood at Genesis 8:21-22, P goes more deeply into the covenant between God and Noah in order to address some of the theological questions of the people of Israel in his time. The first question is whether the first commandment of creation — be fertile (Gen. 1:28) — is still valid. The answer which P gives in chapter 9 is yes. God wants the spreading of humankind. Today we might look at this answer more sceptically, knowing that creation is threatened by the rapid growth of population. But this rapid growth is again the result of sin. Studies have shown time and again that poverty and injustice are the main reasons for what is called the population explosion. As soon as a people's basic needs for shelter, food and work are met, the birth rate goes down. When women are liberated and have income of their own, the rate decreases. As long as both those criteria are not met, many children are needed to support the family and to care for the old.

The second question is: what sort of a relation should creatures have towards one another? How can the violence and the killing be in accordance with God's absolute sovereignty? The answer is that paradise is lost. The groaning of creation (Rom. 8:23) starts here. God allows humankind to kill! The only two exceptions have to do with eating blood, which Deuteronomy 12:23 says is the soul of any being, and with the killing of fellow human beings. The former prohibition is still taken seriously today by Jews and Muslims, while most Christians have forgotten about it. The sentence about the exception of blood is difficult to translate, but what the German Old Testament scholar Claus Westermann infers from it is very important: with the exception of the rule of humankind over animals the blessing is saved. The killing of the animals holds the threat of the lust to kill. Together with the prohibition against killing fellow human beings, to which there is no exception because they are created in God's image and belong to God, this restricts brutality and murder. Even more important, it shows that the behaviour of human beings towards human beings cannot be separated from their behaviour towards animals!

Recognition of this connection may be why, in Western Europe at least, more and more people who care for creation and for others are becoming vegetarians. Consider, for example, how pigs, which have been proved to be highly intelligent and sensitive beings, are raised today — squeezed into huge stalls, three thousand or more at a time. During their few months of life, they live in the dark except for their single daily feeding, since that makes their meat more tender. At all other times the stalls are guarded against light, lest the pigs die of a heart attack from shock. In hysteria and frustration, they sometimes bite one another, and the victim bleeds to death before someone discovers it the next day. Nor can the pigs walk around. Their legs cannot support a body that grows too fast with special food and is bred too long so as to produce more cutlets from a single animal. The horror escalates for those animals that are loaded onto lorries, driven sometimes halfway across Europe — to wherever the market is — and then killed by machines that may start to slice the animal even before it is dead. A society that treats living beings like that — similar stories could be told about cows, chickens, rabbits — has no respect for creation, no respect for God and in the end no respect for human beings.

Thus the new era is a time of God's patience. Even though violence has brought a deep division into the world, God does not withdraw. God retains sovereignty over all creatures, all life in the world. This is the notion of law within the grace of God towards Noah and his kin.

The covenant with which the passage ends differs from those with Abraham and Moses because, without any action on the side of the human partners, God's grace is given, not to one person or one people but to humankind at large. With this, P links the story of creation to the history of all the nations. In spite of violence and destruction, there is order and blessing. God has the "whole world in his hands", as the African-American gospel hymn says. That is the message of P.

God is covenanting not only with Noah but with all human beings — with Noah's wife, with his sons Shem, Ham and Japheth and with their wives. These four women are not named here, which is something that annoys me deeply about the biblical understanding: with very few exceptions women are anonymous. It is especially annoying in this story because it is obvious that without the woman there is no possibility to "abound on the earth and multiply in it" (9:7). Women are an essential part of the covenant whether P would like to acknowledge it or not.

In the history of the World Council of Churches, the notion of covenanting has played an important role. It was already used by the first assembly (1948) to characterize the churches' commitment to one another. For the German churches in particular, this covenanting meant symbolically being readmitted to the Christian community. Although in Amsterdam the covenant was largely limited to white male church leaders from Europe and North America, it has grown in fullness, participation and maturity. Today, 324 churches from all over the world join in the WCC, and its meetings bring together women and men, ordained and lay, from various denominations, of all ages, nations and colours.

At the 1983 assembly in Vancouver, the WCC began to "engage the member churches in a conciliar process (covenant) for justice, peace and the integrity of creation (JPIC)". The idea was in brief that ethical issues are as crucial for the unity of the church as dogmatic questions. While some scholars argued that God is the only one who can covenant, this was met with the response that by granting the covenant God gives the possibility for covenanting with one another on the grounds of this very covenant. The Hebrew part of the Bible knows very well about those covenants among people: Abraham and Abimelech (Gen. 21:22ff.), Isaac and Abimelech (Gen. 26:26ff.), David and Jonathan (1 Sam. 18:3; 19-20). The preparatory document for the Seoul JPIC convocation elaborates covenanting in this way:

> At the heart of the covenant is the promise and challenge, "I will be your God and you shall be my people." Implicit in this is a critical as well as a constructive theological principle: on the one hand, it implies the denunciation of idols ("thou shalt have no other gods!"); at the same time, it holds out the promise and possibility of peoplehood, of becoming under and with the "one God" a true community. [1]

Heino Falcke, a regional bishop and theologian from the former German Democratic Republic, lists five aspects of what he calls the necessary renewal of covenant:

1. *Anamnesis:* the remembrance of the covenant that God has granted, of God's former acts of salvation (exodus from Egypt, new covenant in Jesus Christ);

2. Announcement of God's will translated in the given context, which has at its central point justice, peace and the integrity of creation;

3. Cleansing of idols, renunciation of the covenant with death that today's systems symbolize;

4. Mutual commitment, in which two or more partners agree before God to behave in a new way towards one another;

5. Celebration of the covenant — in the meal, the sharing, the eucharist — signalling that the covenant is open to all, that everyone is invited to the community.

The interconnectedness of justice, peace and the integrity of creation became vividly obvious during a plenary session at the Vancouver assembly during which a delegation from the Pacific told how nuclear testing had forced communities in these islands away from their homes, polluted their environment, the water, the fish, the people. This naming of interconnectedness is perhaps the major contribution of the ecumenical movement to the social-ethical debate of the secular world. The concept of justice, peace and integrity of creation tries to show that we cannot put one concern up against another in some sort of hierarchy. We may pull at different ends, but it is the same complex.

Role play

Each person should receive a coloured card at the beginning of this Bible study. For the final half hour, they should group themselves together with others having the same colour (eight per group), with the following instructions.

You are now the Noah clan. You have seen God's wrath and God's grace, the flood and the rainbow. God has covenanted with you. Read the text again.

What is your answer to God's covenant? What does the rainbow mean to you? What is your covenant with one another in response to God's rainbow?

Take some time initially to reflect individually upon who you are and what you yourself want. Then discuss your response to the questions within your clan group. After about twenty minutes, all the clans will come together, and a spokesperson from each will share the main content of its covenant — if possible in a single sentence — with the other clans.

2. Praise God, all of creation
Psalm 148

Methodology: meditation

The division in natural sciences and theology between humankind and nature — which is best elaborated by the distinction between subject and object in the philosophy of René Descartes — is seen by many in the West as an essential source of the destruction of creation. This distinction has led to disastrous consequences. First, the world of objects had value not of its own but only insofar as it was of use for human beings. Second, men were related to the world of subjects, women to the world of emotion, of nature, and were thus of lesser value, so that up to our times men rule the world and women look after the household and the children.

Philosophers like Martin Heidegger have shown that the division of subject and object absolutizes a special constellation of the process of being. Others have proved that every science has subjective decisions at its basis. But this has not changed the general tendency towards the destruction of creation. In Western philosophy, infinity was taken from God and attributed to the human being. From this arose the idea of unlimited economic growth. A linear thinking began, which alienated human beings from nature because it tried to ignore the circle of birth, life and death.

This is one of the reasons why many people in our societies will talk freely about sex and the most intimate feelings but never about death. People do anything to try to stay forever young: face-lifting, body-building, hair-dyeing. Wrinkles on the face and gray hair are no longer seen as signs of experience, wisdom and maturity; instead, the majority do whatever they can to abolish these signs. Old people are often left alone. Nobody has time to listen to them. And while it is always women who take care of the old ones, their work is not valued by our societies.

When the Club of Rome published its study on the "limits to growth" in 1974, the title itself shocked many people. Coming together with the oil crisis and the Vietnam War, it marked a *kairos* for Western societies to change their ways, in biblical terms a prophetic sign. But the Western industrialized world, unlike Nineveh when Jonah preached there, continued to dance on the volcano. So, for instance, between 1980 and 1990 the use of cars in Germany *doubled*.

Psalm 104:30 makes it clear that it is God's *ruach* — spirit or breath — that creates life, and the rhythm of creation is not indefinite growth but being called into being, growth and growing towards death. The difference between thinking in cyclical ways and thinking in linear ways became vividly clear to me when I met with Aboriginal communities on a team visit before the WCC's Canberra assembly in 1991. I had heard it said that the Aboriginal culture was inferior to the European because they did not know farming. The reality is that the Aborigines have known farming in harmony with the land. They would follow their "dreaming", the path of their ancestors known by the wise and handed on from generation to generation. After living on fertile land for some time and finding all the fruit and seeds it bore, they would burn the land and leave the place. After a few years they came back. The land had recovered, the ashes had enriched it and it could feed the tribe again. By contrast, the European farmers have destroyed the land with their sheep, whose grazing takes out the grass by the roots, creating erosion and desertification.

The writer of Psalm 148 draws on the natural wisdom of the time, using "scientific lists" in a hymnic way, reminiscent of Job 38. This is later taken up in expanded form in the hymn of praise sung by the three young Jewish men thrown into the fiery furnace by Nebuchadnezzar (recorded in the Greek version of Daniel 3, classified in some traditions as the deuterocanonical book Song of the Three). Psalm 148 was probably used liturgically as a sort of creed expressing the certainty of salvation: God has defeated the chaos and will ensure the continuity of creation. Scholars have discovered that it draws on the *Onomastikon* (list of names) of the Egyptian wise man Amenemope, an hierarchical list which gives names to the different categories of living beings and starts to differentiate them. Thus the psalmist uses elements of ancient science to praise God. The main representative of the human being is the people of God at Zion, probably a prophecy of the lifting up of the people of Yahweh at the end of times.

With the whole of creation as its scope, the psalm is constructed magnificently. Like two choirs, heaven and earth stand opposite one another. Like call and echo the praise of God becomes a symphony of a multitude of voices. God is recognized as the almighty creator of all the elements, and the praise of God is the meaning and aim of creation.

Verses 1 to 6 focus on God as creator and show us the praise from heaven. Heaven in this case means the higher, divine part, including the ocean that is seen in the blue over the world. The angels, the sky and its lights, sun, moon, and stars, are called together with the waters above to praise God. Everything is created by God and so everything exists in order to praise God.

Verses 7 to 13 talk about God as the Lord of history and show the other side. The darkness of the oceans and the creatures of the deep are called to praise, as are fire and wind, the mountains, the animals, all that lives and exists. As in the story of creation, one element follows another. In the end there is the human being, who is also called to praise the name of God.

Westermann says this psalm shows exactly the same theological tendency as the two great historical reports of J and P by declaring the God of Israel as the Lord of all humanity, the master of the universe. This is the reason why all services of the Old Testament had an ecumenical and universal touch which is not as evident in Christian services. Indeed, everything that exists can praise God. Jesus picks up the same theme when he takes "small things" as entry points for many of his parables.

If this is the basic belief of our theology of creation, it has consequences for our approach to people of other faiths as well. Who can say where God is and where God is not, if all is created by God? Think again of the Aborigines whom I mentioned earlier. To believe that they lived in heathen darkness until 200 years ago when the first Europeans arrived is blasphemy according to Psalm 148, because this would mean that God had not revealed God's existence to those people. Furthermore, if God only arrived with the Europeans, that implies that God would have been revealed by the sword. I would rather believe that God was there long before Europeans came. The Aborigines know about God's existence; they respect creation; they wait for the cycle to re-create before they use the gifts of creation again. It is God's Spirit that moves in creation, and it is God's Spirit that we can find in other faiths. This is better understood in a multi-faith society like India than in Western countries, where other religions are often seen as a threat and our mission is to convert them.

During the Earth Summit in Rio in 1992, it was evident that care for creation is a common interest for all religions. Wesley Granberg-Michaelson writes about the experience:

> The Global Forum in downtown Rio drew a wide spectrum of religious groups. Most notable was an all-night vigil ending with an inter-religious service at dawn, addressed by, among others, the Dalai Lama. Nearly sixty groups representing different religious traditions gathered in tents in Flamingo Park to pray, meditate, and practise their own forms of worship through the evening. The variety of spiritual practices was so diverse and, depending on one's perspective, bizarre that it stretched the limits of religious tolerance. Evangelical Christian groups from Brazil for instance wanted to participate in the vigil but chose to remain separated on the other side of the fence as they expressed genuine doubts over suspected witchcraft and other "spirits" being worshipped in some of the practices.
>
> Some Pentecostal and evangelical churches in Brazil expressed little faith or interest in all the events surrounding the Earth Summit. But a rally calling such Christians to show their praise for God as the creator drew tens of thousands into the streets of Rio one afternoon.[2]

This draws attention to an important factor: spirituality. Psalm 148 was part of the spirituality of Israel thousands of years ago. Creation has always been a source and inspiration for spirituality. Every manifestation of Christian faith has hymns and prayers that praise God the creator. Day and night, dawn and dusk, the seasons — all have inspired Christian rites and practices. Christmas in Germany is the time when the nights become shorter and the days longer. Easter is the season of fertility. That is why rabbits are a main part of the Easter tradition in Germany — even though they do not appear in the biblical accounts of the resurrection of Christ.

Our spirituality needs our senses, which in industrialized societies are so often suppressed or destroyed. We have lost the ability really to see things because we spend so much time looking at reality through the screen of a television. We have lost the ability to taste because fast food does not taste like anything at all. We no longer know how to touch, to listen, to smell. Thus our creativity shrinks. A recent survey has shown that while children in earlier times knew how to play about a hundred games, in Western societies today they know an average of four to five. A rediscovery of spirituality therefore requires a change in the way we live.

We need to develop what the WCC's Nairobi assembly (1975) called a spirituality of combat — a spirituality that will make us move against destruction in this world rather than silence us to tolerate what we see. Spirituality is not something that can be imported or exported. Surely we can learn from each other. But once Christians in their own context live according to the gospel and take up the challenges before them, their spirituality will emerge. That has been the experience of the peace movement, of the human rights movement and now also the ecological movement.

Our psalm says that everything is created by God and thus everything can praise God. But I would draw on my German context to mention in conclusion two cautions or correctives. One is a reminder of the evil purposes for which the Christian religion and what could be called natural religion were used during the Nazi period. People were told that nature revealed God only in beauty and especially in Hitler. Against this, the corrective is always to look to the suffering of Jesus Christ, the one who died for others, as an example of where to read the signs and where to find God. A second caution has to do with the claim of some people in our societies that they find God better during a walk in nature than in church. We must not neglect the presence of God in the community. Christ has sent us to build community, to relate to others, to care for others, even if we often find it easier to be alone.

Meditation

Each participant is asked at this point to go out and pick up some object — beautiful or ugly, important or useless. The Bible study animator then leads the group in meditation, using these objects.

What you hold in your hand now is created by God. Do not destroy it. Look at how complicated or how simple it is. God cares for both and God cares for the detail. God is an artist. This item that you hold in your hand is able to praise God. It speaks a language that knows what to say about God.

Keep it in your hand while some music is played and some slides projected. Look at the creation in the pictures and in your hand. Feel it. This is God's creation. God is a lover of life and beauty. Relax and see, use your senses: see, feel and smell.

After the slides, place your feet firmly on the ground, close your eyes and breathe deeply. Touch what you hold in your hand. Be conscious of it. Feel your breath. I will read Psalm 148 again...

Now open your eyes slowly. See what you have in your hand. Look at your neighbour and share with him or her, or with the entire group, what creation means to you.

3. Violence — destruction of creation
Genesis 34

Methodology: dialogue

Unlike the writer of Genesis 6:5, humanism declares that the human being is good by nature. God is unnecessary, because the human is good, and evil is in institutions. If only poverty and ignorance were eradicated, everything would be fine. These optimistic theories of sociological progress, beginning with Rousseau and Darwin, consider human improvement as a kind of natural law, almost a technical matter. This myth was destroyed in Auschwitz and with the nuclear bombs over Hiroshima and Nagasaki. We now see much more clearly that the physical power science gives us is absolutely destructive if it is not controlled by spiritual strength. The blessing becomes a curse.

To read the Bible is constantly to be confronted with the reality of violence:
Cain violated his brother Abel.
David violated the Philistine Goliath.
Saul violated David.
The Philistines violated Saul.
David violated the Philistines.
Amnon violated his sister Tamar.
Elijah violated the priests of the Baal.

Holofernes violated Israel.
Judith violated Holofernes.
Herod violated the children.
Christians violated Jews.
Christians violated Christians.
Cain violated his brother Abel.

In both Old and New Testaments, however, we read also of efforts to overcome violence, to find new ways to break out of the circle of violence:

Miriam saves Moses.
Shiphrah and Puah refuse to kill the children.
David loves Jonathan.
Jesus talks to the women.

The entire chapter on which this Bible study focuses is a perfect example of the chain of violence. It shows rape at the centre of violence — rape, which is a term often used to describe the destruction of creation.

Two elements lie in the background of our story. One is the relation of the people of Israel to the people of Hamor. The city of Shechem remained Canaanite, while all of its surroundings became Israelite. This was a constant source of conflict. The other element is a family story: the two tribes of Simeon and Levi, unlike the other ten tribes, are not reported to have land of their own in Israel. Genesis 34 is an explanation of the reasons for this, which are further spelled out in Jacob's last will (Gen. 49:5-7).

The origin of all that happens is rape. The story of Dinah is the only instance in which we hear about a daughter of Jacob. While the names of his sons appear throughout the history of Israel, there is no report about daughters except in this one chapter. Again we see how fifty percent of history is hidden in our religion as well as in our societies.

The story of Dinah is a story of how violence will always produce more violence. Let us start with the rape. This is a constant reality for women all over the world, at all times, in all cultures, in all countries. Sometimes I believe it is easier for women to find words to understand one another because they share this constant threat or reality.

Rape is often used as a weapon of war. During the second world war, German soldiers raped women all over Europe. Russian soldiers raped German women in revenge. Worst of all perhaps — if one can make such comparisons — was the forced prostitution and rape of thousands of Korean women in Japan. Years ago, I attended a peace conference on the beautiful island of Okinawa, where more than 30,000 US soldiers were stationed. This occupation had two consequences: the land and the water are polluted because of the military installation, and one out of four women in Okinawa tries to find a living in prostitution. When the US army began to avenge Pearl Harbor in Okinawa during the second world war, the Korean women forced into prostitution were driven into the sea to drown so that the few hiding spaces and the little food on the island would serve the Japanese soldiers. Standing at the coastline, one can see the destruction of the coral reefs and imagine the cries of those raped and dying women.

The report of a World Council of Churches team of women which visited Croatia in December 1992 offers a horrifying contemporary example of how the use of rape in war can become specialized:

> There is strong evidence of the use of systematic mass rape as an increasingly sophisticated weapon of war being used in this instance by members of the Serbian forces. There is mounting evidence of systematic rape as part of a programme of ethnic cleansing. Survivors speak of "rape on the front line" and "third party rape". These are rapes carried out publicly by Serbian soldiers to demoralize family members and opposition forces compelled to witness them. Many stories refer to village communities being rounded up into camps — perhaps a school or community centre — and a space cleared in the middle. It is in this space that public raping takes place. It is reported as repeated, violent and "procedural". It is claimed that many of the victims and witnesses know the rapists. Many of the survivors and workers with them also claim that there has been persistent rape with the stated aim of impregnating women with "Serbian babies". Women are held until they are at least four to five months pregnant and then let go. Some are repeatedly violated and then killed. Victims include children from the age of ten years and women as old as eighty years... The churches and the international community have an obligation to insist upon greater understanding of the use of rape in this way.

When talking about rape one must also mention international tourist prostitution, which links countries around the globe. People in some Southern countries earn a lot of money by taking advantage of the poverty of women and children and forcing them into the sex trade. Men from rich countries are ruthless in taking with money what one cannot buy. But this also offers a good example of how networking among groups in the North and the South can work. People may be standing at Frankfurt airport to protest when the plane leaves, with others waiting in Bangkok to protest when the plane arrives. Finally, a law has been passed in Germany which provides for punishment of child-abusers even if the act is done abroad, making it clear that the value of a person is the same all around the world.

Amnesty International reports that in some countries, rape of female prisoners is a daily form of torture. Not only do the victims suffer physical violence, but they are also wounded psychologically in their emotions and feelings. Interrogators and other civil servants use rape to extract information or confessions or just to intimidate women.

For a woman, rape is the ultimate humiliation and usually has traumatic consequences for the rest of her life. Whether she is ever able to cope with this experience often depends on the environment and cultural background she comes from and lives in. Especially those women who out of shame or fear try to erase the experience from their memory will suffer from it. But the scars of rape are usually invisible to others. That is what makes it such a perverse weapon against women and girls.

There is much more that could be said about rape. Almost every woman in the world can tell her own story about sexual harassment and rape. But even in this passage of the Bible, as is usual in reports by men, little attention is paid to the pain of Dinah. Instead, the account in Genesis 34 proceeds directly to the wrath of the family to which she belongs. The rape is seen as a violation of them, and that becomes the centre of attention. There is no more mention of Dinah's feelings or wishes. It is as if those who believe that they own the woman are more violated than the woman herself. Dinah's brothers Simeon and Levi kill the men of Shechem. It is a horrible story of how trust is misused. Both brothers will be punished for this by their father in his last will, so that all the family will suffer because they are dispersed all over and thus deprived of a protective environment. The women and children of Shechem also suffer when they are taken prisoners by the sons of Jacob. In the end, Jacob himself fears the revenge of the Canaanites and the Philistines.

This entire story is filled with destruction. The city of Shechem and the fields of its inhabitants are destroyed. One thing we know about war and violence is that destruction of the environment goes hand in hand with the maiming and killing of people. The south of Italy was cleared of wood in the wars of Hannibal and Caesar, which some believe to have caused the expanding of the Sahara Desert. In modern times we are familiar with the results of the use of napalm in Vietnam and of atomic bombs in Japan. And the testing of nuclear weapons has destroyed nature, especially in the Pacific, in immeasurable ways.

Violence always starts in a certain context. Reasons for it are often taken from long ago. The combatants in the former Yugoslavia date their hatred back as far as 1389 when there was a famous battle on the Amselfeld. Some right-wing youths who violate foreigners living in

Germany feed their hatred with the ideologies of Germany in the 1930s. Very often ideologies nourish violence: apartheid, racism, militarism, sexism. Their language becomes the language of violence. In our text, this language first reaches Dinah, then her brothers, then the men of Shechem and their familes, finally leading to the possibility of genocide.

Usually society knows only one way to stop violence: violence. Sometimes we seem to despair of finding other ways. Or is it just that we do not have enough imagination and creativity to find new ways to break the spiral? Today we talk about the rape of nature. Again, if we want to stop this destruction, we have to invest in the search for new ways. You do not deal with rape by being silent about it but by talking about it, by expressing the source of the wound. We need the courage also to talk about the rape of nature and the creativity to find new ways — I think of ecological farming, the reduction of energy use, particularly in Western societies, overcoming the ideology of the automobile society, bringing production and consumption back into relationship.

To stop the raping of nature, we have to stop violence. Justice, peace and integrity of creation are interconnected. With a world at war there is no chance for the preservation of creation.

Dialogue

Look at the six people in our story and their thoughts. Think about the story and then choose one person on whom to focus. Try to find a way out of the conflict. Then share your line of thought to help us on the path of finding a spectrum of non-violent approaches to conflict resolution.

The six people in the story are:

Hamor: I did my very best to stop an escalation of the conflict. But the destruction of a whole city because of one single rape — that I cannot forgive.

Dinah: The rape was horrible. But the revenge of my brothers made it even worse. Nobody asked me. My life is totally destroyed. Both sides made me an object of their violence.

Shechem: I raped Dinah, but I really wanted to make up for it. I tried everything: paying the bride's price, offering peace, even being circumcised. I trusted them but they have betrayed me.

Simeon: They have raped my sister. People like that do not deserve justice. Cheating is the least they deserve. They all have to die.

Levi: Really, we just wanted to punish Shechem. But then it went on, and one thing led to another. In the end, though, we are right; that is obvious.

Jacob: My daughter was raped. I didn't talk about it because I know the wrath of my sons and I did not want trouble. But I could not stop them. Now I fear the revenge of the others.

4. Justice — about sharing creation
Luke 12:16-34

Methodology: writing a letter or testament

Of the four gospels only Luke includes this parable. The farmer seems to be quite a sensible man, carefully and successfully planning his investments. He is an entrepreneur who knows the market, a self-made man. This text is often preached in Germany at the harvest festival in October and is supposed to remind people that we should not think of the harvest selfishly but for others, that in the end the viewpoint from which success and failure in life are judged is God's. Many people have problems with the text because it seems so critical of farmers; and a colleague of mine has written about it, "as a rich person with the security of thinking of a rich person, I would say that I am too prejudiced to preach about it".

The Russian writer Leo Tolstoy gave a name to our farmer: Pachom. One of his stories tells about the Russian farmer Pachom, who has the opportunity to get as much land as he can walk around during one day. Breathless, he tries to walk around more and more. In the end, he is not able to complete the circle, and his greed keeps him from attaining what he wants. Human greed is the source of most of the ills of the world. But human greed is what is needed in the industrial society if you want to make it according to the law of the market.

Luther called the farmer superstitious, a magician, an opponent of God. In the end, he gave him the name Mammon. Looking at wealthy people in the North or the South, you begin to realize how easily being wealthy can become the main purpose of life. Replies to a recent survey in Germany on the meaning of life showed how many people equate the "good life" with such consumer aims as vacation, eating, drinking, leisure, erotic and social life.

Luke's story bears directly on such attitudes. What is to be condemned is not being rich as such, but not realizing God's will even when it is obvious. Jesus seems never to have condemned wealth as such, but he pointed to its risks and he always judged its misuse. Like any other power, money can be used for good or bad. Wealth as such is not bad and poverty as such is not good. For instance, was not Joseph doing God's will when he filled the barns and built new barns to store the harvest in Egypt (Gen. 41)? But the fundamental difference between Joseph and Luke's farmer is that Joseph planned and stored so that others might live. The man in Luke's story was a fool because he mixed up the means for living with life itself. The sixty or so words of his which are quoted in the parable constantly repeat "I" and "me". Never does he say "we" and "our". He was so caught up in himself that he did not realize that personal wealth always has its roots in collective wealth. He acted as if he himself were doing all the work, as if he were not standing in a long line of other people who had worked the land before him. Growing awareness of ecological farming today gives us a new realization of what it means to be grateful to generations before us and responsible for generations to come. When chemical fertilizers are used, it takes at least three years before the land cleans itself in a way that you can talk about ecological farming and several more years before the land has truly recovered.

In 1992 I was part of a WCC team that went to Brazil, where we visited the Xurcuru tribe. They have been living on their land in the northeast, about ten hours' drive west of Recife, for hundreds of years. When the Europeans reached their part of the country about two hundred years ago, the people were destroyed by weapons, by diseases brought by the invaders, by alcohol and, worst of all, by the destruction of their land. Shortly before our visit, the chief of the tribe had decided to go back to their traditional grounds. After passing several guards, we finally reached sixty little huts — sixty families, full of fear and pain and pride. They had no clothes, no grain, no food. But they were back on their land. And they showed us a baby that had been born, the first Xurcuru to be born on Xurcuru land in more than two hundred years. When we saw this vulnerable creature we were reminded of the child in Bethlehem two thousand years ago.

"We try what we can to help with the little means we have," said the man from the church who accompanied us. "But the owner of the land will probably just drive them off or kill them — that's the usual story."

What does the owner do with the land? He has used poorly paid workers to till the land for sugar cane to export. That is not only unjust; it is destruction of creation. Growing sugar there year after year will kill the soil. More rain forest has to be destroyed adding more greenhouse gases to the atmosphere. Who is the owner of the land? God gave the land. No one person can ever own it. That belief lay behind the jubilee legislation in Israel (Lev. 25), which provided that after fifty years, slaves should be freed and land given back to the original owner.

When a person or a people starts to forget these connections between justice and ecology, the consequences can be tragic. Many rich people, like Luke's successful farmer, begin to lose their sense of reality. For Luke sin is related to exalting oneself; and salvation is not so much moral improvement as the liberating insight that it is God's grace and being part of the community that will save us. So this parable is part of Luke's soteriology: an insight into liberation at a time in the early church when rich and well-educated people were beginning to play a role.

It is very easy to apply this text to the perverse situation of the world today. While people are dying of hunger in other parts of the world, Western Europe destroys surplus food and obliges farmers to produce less milk and less meat in order not to lower the prices. Because of such legislation, farming is no longer economically viable for many of them. At the same time, the banana that my daughter eats for breakfast comes from Latin America, the tea I drink comes from India, the cocoa for my older daughters comes from West Africa and my husband's coffee is from Brazil.

The sin today in the rich world is to ignore these connections, to say "Foreigners out!" and "Germany for Germans only". A colleague of mine has written a story in which he imagines what would happen if all the foreign products in Germany started to take these slogans seriously: the automobile tires went back to the country of the rubber trees, the tea to India, the cocoa to West Africa, the coffee to Brazil, the bananas to Panama, the wood to the rain forests in Africa, Asia and Latin America. Finally Germany is empty of all foreign goods, and people begin to realize that they are truly dependent on others and that their wealth comes not from their own labour but from cheap labour abroad and unjust terms of trade. The story caused a good deal of debate — a debate that is desperately needed to force us to realize that we are one people who have to take care of this world and we cannot do that as long as a minority lives at the cost of the suffering of the majority.

The crisis of the farmer in Luke's story is touched off by the fear of death. It is a crisis in his relationship towards property because he did not use what he had for what it was meant: to care that others may also live. Anyone who aims solely at the growth of his or her own property because he or she thinks that this is the way to attain security is living like a fool — which is what God calls the farmer in Luke's story. Wouldn't we often like to call those who consider themselves so important, who believe the world cannot exist without them, fools? Those who killed the students in Tiananmen Square, those who boast about the "mother of all battles", those who try to silence their critics with bannning orders. This judgment of God, announced by Jesus and recounted by Luke — "You fool!" — is good to hear, because history so often seems to reward the other side, the "important" people who bring development and technology and claim that it is for the good of the people, because transnational corporations bring jobs — but neglect to mention that wages are low and working conditions so miserable that two hundred people can burn to death in a factory where there is no preparation for any kind of emergency. It is the other side of history, from below, the perspective of those without power, that comes out into the open through Luke's story. You fool!

We need a new awareness of the *social responsibility* of property and of the *generational accountability* of whatever we do. The good life is no good life if it has disastrous consequences for nature, for myself and for the generations to come. A major issue of social responsibility in my part of the world relates to driving a car. In a single German state, North Rhine-Westphalia, there are more cars than on the whole continent of Africa. Here is an example of social responsibility being totally neg-lected. The world could not sustain it if everybody were to own an automobile. Yet even though it has been well established that what comes out of the exhaust pipe of a car is one of the major contributors to the accumulation of the gases which cause climate change, people in the North mainly decry the destruction of the tropical rain forests. The prime minister of Malaysia once observed that the richest 25 percent of the world's population consume 85 percent of its wealth and produce 90 percent of its waste. "Mathematically speaking, if the rich reduce their wasteful consumption by 25 percent, worldwide pollution would be reduced by 22.5 percent. But if the poor 75 percent of the world's population reduce consumption totally and disappear from the earth, the reduction in pollution will only be 10 percent."

For generational accountability the example of energy consumption is a key issue. Our generation is using energy at a rate that will not leave enough for our children. We try to find a way out by using nuclear power, which is full of risks and leaves waste that will remain radioactive for thousands of years. The catastrophe in Chernobyl should have taught humankind the energy lesson, but it seems not to have succeeded. Some experts estimate that 40 percent of the territory of the former Soviet Union is polluted by nuclear testing, accidents and dumping of wastes. This is a disastrous heritage for generations to come.

German New Testament scholar K.H. Rengstorf writes:

> The mistake of the farmer is that nature and its produce are no longer in a reasonable relation to God, that there is no value in life for him except for filled barns and, especially, that the blessing of harvest does not include any responsibility for him. Thus he must die in order to realize that it is not nature that gives and protects life.[3]

Luke's farmer may be seen as a parable of Western civilization, rich outside and dead inside. The German theologian Dorothee Sölle described this in her address to the WCC's Vancouver assembly in 1983:

> In the rich First World, there is little life in its fullness... and instead of that a constantly growing void. It is not material deprivation but a psychic void that comes between Christ and the middle class. Life without meaning is the experience of the masses. Nothing makes you happy, nothing really hurts. Relations to others are on the surface and interchangeable. Hope reaches out only to the next trip or vacation. One's work is senseless, boring.

Philip Slater offers a similar picture of this emptiness:

> We seek a private house, a private means of transportation, a private garden, private laundry, self-service stores and do-it-yourself skills. An enormous technology seems to have set itself the task of making it unnecessary for one human being ever to ask anything of another. Even in the family, each member should have a separate room, separate telephone, TV and car, if possible. We seek more and more privacy and feel more and more alienated and lonely when we get it. What accidental contacts we do have seem intrusive not only because they are unsought but because they are unconnected with any familiar pattern of independence.[4]

In the end, Luke says, it is God the creator who will care for what he has created. God's kingdom will come, and the main thrust of one's life therefore is to give reality to that kingdom during one's lifetime in whatever way is possible in the very different contexts in which we live. In the end that means a fool will be a fool and God's justice will prevail. Until then, we have to force the "rich farmers" to store in order to share, to till the land in order to feed people, to work the land and not to destroy it but to care for God's creation. Whoever works the land must take account of the social responsibility of the land and pay attention to the generations to come who will need it.

Letter-writing

Reread the passage from Luke and meditate on what it means to be rich before God. Meditate also on what the subsequent verses say about the birds and the lilies, the right and wrong things about which to worry. Then write a letter to children fifty years hence about what we will have left behind for them. This might be a letter of hope or despair, of encouragement or confession.

5. In Jesus Christ — a new creation
Romans 8:18-23

Methodology: painting

A biblical passage cited often when Christians discuss ecology is Revelation 21, which speaks of a new heaven and a new earth, where there will be no more suffering and God will wipe all tears from our eyes. Certainly a Christian approach to ecology must include hope and a confession of faith in the end, because the eschatological aspect is essential to our faith. This text from Romans 8 by contrast focuses more on the christological connection with creation. It is the main New Testament text in which creation itself is the subject.

In Germany this passage is often read during funerals. It is supposed to show the longing for heaven and the forgetting of this world. It is also used for sermons on *Volkstrauertag*, the day we remember those who have been killed in wars. At the same time, the text is of high theological interest and many famous German theologians and even philosophers (Bloch, Horkheimer, Adorno) have commented on it. It is a key passage for a theological approach towards nature, with its reflections on suffering and on longing. The experience of the human being and hope come closely together in a brilliant linguistic form. In the various interpretations that have been given of the text we can identify two lines of hermeneutical approach.

Karl Barth, in his 1921 commentary on Romans, interpreted it in connection with Paul's christological and eschatological teaching of salvation. Following Luther, Barth interprets the connected terms of expectation and revelation, slavery and freedom, suffering and glory, this reality and hope as the christological definition of humankind and the world.

Rudolf Bultmann stresses the other line: the existential and historical approach. He sees the text as using a gnostic-mythological language that reinforces an existential interpretation. In a sermon in Marburg in 1938, he states, "We are not what we now seem to be, but what we hope. We are not what we make of us, but what God has planned for us."

Paul Tillich followed this second line, but stressed the historical element, concluding that salvation will be the end of the discrepancy between nature and spirit, nature and culture. For him, there is no salvation of the human being without salvation of nature. The human being is within nature and nature is within the human being. A new heaven and a new earth is the meaning and aim of all life.

Jürgen Moltmann draws out this line further in his theology of hope, for which this text is a key passage, seeing it as a prophetically proclaimed hope of salvation for the world, for history, in a real future. This line of interpretation is expanded today to the hope for salvation of the world from ecological destruction.

Ernst Käsemann, in his commentary to Romans, shows the danger in both ways of interpretation: the existential approach risks individualizing salvation and shrinking Paul's message by describing freedom formally as openness to the future; the historically oriented exegesis risks becoming *theologia naturalis*, cosmological speculation, secular utopia. Käsemann tries to hold both aspects together: eschatological freedom is understood by Paul as salvation in a cosmic dimension. The justification of non-believers is described cosmologically as the salvation of the world. The text wants to point out the presence of salvation in the framework of a *theologia crucis*, a theology of the cross.

Creation in this text is the subject of groaning as a woman in labour (v.22). The main point of the text is that to believe in Christ in this world is a belief against reality. While Christ himself has risen, those who follow him are still in the world which he left, a world of suffering, pain and destruction. They have to live hope in the midst of despair. As Käsemann says, "within the world... and by contrast in the community which suffers with Christ, eschatological freedom as salvation for all creation appears in outline."[5]

This creation *is* suffering. There are thousands and thousands of examples: ozone depletion, climate change, land degradation, water pollution, deforestation, habitat destruction, species extinction, use and misuse of biotechnology. Every day seems to bring news of some new environmental deterioration.

This suffering is described as labour pains. Being in labour is an impressive experiences. The pain starts and you can no longer stop the process. The woman may scream — or, if her patriarchal tradition forbids it, she will use all her energy to avoid screaming. There is sweat and blood, there are tears. At the high point of pain, when it becomes unbearable and you have the feeling that you are about to die, the child is born. There is new life just at the moment when you feel that there is no sense in this suffering, no longer any use in trying.

It is like this with creation. It screams. There is blood, sweat and tears from what God has created. As far as we can see, there is no future on this planet. But our hope is for new life, that this process may be a fertile one.

The first difficulty with this image is that it might tempt us to say, well, if in the end there is new life, why worry during the process of pain? But there are dead children born. Children are born with genetic defects from radiation in the Pacific, children are born with asthma in the big cities, children are born with drug addiction, children are born who have no chance to live. The destruction of creation may go too far. There is no cheap hope just as there is no cheap grace, as Bonhoeffer has put it. Such an interpretation falls into the first trap we mentioned — now there is suffering, then there will be glory. But Paul sees a tension, a dynamism. Creation waits for the revealing of the children of God. That means to act in hope, not to despair and say there is no longer any way to save life on this planet because the destruction has gone too far. Nor can we simply relax and say, "There is always hope; God will save life." No, we have to live with the dialectic of the real threat and the real hope, with the knowledge that God wanted us to be co-creators. This is not always easy to maintain. A great deal of spiritual strength is needed to face reality and still maintain hope.

The second difficulty is that we might interpret the text as some sort of metaphor for the salvation of humankind. It is only in the last few years that we have learned to accept that there is a history of nature, a suffering of nature. Nature is not object but subject. Thus we come back to the insight from our earlier Bible study that we are part of creation.

The Native American Cree people have a saying: "Only when the last tree has been cut, the last river poisoned, and the last fish caught, only then you will realize that one cannot eat money." In this text from Romans, Paul is speaking about those who live in the age of the Spirit of God. Before the last tree has been cut, this Spirit can lead us to the insight that we cannot eat money. It is the Spirit that gives us the possibility to be what we are to become, children of God.

A woman from another North American indigenous people, the Wintu, has said:

> The people do not respect the land. They kill everything. The spirit of the land hates them. The Indians do not destroy anything, but the whites destroy everything. How can the spirit of the land love the white man? Wherever he touches the earth it becomes sore...

Whether this "spirit of the land" and the Holy Spirit about whom Christians talk are connected is an interesting and important debate that has been reactivated in the ecumenical movement since the presentation by Professor Chung Hyun Kyung at the WCC's seventh assembly in Canberra. In any case both reveal the same reality: the respect for nature and the knowledge that in the midst of our longing and suffering we are between the times. As children of God, we have the duty and blessing to see our salvation in conjunction with the salvation of creation. We are part of creation. In destroying what God has created we destroy ourselves. Thus ecological issues are not "non-theological factors" but of eminent theological interest. With the Holy Spirit God has given we know that we have hope without neglecting the reality of the sin in which we live.

While Paul interpreted the curse of creation as the lack of relation to God, we confess that it is humankind which causes the most horrible suffering of creation. While Paul saw the groaning of creation as a sign of hope for its final redemption, we hear it as a final groaning before death, the end of the world. While Paul saw the labour pain of creation as a sign of rebirth, this pain drives us to the confession of guilt. So we have to recognize the connection of human beings and nature as a whole because there is common salvation or common condemnation. This starts with how we look at our own bodies and it goes on to the way we look at nature and treat it. It will have to reach the point soon where we change our life-styles. God's covenant is valid; the rainbow is still up in the sky. The question is whether we will destroy the earth which God has promised not to destroy again.

Painting

We will finish our Bible studies together with something creative. While we listen to some music, materials are available to paint the labour pains of creation and the hope you have for creation and for all of us. Paint what you feel, the colours that come to your heart or to your mind. Let go of the idea that others will look at it and judge it. This is your picture. These are your feelings and imaginations.

* * *

A closing blessing comes from the worship materials in the WCC book *An Ecumenical Response to UNCED: Searching for a New Heaven and a New Earth*:

May God Almighty bless you,
blessings of heavens above,
blessings of the deep lying below,
blessings of the beasts and the womb,
blessings of the grain and the flowers,
blessings of the eternal mountains,
bounty of the everlasting hills,
be with you and go with you,
in the name of the Father, Son and Holy Spirit.
Amen.

NOTES

[1] "Between the Flood and the Rainbow", 2nd draft document for the WCC world convocation on JPIC, Seoul, March 1990, p.21.
[2] Wesley Granberg-Michaelson, *Redeeming the Creation: The Rio Earth Summit*, Geneva, WCC, 1992, p.37.
[3] Karl Heinrich Rengstorf, *Das Evangelism nach Lukas*, Göttingen, Vandenhoeck & Ruprecht, 1949, p.156.
[4] Philip Slater, *The Pursuit of Loneliness: American Culture at the Breaking Point*, Boston, Beacon, 1976.
[5] Ernst Käsemann, *Commentary on Romans*, tr. G.W. Bromiley, Grand Rapids, Eerdmans, 1980, p.234.

Creation and Restoration
Three Biblical Reflections

Renthy Keitzar

1. "The maker of heaven and earth" (Gen. 14:17-24)

When Christians reflect on the creator or creation, the first article of the Apostles' Creed comes to mind: "I believe in God the Father Almighty, Maker of heaven and earth." According to Martin Luther, this means:

> I believe that God has created me and all that exists. He has given me and still preserves my body and soul with all their powers. He provides me with food and clothing, home and family, daily work and all I need from day to day. God also protects me in time of danger and guards me from every evil. All this he does out of fatherly and divine goodness and mercy, though I do not deserve it. Therefore I surely ought to thank and praise, serve and obey him. This is most certainly true. [1]

This opening affirmation of the creed presupposes our relationship to God, the maker of the whole universe. We believe that the world (*oikoumene*) and humanity (*adam*) were created at the beginning of time and space. The writers of the Old Testament do not look for a scientific explanation of the origin of the world and humanity. Rather, as Luther explains, we see there how the people of God, Israel, encountered their God as a saviour and responded in praise. Such praise of God the creator may be seen in the creation stories of Genesis, in the Psalms, in Second Isaiah, in the book of Job.

Our passage from Genesis 14 has a special context of its own in the firmly formulated belief in creation which Israel encountered in Canaan. Abraham, returning from a campaign against the kings of the east, meets Melchizedek, the priest-king of El-Elyon, the "Most High God", in Salem (i.e. Jerusalem or Zion). In this context the title "maker of heaven and earth" is used in verse 19. It is significant that Abraham's oath in verse 22 speaks of Yahweh, God Most High, maker (*qnh*) of heaven and earth. A similar title was applied to Baal in the Ugaritic texts. Abraham acknowledged the blessing of Melchizedek and gave one-tenth of his possessions to the god of the Jebusite city Salem, who was called El-Elyon, maker of heaven and earth.

Israel's understanding of creation and the creator came from the wider context of their time and region. According to Claus Westermann, "not one of the motifs of the Old Testament story of creation is absolutely new; they all have close or distant parallels".[2] The Hebrews were familiar with the cosmogonies and theogonies of the Canaanite-Phoenician *Sanchuniaton* creation myth, the Babylonian creation myth and many others. But although they might have been externally influenced by such myths and traditions, what made the Israelite understanding unique was a "Yahwization" — a contextualization in terms of their faith in Yahweh. So much so that Yahweh, the God of the people of Israel, is called "maker of heaven and earth".

In the light of Abraham's affirmation of God as maker of heaven and earth let us look at some other selected passages of the Old Testament.

Deutero-Isaiah (Isa. 40-55). These chapters offer an abundance of statements about the creator. The author, an unknown prophet who lived during the exile, had experienced the fall of the monarchy and the kingdom. The exile deprived the people of their land, the concrete sign of God's blessing; their king and kingship, which guaranteed national unity; and the temple in Jerusalem, the place of the divine presence. But the prophet proclaims that their creator-redeemer-king will deliver them from the exile through a second exodus, a liberation from Babylonian bondage. Through the books of Deutero-Isaiah, Jeremiah and Ezekiel, the message of restoration echoes. Deutero-Isaiah proclaims imminent deliverance. Creation is one of the great acts of Yahweh, proving the worthlessness of the gods so that all eyes will see the sovereignty of Yahweh.

Note these passages: Yahweh created (*bara* — 40:26,28; 42:5) the stars, the ends of the earth and the heavens; he formed (*yatzar* — 45:18) the earth like a potter; he made (*asa* — 44:24; 45:12,18) all things; he stretched out (*natah* — 40:22; 42:5) the heavens; he hammered down (*raqa* — 42:5; 44:24) the earth; he called (*qara* — 40:26) the stars and led forth (*hoshia* — 40:26) the host of them by number. The author also brings out the concept of creation in a more radical manner: "I make (*yatzar*) light and create (*bara*) darkness, I author prosperity (*asa*) and create (*bara*) trouble — I Yahweh do (*asa*) all this" (45:7). Nothing in the created world lies outside his creative realm.

Yahweh's creative act is liberative and redemptive. Yahweh is the redeemer and creator of Israel (44:24; 45:8; cf. also 41:20; 48:7). The

Babylonian creation myth of the slaying of the sea monster is reflected in Yahweh's act of deliverance (51:9-10). The *Enuma Elish* tells how the creator god cut the sea monster (Tiamat) into halves, from which he formed heaven and earth. Note the division of the waters of the Sea of Reeds in the deliverance of the first Exodus (Ex. 14). The creator God is none other than the God who brought Israel out of Egypt.

The Psalms. Behind the litany of God's wonders in Psalm 136 is a very similar salvific understanding of creation. This Psalm is a hymn of praise which may be classified as an historical psalm. Like the Genesis accounts of creation and Deutero-Isaiah, it combines the tradition of Yahweh as creator with his saving deeds for Israel. Another hymn of praise is Psalm 104, which sings of Yahweh who created and providentially maintains the habitable world, bringing out the ecological dimension. Similar reflections are seen in Psalms 8, 19 and 24.

Psalm 139 is unique: verses 13-16 offer a reflection on how an individual gives thanks to Yahweh for his creation (*qnh*). Mythological references to the battle with the sea monster at the beginning of the world (cf. Isa. 51:9-10) are also found in the Psalms (74:13-14; 89:10-11). Yahweh's creative work is also extolled in the context of his royal sovereignty and creation (Pss. 95:4-5; 96:5).

Wisdom Literature. The books of Job, Proverbs, the Wisdom of Solomon, Ecclesiasticus (Sirach) all stress how God performed the act of creation "in wisdom" or "by wisdom" (cf. Job 38:4ff.; Ps. 19; Prov. 3:19; 8:22ff.; Sir. 16:24-17:14; Wis. 9:1ff.).

2. A garden in the east (Gen. 2:4b-25)

One of the important consequences of the establishment of a united monarchy in ancient Israel was the flowering of literary activity. The oral traditions were reduced to writing in the courts of the kings by the wise men or courtiers who had the leisure and ability, along with the education, to engage themselves in wisdom reflection and raise questions on the origin of everything on earth. Who created the earth and heaven? Where do we come from? Where are we going? What is the reason for life, suffering, death? Why does the snake crawl rather than walk or fly? Why does the woman suffer at the time of delivery? What is the relationship between humanity and God? What is the relationship between humans and nature? Why are there different peoples and races? What about the animals, plants and birds of the air?

The wise men tried to answer all these etiological questions. Their answers are reproduced in different forms and genres. The text before us is a wisdom text from an older writer, often referred to as the Yahwistic writer because of the use of the divine name Yahweh. Since its origin was in the southern kingdom, Judah, at Jerusalem, the siglum J is also used. This J source-document or Yahwistic tradition is dated around 950-850 B.C. Genesis 2:4b-25 is thus an older account of creation than the first chapter (Gen. 1:1-2:4a).

This J account came originally from the desert lands of the Middle East, perhaps from a Palestinian environment and ecology. The environment in the beginning of time appears as dry: "When Yahweh God made the universe, there were no plants on the earth and no seeds had sprouted, because he had not sent any rain, and there was no one to cultivate the land" (Gen. 2:4b-5, GNB). Unlike the Mesopotamian valley, where the alluvial plain flooded annually, the environment of God's creation in this narrative is a desert, and when God makes an habitable environment it is an oasis, like a paradise in the desert. We also see reflected here the experience of the nomad.

So God prepared an environment for the human community: the focus is on the people. God formed human being (*adam*) from the soil of the ground (*adamah*); he breathed into the human's nostrils the breath of life; and the human became a living being (*nephesh haya*). It is by the breath of God that a human being lives. If that breath is taken away, the human being returns to soil again (cf. Isa. 2:22). The very being of God is in human nature, not just a spark of Ultimate Reality or the blood of Nintu or Kinku. It is not just *something* divine; the human being is created in the image of God and after his likeness (cf. Gen. 1:26ff.) or, as the Psalmist says, "a little lower than God" (8:5).

What is the role of the human towards nature? Yahweh prepared a garden in Eden (Gen. 2:8). Notice that this account is written from the Palestinian geographical standpoint: the garden is located "in the east". Eden is not the name of the garden but of the region where it is set. The first human being is placed in the garden to cultivate it and guard it, and is entrusted with responsibility of keeping God's world (2:15). This responsibility is then extended to a proper management of the animal world as well (2:19).

The first human being, Adam, lived in the Garden of God (cf. Gen. 13:10; Ezek. 28:13; 31:8; 36:35; Joel 2:3) in an environment of peace and harmony with all God's creations and nature: eco-balance in a state of symbiosis. He is to cultivate and keep the garden as a responsible steward. A limit is also set: he is not to eat of the fruit of the tree of the knowledge of good and evil, "for in the day that you eat of it you shall die" (2:17), says God. This threat is difficult to understand, because although he did eat of it, he did not die. Perhaps it is an order not to destroy the trees and fruits in God's garden, the world. Or "to die" may here mean "to be cut off" from having communion with God. Later Adam and Eve were driven out of the garden for having eaten of the fruit of the forbidden tree, but not killed. The original innocence and incorruptible nature of primeval humans was a later concept (cf. Wis. 2:23; Rom. 5:12), and from this arose the understanding that death is a result of sin.

Finally, God created the woman from one of the ribs of man himself, because it is not good for man to be alone (2:18). The woman is not to be understood as subordinate to man; the two verses, 2:18 and 2:23, clearly signify their equality. These passages also signify that man becomes a man only in loving relationship and companionship with woman. Consequently, a man and a woman enter into the institution of marriage as one flesh. Marriage is a divine institution, not just a social contract; it is created by God. It is also meant to be monogamous and inseparable, because the man and woman are no longer two, but one. No one must separate what God has joined together (cf. Matt. 19:4-6).

The Yahwistic account of creation is didactic in the sense of being a critique of the practice of marriage in the time of monarchy, particularly in the court of Solomon. An abuse of the status of women in the form of concubinage (or harem prostitution) and polygamy prevailed during that time, making women mere sex objects and playthings in the hands of men. In this context the wisdom teachers taught that woman was created out of the very bone of the man as a suitable companion, and so equal with man.

In reading this Yahwistic account of creation, we see the Garden of God, a paradise, as a symbol of the *oikos*, an ecosystem in which the different species of organisms in God's creation, from the smallest to *homo sapiens*, co-exist in a state of symbiosis, fulfilling God's plan and the purpose for which they are created. The Psalmist writes: "The heavens are telling the glory of God; and the firmament proclaims his handiwork" (19:1) and "The earth is the Lord's and all that is in it, the world and those who live in it" (24:1). In the Garden of Eden the first human beings, Adam and Eve, lived in close relationship to every living creature, the birds of the air and the beasts of the field, in an environment of natural beauty and splendour unspoiled by ecological degradation. Such a beautiful description of the Garden of God is visualized further in Ezekiel (28:13f.; 31:1-9; 36:35ff.). God himself is very much present with the whole of his creation in a human (anthropomorphic) way.

Hence, any ecological degradation, whether in the form of imbalance in nature created by humans, discrimination and inequality in human relationships, injustice, wanton destruction of the ecosystem, depletion of the ozone layer, is a destruction of God's creation. All these affect human existence and subsistence in God's own *oikoumene* and interfere with God's order of creation. God's creation and ecosystem must be saved if humans are to survive.

3. Through him God made all things (John 1:1-3)

The gospel of John, a devotional favourite of many Christians, differs from the other three gospels in that it "starts with a philosophical statement" (1:1-18).[3] Barnabas Lindars goes on to relate this to the special character of the gospel's first readership:

> At the very least, the Prologue suggests that the readers include people who would wish to relate the gospel's claims concerning Jesus to a philosophical account of the nature of God and cosmology. This could imply a Greek or Gnostic readership. But it will also turn out that the disputes of Jesus in Jerusalem, which form the bulk of chapters 3-13, are concerned with issues between Christians and Jews opposed to them at the time when relations between church and synagogue had reached breaking-point. This suggests that the readers are actually involved in such disputes.[4]

The community John was addressing is generally thought to have been at Ephesus, where it was subjected to various influences:

Greek philosophy. The leaders in Hellenistic culture drew on philosophers like Socrates, Epictetus and the Stoics. More importantly, they were influenced by the Alexandrian Jewish philosopher Philo, who tried to make a synthesis between Greek philosophy and his Jewish faith. That John's audience lived in such a context is suggested by his use of such themes as the Logos (the Word) to interpret Jesus to them.

Gnosticism. While this can take various forms, its basic doctrine is that matter is essentially evil and spirit is essentially good. On this basis it is believed that God did not create the world, for God is good and cannot be the creator of the world, which is evil. To such a context John announces in his gospel that "through him [the Word] God made all things; not one thing in all creation was made without him" (1:3, GNB). The Gnostics also think that they can acquire salvation by gnosis (compare *jnana marga* in Hinduism), knowledge which is reserved for those who have been initiated. The gospel of Thomas, discovered in 1946, gives an example of this. John had to fight against such tendencies in his community, and it is certainly no coincidence that he presents Christ primarily as the one who reveals God's secrets (1:18).

Judaism. There were Jews and Jewish Christians among John's readers, and he draws primarily upon Jewish faith. Although direct citations from the Old Testament may not be many, it is clear that the author has assimilated the great themes of the prophets and the wise men of the Old Testament. The exodus motif, like the paschal lamb, manna and water all feature significantly to interpret Christ. Jesus is the Messiah, the Shepherd, the vine, the light, and above all the very "I AM" (an equivalent for Yahweh). All these images or titles for God in the Old Testament are used extensively by John in reference to Jesus. Sometimes John appears to be anti-Semitic (1:11; 8:31-47); however, I think this is not actually a case of anti-Semitism but an indication of John's evangelistic thrust to convert Jews to Christ.

Qumran. The Qumran covenanters belonged to a Jewish sectarian group often referred to as the Essenes. They have become much better known since the discovery of the Dead Sea Scrolls in 1946. The points of contact between John's teaching and theirs are worth noting: ideas like light and darkness (1:4-5,9; 3:19-21), Jesus as the truth (14:6) and, perhaps most striking, "By his understanding things are brought into being, by his thought every being established, and without him nothing is made" (*The Scroll of the Rule*, 1QS 11:11). These points of contact may have arisen because both John and the Essenes drew on the same Old Testament texts.

There is much uncertainty as to the identity of the writer and the date of composition of the fourth gospel. John Marsh located its original environment as the first or second century.[5] Lindars writes:

> If the late date is accepted, the length of time available allows for the formation and reworking of traditions over a long period before the actual writing of the gospel. One possibility is that the apostle John was the originator of the special traditions which lie behind the fourth gospel, and these were preserved and developed in the Johannine church until someone else wove them into the finished form of the gospel.[6]

Thus, we may say that the source of the fourth gospel can be traced back to the apostle John, even if the work itself went through several stages of redaction before the final form as we have it took shape.

Whoever he was and in whatever circumstances he lived and taught, John was an interpreter and theologian in his own right, regardless of how or by whom he was influenced. It is possible that he was familiar with the synoptic traditions and had the background of the *paradosis* of the kerygma. Hence, he knew the teaching of Jesus and he interpreted the message of Jesus to his community in their context. His gospel is a contextualization. What John Marsh says is relevant here:

> His tremendous gift has consisted in his ability to put each and all of them completely at the service of Jesus Christ, Son of God and Saviour of the World. The very fact that the fourth gospel can be claimed as Gnostic, Hermetic, Mandaean, Hebraic, etc., is itself an indication not only of a hospitable mind, which might have produced merely syncretism, but of a uniquely creative spirit that could in the crucible of his own profound religious experience fuse all the diverse elements of his contemporary world into one magnificently effective instrument of Christian proclamation. [7]

Similarly, the gospel of John can be interpreted to different communities in the contemporary world using their language, ideas and thought forms. As John contextualized the message of Jesus and proclaimed to his community in the context of their life and culture, we too have the same task of contextualization.

John 1:1-3 interprets the creation of the universe by the Word of God (Gen. 1; Isa. 40:21; Ps. 33:6). Let us look at this in two ways: (1) Who is this Word? (2) What is the function of this Word?

The identity of the Word. It is useful to compare the translation in several versions, especially in the RSV and GNB, to see how various translators have interpreted this passage. Note especially the capitalization of the initial letter "W" in "Word", at least in English, which means it is personified. Perhaps the Greek term Logos was already understood that way in the time of John, and so he used it naturally. Or are we reading this into the text? In many Indian languages it is not capitalized. At any rate, with the understanding reflected in English versions, let us now reread this passage replacing the words "the Word" by "Jesus", as John would have had in the back of his mind when he wrote.

The expression "in the beginning" (RSV) is dynamically rendered in the GNB as "before the world was created". Perhaps this is an over-translation, reflecting the theological bias of the translator. The phrase can be understood in different ways: as referring to pre-creation or to the beginning of time and space in the sense of the history of time. John may have borrowed this phrase from the Greek Septuagint translation of Genesis 1, because the Hebrew *bereshith* can be construed temporally as "When God began to create..." (cf. Gen. 1:1, marginal note in NEB, RSV, GNB). For John this is definitely a reference to the pre-existence of Christ, as explained in the subsequent statement, "the Word already existed" (GNB); and he continues, "he was with God, and he was the same.as God" (GNB). The statement does not only specify the pre-existence of the Word (Jesus) but also spells out the identity of the Word. This means he is God; John affirms the divinity or deity of Jesus. Later in the gospel, this is attested to in Jesus' own answer to Philip:

> Philip said to him, "Lord, show us the Father, and we will be satisfied." Jesus said to him, "Have I been with you all this time, Philip, and yet you do not know me? Whoever has seen me has seen the Father. How can you say, 'Show us the Father'? Do you not believe that I am in the Father and the Father is in me? The words that I say to you I do not speak on my own; but the Father who dwells in me does his works. Believe me that I am in the Father and the Father is in me; but if you do not, then believe me because of the works themselves" (John 14:8-11; cf. 16:25-28).

Jesus reveals God; he himself is Son of God (1:18; cf. 1:14). The use of the formula "I AM", which appears frequently on the lips of Jesus in John, and is even used as an absolute on four occasions (8:24,28,58; 13:19), testifies to the divinity or deity of Jesus. This term corresponds to the name Yahweh, God's own name, in the Old Testament (Ex. 3:6,14; Isa. 41:4; 43:13,15; 47:12). John stresses the pre-existence and deity of Jesus, as it is written, "Before Abraham was born, 'I AM'" (John 8:58, GNB). Jesus also speaks of his coming down from heaven (6:33-38). Hence, according to John, Jesus is God. He is the Word become flesh (1:14), the one who reveals God. He has made himself equal with God (5:18; cf. 10:33). He is the creator God. As Colossians says, "He is the image of the invisible God, the first-born of all creation; for in him all things in heaven and on earth were created, things visible and invisible, whether thrones or dominions or rulers or powers — all things have been created through him and for him. He himself is before all things, and in him all things hold together" (1:15-17).

The Word and creation. The function of the Word is spelled out thus: "All things came into being through him, and without him not one thing came into being" (1:3). This verse reminds us of Isaiah 44:24: "I am Yahweh, who made all things, who alone stretched out the heavens, who by myself spread out the earth" (cf. 1QS 11:11; Col. 1:15 ff.). The one who was with him was the Word, Jesus (cf. John 1:1-2).

Notice that the noun "Word" is replaced by the personal pronouns "he" and "him", not the neuter form "it". John understood the Word as a person; and Jesus the Word is the maker or creator of all things, because he is the same as God (1:1-2). The Greek word *egeneto* ("came into being") — "all things came into being through him" — signifies the fullness of God's creation (Isa. 44:24), equating this with the fullness of creation in Jesus (cf. also Rom. 9:36; 1 Cor. 8:6; Col. 1:16).

The Old Testament includes many references to this idea of the powerful creative word (Gen. 1:3ff.; Ps. 33:6; 107:20; 147:15; Isa. 55:11; Jer. 23:29). Against this background of the Old Testament understanding of the dynamic, acting and creative power of the Word, John appropriated and contextualized the *paradosis* of the *kerygma* of Jesus. Jesus is that Word; in him the Word becomes a person; and he himself is God. He is the creator. To quote Raymond Brown, it is through Jesus that

> all things came into being, and not from a demiurge or one of the emanations of God who is responsible for material creation, which is evil. Since the matter is evil, according to Greek philosophy, God could not have created the world. But the Bible says that God created the world, which "was very good" (Genesis 1:31). The Word, that is Jesus, who is related to and with God, created *all things* in the universe. Thus the material world has been created by God and is good. [8]

What is important here is John's contextualization. He uses a contemporary term, not compromising with his readers' understanding, but rather explaining the biblical view of the Word and its function through the use of language that can make his theology understandable to his readers. Two aspects are evident: (1) an evangelistic thrust — Jesus is the same as God the creator, who gives eternal life to believers (cf. 20:30-31); the image of God is restored in him, making the believers "a new creation" (cf. 2 Cor. 5:17); and (2) an ecological relevance — the world (*oikoumene*, cf. Heb. 2:5) is created by God and is subjected to the control of Jesus (Heb. 2:5-9). This is God's world, which is good. God sends his Son Jesus Christ into the world (cosmos) because he loves it so much (3:16).

NOTES

[1] Translation in Martin Luther, *The Small Catechism in Contemporary English*, St Louis, Concordia, 1960.

[2] Claus Westermann, *Elements of Old Testament Theology*, tr. Douglas W. Stott, Atlanta, John Knox, 1982, p.86.

[3] Barnabas Lindars, *John*, New Testament Guides, Sheffield, JSOT Press, 1990, p.9.

[4] *Ibid.*, pp.11ff.

[5] John Marsh, *St John*, Harmondsworth, UK, Penguin Books, 1985, p.26.

[6] *Op. cit.*, p.19.

[7] *Op. cit.*, p.40.

[8] Raymond E. Brown, *The Gospel According to John*, The Anchor Bible, New York, Doubleday, 1975, p.26.

3.

Theological Challenges

A Theological Response
to the Ecological Crisis

K.C. Abraham

There was a time when we in the poorer countries thought that the ecological crisis was not a serious problem for us. Our problem, it was assumed, was poverty and economic exploitation; the environmental issue was a "luxury" of the industrialized countries. Social action groups and people's movements in Third World countries thus showed relative indifference to the problem of ecology. Today, we realize how urgent this issue is for the whole world — rich and poor countries alike. The threat is to life in general. The life of the planet is endangered. The ecological crisis raises the problem of survival itself. Moreover, there is a growing awareness of the organic link between the destruction of the environment and social, economic and political injustice.

The interconnectedness between commitment to the renewal of society and to the renewal of the earth is clearly seen in the struggle of many marginalized groups all over the world. Indigenous peoples (Native peoples in the USA and Canada, Maoris in Aotearoa-New Zealand, Aborigines in Australia, tribal people in many countries of Asia) and groups who have traditionally depended on the land and the sea (small farmers, fisherfolk, agricultural labourers) have kept these two dimensions together in their movements for liberation.

A majority of the poor are also landless. Agricultural development helps the rich landlords and not the poor. The poor in the slums of our cities are squeezed into small hovels, and their struggle is simply for living space. Meanwhile, to enhance and expand their own comforts, the rich continue to destroy whatever is left for the poor: their villages, their forests, their people. The stubborn resistance of poor tribal women in the now-famous Chipko movement against the Indian government's decision to turn their habitat into a mining area has helped to make us aware of the inseparable link between the struggle of the poor and ecological issues.

Today, the cry of the poor in the Narmada Valley in India is not only to preserve their own habitat but to protect forests everywhere from wanton destruction. The ecological crisis is rightly the cry of the poor. Their experience of deprivation and exploitation is linked with environmental degradation, and their perspective on these problems should thus be the starting point of our discussion. It is not a problem created by scientists or by a group of people who fancy growing trees around their houses. It is the problem of the poor. It is integral to their struggle for justice and liberation, and basically it is about preserving the integrity of creation.

Of course, committed scientists and other ecologists have helped us to deepen our understanding of the ecological problem. In the past, nature was seen as an object for ruthless exploitation by "developers" and scientists for the "good" of humans. Little thought was given to the perils of environmental destruction. A sense of optimism prevailed about the capability of science to tame nature, and those who raised any voice of concern about it were branded as "prophets of doom". But today more and more scientists are among those crusading to make people aware of the ecological disasters. They marshal convincing scientific data to demonstrate that the environmental degradation caused by massive pollution of air, water and land threatens the very life of the earth. Rapid depletion of non-renewable resources, indeed of species themselves, the thinning of the ozone layer, exposing all living creatures to the danger of radiation, the buildup of gases exacerbating the greenhouse effect, increasing erosion by the sea — all these are documented by scientific research. Related to these are problems of rapidly increasing population, the spread of malnutrition and hunger, the subordination of women's and children's needs to those of men, the ravages of war, the scandal of chronic poverty and wasteful affluence.

These problems are well known, and much literature is available on them. My purpose here is to highlight the theological and ethical issues involved in the ecological crisis and to suggest a possible response from the church and people's movements. To do this we need to clarify some perspectives on the ecological problem.

Some perspectives on ecological issues

The growth model must be changed. The ecological crisis is created by modern industrial and technological growth and modern life-style. One paradigm of development, the Western industrial growth model, is almost universally accepted. It is a process using enormous capital and exploiting natural resources, particularly non-renewable ones. The inevitable consequence of this pattern of development is ruthless exploitation of nature and fellow beings. Decisions about the kind of goods to be produced and the type of technology to be used are influenced by the demand of a consumerist economy, whose controlling logic of growth is greed, not need.

The growth model creates imbalances between different sectors and allows massive exploitation of the rural and natural environment for the benefit of the dominant classes. Much of the profit-oriented growth, which destroys the ecological balance, is engineered and controlled by multinationals from the USA, Europe and Japan. For example, Japanese multinationals indiscriminately destroy forests and other natural resources in the Philippines, Indonesia and other Asian countries. Thus Japan can preserve its own forests and trees because countries in the surrounding region supply what is needed to maintain its life-style.

Industrial pollution has risen alarmingly. The havoc created by the gas leak in Bhopal is vivid in our memory. Overuse of fertilizers is turning our farmlands into deserts and killing the fish in our seas and our rivers.

Human demands for food and energy are increasing faster than the resources, which are, in fact, dwindling. The negative impact of people on environment is recognized to be the product of three factors: the total population, the amount of resources consumed by each person and the environmental destruction caused by each person. All three continue to increase, with the wasteful life-style of the rich and its irresponsible use of natural resources adding a particular burden on the ecosystem.

An Indian conference on ecology and development has stated:

> While all are affected by the ecological crisis, the life of the poor and marginalized is further impoverished by it. Shortage of fuel and water adds particular burdens to the life of women. It is said that the tribals are made environmental prisoners in their own land. Dalits, whose life has been subjected to social and cultural oppression for generations, are facing new threats by the wanton destruction of natural environment.[1]

If we in India ask whether the present policies of the government will help us alter this form of development, the answer is likely to be that nothing short of a rejection of the dominant paradigm of development and a commitment to an ecologically sustainable form of development will reverse the present crisis.

Ecological crisis as a justice issue. Our ecological crisis should be seen as a justice issue. This is a fundamental perspective distinguishing the people's view on ecology from "establishment" and "expert" viewpoints. Political and social justice are linked to ecological health, as Jürgen Moltmann has said: "We shall not be able to achieve social justice without justice for the natural environment; we shall not be able to achieve justice for nature without social justice."[2] Several dimensions of this eco-justice are coming to the fore through experiences in the struggle of the marginalized.

First is the connection between economic exploitation and environmental degradation. This has become clear in deforestation. The massive destruction of forests due to avarice and greed has resulted in atmospheric changes. The poor are driven out of their habitat for the sake of "development". A typical example is described in a paper prepared by the trade union of fisher people in Kerala, which notes that a massive fish epidemic caused by the pollution of water from pesticides has led people to refuse to buy fish, making the fisherfolk jobless. At the same time, the use of mechanized trawlers has resulted in threatening all fish life, and traditional fisherfolk still have not recovered from the losses suffered for that reason.

Second, justice is actualized in just relationships. Unequal partnerships and patterns of domination are unjust. It is obvious that the human relationship with nature today is not that of equal partners, but of domination and exploitation. Unjust treatment of the planet by humans is one of the principal causes of the ecological crisis.

Third, the uneven distribution, control and use of natural resources are serious justice issues. For example, it is estimated that the natural resources needed to maintain the life-style of one person in the USA are equal to what is required by 200-300 Asians. Imagine what would happen if the same North American life-style were to be extended to people everywhere.

Fourth, the rapid depletion of non-renewable natural resources raises the question of our responsibility to future generations. If we extend the five-star culture to all countries and all segments of people, pressures on these resources will become intolerable. For example, we are warned that we cannot go on exploiting the deep-level water without disturbing the ecological balance. Someone has compared the function of deep water to the fluid in the middle ear which helps the human body maintain its balance. The question therefore, is how to use natural resources in a way that sustains life and does not destroy it.

Ethics of care, alleviation of poverty. The logic of justice as developed in the West emphasizes rights, rules and respect for the other. It can be applied only to human beings — supposedly equally. It is a balancing of rights and duties. In order to include the cosmos in the justice enterprise, we need to affirm an ethics of *care*. Justice cannot be accorded except through care. Justice expressing compassion is the biblical emphasis. The prophets did not talk about balancing interests and rights, but about the righteous God's caring for and defending the poor. And defending the vulnerable and defenceless should also include defending our weak and silent partner, the earth.

> We can no longer see ourselves as rulers over nature but must think of ourselves as gardeners, caretakers, mothers and fathers, stewards, trustees, lovers, priests, co-creators and friends of a world that while giving us life and sustenance, also depends increasingly on us in order to continue both for itself and for us.[3]

Poverty is also a source of ecological degradation, and the alleviation of poverty by the poor through their struggle for justice is an ecological concern. We cannot separate these two concerns. Unless the poor have alternate sources of food and basic needs like fuel, they too will wantonly destroy whatever natural environment is around them.

Justice in relation to ecology has a comprehensive meaning. Negatively, it is placed against economic exploitation and unjust control and use of natural resources. Positively, it affirms responsibility.

A new sense of interdependence. The ecological crisis has impressed on our consciousness a new awareness of our dependence on earth. We belong to the earth. We share a common destiny with the earth. This awareness poses a sharp challenge to the modern view of reality and demands a re-evaluation of our previously held scale of values. The modern perception of reality, thanks to the all-pervasive influence of Western rationality, follows a mechanistic model. It is functional and dualistic — spirit/flesh, objective/subjective, reason/passion, supernatural/natural. The ecological view is organic, emphasizing interconnectedness and mutual interdependence. It adopts a view of the world captured well in Martin Buber's famous distinction between I-Thou and I-It relations. All entities are united symbolically.

Sallie McFague has expressed this challenge:

> Ecological perspective insists that we are, in the most profound ways, "not our own": we belong, from the cells of our bodies to the finest creations of our minds, to the intricate, constantly changing cosmos. The ecosystem, of which we are a part, is a whole: the rocks and waters, atmosphere and soil, plants, minerals, and human beings interact in a dynamic, mutually supportive way that make all talk of atomistic individualism indefensible. Relationship and interdependence, change and transformation, not substance, changelessness

and perfection, are the categories within which a theology for our day must function.[4]

We cannot here go into the implications of this rather provocative suggestion, which calls for nothing short of a "paradigm shift" in theology, far beyond the mere critique of theology as too anthropocentric.

Challenge to ethics. In addition to calling for this theological shift, the ecological perspective also challenges our notion of ethics. In fact, the ecological model of mutual interdependence can provide a new orientation in ethics that can be the source of human renewal. Our Lord asks us to learn from the birds of the air, the lilies of the field. Values that are essential for the survival of life are those of caring and sharing, not domination and manipulation. The pattern of domination and exploitation can only lead to the silencing of nature and to the ecological death of both nature and humans. The new perspective affirms our inter-relatedness one to another and to nature.

The scale of values essential for sustaining the inter-relatedness and wholeness of creation differs from the dominant value system of modern society. One may state them as follows:
• conservation, not consumerism;
• need, not greed;
• enabling power, not dominating power;
• integrity of creation, not exploitation of nature.

We need to build structures and adopt new life-styles that nurture such values. Devising social mechanisms and political structures that encourage genuine interdependence, in order to replace those which sustain domination and subservience, is an urgent task facing humanity.

The emphasis on holistic reality and the ethics of solidarity or communitarian ethics is very much ingrained in Indian culture and religions. But the onslaught of Western rationality and science has made us insensitive to those dimensions of indigenous wisdom. What is called for is a recovery of this vision and the expression of it in concrete forms and relationships.

The ecological crisis compels us to choose a sustainable form of development. It challenges us to be committed to values enshrined in eco-justice. It makes us aware of a new way of approaching reality which influences our faith-articulation.

The church's response

With some notable exceptions, the theology and practice of the churches in India have been heavily influenced by Western missionaries, with the result that, at least among Protestants, little thought has been given to linking faith with ecology. Indeed, we are inclined to view with suspicion any talk of nature in theology. Occasionally churches have adopted symbols and customs from our natural environment, but seldom have these been integrated into mainstream thinking or practice.

But the church's record is not altogether dismal. There have been bold experiments, responses which have the potential for challenging us. We need to examine them critically and affirm whatever is helpful and relevant. Mention must be made of the world convocation on Justice, Peace and the Integrity of Creation in Seoul, Korea, in 1990, with its affirmations and covenants on responsibility to creation, perhaps the first time in the history of the churches that such a significant step was taken to express concretely the church's response to the ecological crisis.

There are at least three models for this which the church can follow.

1. Ascetic, monastic model. This is perhaps the oldest form of response to some concerns related to ecology as well as the crisis created by the misuse of the natural environment. Renunciation is the key. Greed is identified as the source of the problem of ecology, and adopting a simple life-style is a way to suppress greed. "Small is beautiful" is the slogan coined by moderns who have been highly impressed with the monastic model of life. Living in harmony with nature and keeping their needs to a minimum, monastic communities proclaim the message that the earth is the Lord's and that it should not be used indiscriminately to satisfy human avarice and greed. They register a powerful protest against a wasteful life-style devoid of any sense of responsibility to the world of nature.

We see a similar response in the characteristic Indian or Asian model of relating to the concerns of ecology. Sanyasins and ashrams are centres where life in harmony with nature is consciously promoted. One is reminded of a scene in Kalidasa's *Sakuntalam*: when Sakuntala has to leave Kanva Muni's ashram to join Dushyanta's household, the plants and creepers of the ashram, and also its birds and beasts, mourn her imminent departure. Their hearts bleed at the idea of being separated from her.

In the church, this model has been instrumental in calling people to their responsibility to lead a life that is in tune with nature. The problem with this model is that it is addressed solely to individual life-styles. While the values enshrined in it are important, they are not adequate to effect structural changes and radically alter relationships that have assumed a systemic character. Today, we face a situation in which individual greed is organized in the structures of capitalism and the market economy, forces deeply entrenched in society and operating according to a logic of their own. A constellation of powers — ideology, multinational corporations, market and media control — influence our collective life. Individuals at best can only raise a voice of protest. Only collective action and countervailing power can alter the course of these trends. The monastic ideals could certainly inspire us in that effort.

2. Sacramental/eucharist model. Life and all its relationships are brought to the worshipful presence of God, where they are constantly being renewed. All things are received as gifts; therefore, they are to be shared. The cup is offered, blessed and shared. Psalm 148 is a beautiful poem that affirms the cosmic setting of our worship. We praise God in the presence of and in harmony with all creation.

In the tradition of the church, the human person realizes his or her cosmic being through contemplation. Cosmic power can be absorbed by humans. Particularly in the Protestant tradition, however, we have neglected this tradition of cosmic contemplation as a source of renewal.

A problem with this model comes at the level of practice. For many Christians, the meaning of the eucharist is confined to ritual observance, and it is not seen as a way of active engagement with the world. The body broken is rarely taken as an imperative for sharing. We need to recover the dynamic character of eucharist which can motivate people to be open to God's creation and re-creation.

3. Liberative solidarity model. According to this model, the church must be in solidarity with the weakest part of the whole creation. The roots of this contemporary model are in the Bible. Liberation theologians have forcefully articulated the biblical motif for liberation in Exodus and other passages. Salvation is liberation. Because of the immediate context, liberation theologians have primarily emphasized political and economic liberation. What must be affirmed today is that the liberation witnessed to in the Bible includes liberation for creation. Paul makes it clear in Romans that the work of the Spirit — freedom — extends to the total renewal of creation. Christ's work of redemption takes in the whole universe (Rom. 8:19-23). Christ the Lord of history initiates a process of transformation that moves towards cosmic release (Eph. 1:1-10; Col. 1:15-20). There is a unity between the hope for the inward liberation of the children of God and the hope for the liberation of the entire physical creation from its bondage and oppression. The work of the Spirit is to renew all of the earth. The Greek word *ktisis*, translated as creation, includes not only women and men, but all created things, including demonic powers. It is in the search for liberation of all aspects of human life — histories, cultures and the natural environment — that we can truly affirm that salvation is the wholeness of creation.

There is something common to the interpretation of liberation as a historical process in the exodus and the liberation process of creation in Romans. The former is linked to the cry of the oppressed (Ex. 3:7ff.); the latter is promised in response to the groans and travails within us and in creation (Rom. 8:22f.). God has heard the cry of the poor, and God is taking sides with the poor. In the same manner, the renewal of earth comes in response to the cry of the poor and of the dumb creatures and of silent nature. When God decided to spare Nineveh (Jonah 4:11), it was out of pity for the "more than 120,000 persons who do not know their right hand from their left" (the reference is to babies) — "*and also many animals*". God is not interested in preserving great cities for the sake of their skyscrapers, supermarkets and giant computers!

We are committed to a vision of human wholeness which includes not only our relationship with one another, but also our relationship with nature and the universe. We are also committed to the struggle for the transformation of the poor, the weak and the disfigured and over-exploited nature. Both mission and spirituality together are decisive for our faith.

The covenant idea in the Bible has also influenced this model of liberative solidarity. Both the covenant with Abraham, set within the framework of history, and the Sinai covenant, which affirms God's continued care and commitment to human structures and law, have assumed great significance in our theological construction and biblical interpretation. But the covenant with Noah and its cosmic setting are often forgotten. God is faithful in his promise to the whole of humanity and all of his creation.

This broader meaning of covenant was reflected in the 1990 world convocation on Justice, Peace and the Integrity of Creation organized by the WCC, which called all the churches to make a covenant based on God's covenant for the well-being of his total creation. The convocation called the churches to translate their response to God's covenant into acts of mutual commitment within the covenant community. Four areas were selected for specific "acts of covenanting", expressing concrete commitment to work for

— a just economic order and for liberation from the bondage of foreign debt;
— the true security of all nations and people;

— building a culture that can live in harmony with creation's integrity;
— the eradication of racism and discrimination, on national and international levels, among all people.

In India, churches should enter into an act of covenanting, and commit themselves to fight for the marginalized — Dalits, tribals and women — to build a just economic order, to commit themselves to sustainable development, justice, peace and integrity of creation in our context.

A new spirituality

We need to evolve a form of spirituality that takes seriously our commitment to the earth. Matthew Fox has coined the phrase "creational spirituality" and even initiated a new movement among the Western churches. Its hallmark is a deep awareness of God's gifts and presence in creation.

> Awe is the starting point — and with it, wonder. The awe of being part of this amazing universe... The awe is not of a pseudo-mysticism about a state or a political party but of our shared existence in the cosmos itself.[5]

In the Buddhist tradition, greed and acquisitiveness are identified as the source of bondage. Material progress is to be tempered by non-acquisitiveness and sharing. According to Aloysius Pieris,

> In the Asian situation, the antonym of "wealth" is not poverty, but acquisitiveness and avarice, which make wealth anti-religious. The primary concern is not eradication of poverty, but struggle against Mammon — that undefinable force that organizes itself within every person, among persons, to make material wealth anti-human, anti-religious and oppressive.[6]

Unfortunately, Asian spirituality has developed in ways that emphasize either individual moral behaviour or forming an exclusive community — a spiritual aristocracy. In either case, the spirituality of non-acquisitiveness, sharing and harmonious relationship between humans and nature, which are the hallmarks of true Asian spirituality, lose their neighbourly thrust.

This is also the spirituality of the poor, derived from their closeness to earth and sea and their communitarian mode of existence. It sustains them in their struggle. How else can we explain the staying power of the marginalized and oppressed who are being continuously crushed by the onslaught of violent forces? Alas, in our activist mode we pay little attention to this and thus fail to learn from it.

A conscious effort is needed today to express the biblical insights on creational spirituality. Materials for Bible study, worship and Christian education to help us celebrate and learn God's design for creation and human responsibility should be made available. "Steward" images that emphasize our responsibility, accountability and answerability ought to be studied. Many Psalms praise God the creator. The prophets unfold a vision of *shalom* as the fullness of creation, in which harmony is the characteristic mode of existence — beasts and humans dwell together, the lion and the child play together, swords are turned into plowshares. The prophet Amos asserts that to shed blood is to commit violence to the earth. All these establish a connection between social injustice and ecological degradation.

We should listen to our Lord himself: his closeness to the earth, asking us to learn from the birds of the air and the lilies of the field; his commitment to a kingdom that grows as a seed which germinates and sprouts, his response to the hungry, his breaking the bread and pouring out the wine. Finally, the salvation he achieved includes the liberation of all, and we hope for a new heaven and a new earth. To be sure, there are passages that talk about the complete destruction of all, but these are spoken in a way which will help us to turn to God and to reject and renounce our ways of violence towards one another and to the earth. To read them in a fatalistic way is to miss the central thrust of the gospel.

A new scale of values

An ecological perspective on theology and spirituality challenges us to re-evaluate our present value system and adopt a new scale of values. Some suggestions along these lines have come from a WCC consultation on "Sharing Life", which asks us to commit ourselves to the following:

— to putting the marginalized at the centre of all decisions and actions as equal partners;
— to identifying with the poor and the oppressed, and their organized movements;
— to mutual accountability and power.

In adopting a new value system we need to follow guidelines suggested by two decisive questions: To whom are we listening? Whose interests do we represent? Are we listening to planners, bureaucrats and technicians or to the poor tribals who are displaced? In the struggle of the fisherfolk, are we carried away by financial wizards who tell us about the importance of the export market and of competing with other countries?

One of the basic elements in value formation is the use of power. In Jesus we see that power values are transformed into bonding values. The New Testament clearly shows that Jesus was confronted with two opposing views of power: self-aggrandizing power and enabling power.

The former is the power that dominates, manipulates and exploits. This is the power of the autocrats; it can also be the power of the ardent crusader for the gospel. It is the power of the profit-conscious industrialist and of the party boss who strategizes against the opposition; it can also be the power of authoritarian bishops or clergy. Some use it blatantly, others subtly. Some use it for ends which are evil, others to achieve supposedly noble objectives.

Enabling power, by contrast, is the power that serves, cares for others and builds people up. Its strategy is an end in itself. The temptations of Jesus, his constant struggle with the disciples, the Last Supper, the washing of the feet — all these vividly show Jesus' own conscious rejection of the power that manipulates and his willing acceptance of the power that serves, the power that strengthens our bonds. The bonding values are integral to the ecological view of reality.

Values are expressed in life-styles, practices and structures. While we cannot agree upon a uniform life-style, a conscious and judicious rejection of extravagant and wasteful use of natural resources is a possibility and should be a priority for all. We need to put a limit to our needs. Slavish acceptance of everything the consumerist economy produces and the market dictates is contrary to ecologically responsible living.

In this connection, it is important to raise the question of responsible use of the church's own resources of property and investments. Property development is an easy option for many urban churches. Here we do not seem to follow any guidelines that express our responsibility to ecologically sound development. I am not referring here to the aesthetics of the building — although in this area too we could do better! By commercially developing our church property, are we not endorsing the logic and value system that governs much of commercialization which is ecologically harmful?

A few years ago, we addressed this issue at St Mark's Cathedral in Bangalore, situated in the heart of the city. Many commercial developers had an eye on this precious piece of land that belonged to the church. A great deal of pressure was brought to bear on the pastorate committee, which decided to turn for advice to architects and developers. At that juncture a colleague suggested that we discuss the "theology of the building" as well. His suggestion was received with derisive laughter by company executives and business magnates in the congregation. Nevertheless, he made his point. "What is our Christian witness when we enter into such an activity?", he asked. "By this activity can we raise any questions about the exploitative mechanism that underlies commercialization?" Although the ecological dimension was not explicitly present in that discussion, perhaps today we should add that too when we discuss our plans for the "development" of church properties. The eviction of the poor for the sake of development even from church properties is common. What is most surprising is that in such matters we seem uncritically to accept the logic of profit-oriented developmentalism.

A concern of all religions

Ecological concerns should be taken up as a common cause of people of all faiths. To protect our common home, we must mobilize the spiritual resources of all religions. The United Nations Environment Programme has called all religions to celebrate together the "Environment Sabbath/ Earth Rest Day" and has provided resources for worship drawn from Buddhism, Christianity, Hinduism, Judaism, Sikhism and Islam. It begins with declarations drawn up by representatives of different religions which together affirm that "the religious concern for the conservation and ecological harmony of the natural world is our common heritage, our birthright and our duty". Listen to some of the excerpts from the prayers:

Supreme Lord, Let there be peace in the sky and in the atmosphere, peace in the plant world and in the forests;
Let cosmic powers be peaceful:
Let Brahma be peaceful;
Let there be undiluted and fulfilling peace everywhere.

Atharvaveda

May every creature abound in well-being and peace.
May every living being, weak or strong, the long and the small, the short and the medium-sized, the mean and the great,
May every living being, seen or unseen, those dwelling far off, those near by, those already born, those waiting to be born,
May all attain inward peace.

Buddhist prayer

O God! The creator of everything!
You have said that water is the source of life!
When we have needs, you are the Giver.
When we are sick, you give us health.
When we have no food, you provide us with your bounty.

Muslim prayer

Be praised, my Lord, for Brother Wind
And for the air, cloudy and clear, and all weather!
By which you give substance to your creatures!
Be praised, my Lord, for our sister Mother Earth,
who sustains and governs us,
and produces fruits with colourful
flowers and leaves.

St Francis of Assisi

All these worship resources can be shared among people of different faiths. People can unite on Environment Day in praying for the earth.

Worship is not the only possible common action by different religions. They can also unite in measures that prevent ecological degradation through deforestation, pollution of lakes and rivers and the like. Every congregation may be challenged to undertake a specific programme on environmental protection in co-operation with people of other faiths in its area.

NOTES

[1] Daniel Chetti, ed., *Ecology and Development*, Madras, BTE/SSC & Gurukul, 1991, p.96.
[2] Jürgen Moltmann, *The Future of Creation*, Philadelphia, Fortress, 1979, p.128.
[3] Sallie McFague, *Models of God*, Philadelphia, Fortress, 1979, p.13.
[4] *Ibid.*, p.8-9.
[5] Matthew Fox, "Creation Spirituality", in *Creation*, vol.II, no.2, 1986.
[6] Aloysius Pieris, *Asia Theology of Liberation*, Maryknoll, NY, Orbis, 1988, p.75.

Social Ecology

A Timely Paradigm for Reflection and Praxis for Life in Latin America

Tony Brun

During a period when many of the academic activities of the Latin American Biblical Seminary in San José, Costa Rica, were emphasizing the theme of ecology and the problems posed by the environmental crisis, some friends asked us whether ecology had become the "new intellectual fad" at the seminary.

Our response was No. Ecology is not a fad; it has to do with a paradigm, a model for interpretation that is useful and urgently necessary for biblical theological reflection and pastoral praxis. In reality, ecology is a new worldview. There is no human discipline that is not challenged by ecology to question and even reformulate its basic principles.

At the same time, ecology is a novelty. As a human science and concern it is relatively new. In theology and ecclesiology, its newness is even more evident as the ecological perspective begins little by little to influence these disciplines. It is still missing from the majority of the well-known theological dictionaries and encyclopaedias.

Ecology offers us a timely paradigm, capable of producing a fruitful revision of some of our so-called "truths". However, the specific intent of this paper is to provide a motivation for dialogue and community praxis in which our concern with social and environmental issues can be integrated into our Christian testimony.

The paper is divided into three parts. The first, concerning social ecology and its contributions, serves as a theoretical framework. The second and third have a more practical orientation, offering some reflections and examples about humour, social ecology and Christian faith which we hope will be useful for church life.

Social ecology

In 1869 ecology was defined by Ernest Haeckel as "the study of the relationship between a living being and his environment, both organic and inorganic". At the outset, therefore, ecology as a science concerned itself almost exclusively with the study of animal and vegetable species, their environment and inter-relationships. Restricted to this biological realm, ecology was at first associated almost exclusively with the natural sciences. Towards the beginning of this century, however, many thinkers began to consider that this perspective could also be useful for the study of the human being; and different disciplines began to pay more attention to the human environment.

From the 1930s to the 1950s, human and urban ecology developed. Anthropology borrowed these perspectives in the development of cultural and anthropological ecology. Psychology developed "environmental or ecological psychology"; economics, geography and philosophy also made significant contributions towards helping to understand human behaviour and environment. But despite certain important contributions, this research was enclosed within its own epistemological matrices and its proximity to reality was only partial.

Many of the phenomena that have become evident since the 1960s, however, have demonstrated the close relationship between social and environmental issues. Nuclear radiation, increasing air and water pollution, the effects of uncontrolled chemical experiments, the reduction of the ozone layer and the deforestation of the earth stem from a reality that makes it inadequate to consider ecology as only a science of nature. "The social implications of the environmental crisis make necessary a type of ecology that can see and analyze the relationship between these two dimensions. As of the 1970s a social ecology begins to develop that seeks to overcome the break between the natural and the human sciences."[1]

Social ecology is the study of human systems in interaction with their environmental systems. This brief definition demonstrates the pertinence for Latin America and the Caribbean of the ecological perspective. During the past few years we have sought to bring to light practices and ideologies that are at the service of death.[2] The ecological perspective broadens our understanding of these practices of death, such as the damage caused to ecosystems by the disruption of their equilibrium.

Faced with this disturbing and unsustainable reality, our reflection and praxis need alternative paradigms that are more holistic and integrating. Even with the critical and intellectual progress resulting from the famous theory of dependence and its relationship to the social crisis, little attention has been paid to the environmental crisis in Latin America. Something similar (although it is being overcome) could be said about analysis of the foreign debt which is limited to a study of financial and economic mechanisms. Is this not the result of a dichotomy between human systems and environmental systems? The resulting inflexibility and the exclusion of the ecological consequences of the social crisis have reduced our clarity in proposing global solutions to our problems. From our America — not poor, but impoverished — we can no longer speak of social crisis on the one hand and environmental crisis on the other. We must speak rather of a socio-environmental crisis.

Human-environmental interaction has a long history. Throughout, the position of domination over nature has always been associated with the domination of man by man and of woman by man. In our species we find predatory as well as co-operative relationships.

In this sense we become aware that we have all incurred an ecological debt to nature due to the violence we have inflicted on it. But this generalization can be subtly reactionary as well as useful and necessary. Reflection on the theme of the 500 years of conquest has pointed out that with the invasion-conquest, an economic-political-military-cultural and religious system began to function that has allowed the nations of the North to exploit and plunder the peoples and resources of the South in order to secure their own wealth and well-being.

> This historic exploitation acquires today new and global dimensions and places responsibility particularly on the peoples of the North, whose model of economic development, characterized by idolatrous consumerism and industrialism, produces the greatest percentage of the contamination and destruction of the biosphere (80%) that reaches and affects all nations.
>
> In other words, the socio-environmental crisis has its origin in the crisis of the economic processes of industrialization in the North and to a much lesser degree in the South, but it affects the entire planet. [3]

It seems strange therefore, that during the United Nations Conference on Environment and Development in Rio de Janeiro in 1992, the issue of financing for a sustainable social and environmental development was the greatest point of tension between North and South.

> The programmes of Agenda 21 demand more than US$600,000 million a year, and this only for the developing nations. The conference itself considered that an annual financial transfer from the North to the South of US$125,000 million was needed in order to implement a different type of development. Meanwhile, only 10 percent of this total was found and only US$2000 million committed. This is nothing compared to the US$200,000 million a year that are captured from the debtor countries of the South by the creditor banks of the North. [4]

It seems difficult to accept that the remedy for this problem will come from the same place as the disease did. But it is insulting to accuse the peoples of the South of producing the environmental crisis, even worse if, by omission or intention, we pardon the system that creates social and environmental poverty.

As opposed to the North, where the environmental crisis is felt in a context of social well-being, in the South it is closely related to poverty. In Latin America, the dramatic situation of its natural ecosystems is related to the profound social problems.

This same Latin American perspective was raised thirty years before UNCED at the UN Conference on the Human Environment in Stockholm in 1972. In the words of Josué de Castro:

> Poverty is the greatest environmental problem of the region. To maintain that poverty is a primary environmental problem does not mean that the poor are the problem. On the contrary, we see in them those who suffer the effects of social-environmental deterioration.[5]

We must make way for a new language, a new method, a new paradigm and certainly a new praxis capable of recognizing the close "connection between the social issue (the survival of the peoples) and the environmental issue (the conservation of the biosphere)".[6]

Social ecology has emerged to challenge the dualism between the human sciences and the natural sciences in recognition of their connectedness. It continues the richest traditions of the environmental sciences with those of the social sciences which are committed to the human being. From a Latin American perspective, it reappraises the wisdom and culture of the original peoples with ethical respect for their diversity and a utopian and praxiological option for life, in which the goal of our knowing is not simply "knowledge", but how and how much it can contribute to creating broader spaces of freedom. Does it favour the effective expansion of life or does it limit and thwart the yearning for liberty?

Social ecology offers us one of the most timely paradigms for the search to reorganize society from a human and ecological perspective, starting with the interests of the impoverished majorities. This discipline reminds ecologists that there is a social component; it reminds sociologists and anthropologists that there are non-human components; and it reminds theologians that God's saving revelation has natural components capable of inspiring a spirituality that is less settled in the empire of reason.

Humour and the socio-ecological education of the church

Some years ago, on a wall in a densely populated barrio of Montevideo, I read these words: "Even the rivers, when their flow is enriched, wash away the poor."

This is popular humour — concrete and direct, but profound and full of possibilities, immediately evoking a chain of ideas, opinions and questions on political, social, economic, ecological and existential issues. This writing on the wall aptly expresses the connection that social ecology seeks between social and environmental issues and reminds us that social practice must never be isolated from environmental practice.

The educational environment of the church — formal or informal — is a place where a process of learning and integration between persons and between persons and the environment can take place. Because of its family and community feeling, the church can recover with evangelical spirit the value of daily life, the value of play and of humour.

In the following pages we look at the usefulness of humour as a tool for teaching the socio-ecological perspective in the church. But what relationship is there between humour and social ecology? In the face of so much dramatic socio-environmental violence, isn't humour evidence of a lack of seriousness, even an insult?

In spite of some warnings in Old Testament wisdom literature against "laughter and joy" (cf. Eccles. 2:2; 7:3), I want to affirm an authentic appreciation of the healthy psychological effects of humour and laughter. The constant effort for a socially and ecologically sustainable world demands a balanced "mental ecology". An indispensable ingredient is humour.

1. Humour is a way to speak about God. Humour is the sign of the presence of God, indicating his transcendence and manifestating his grace in us. We believe that God not only has love, but also a sense of humour. Karl Barth once wrote that "theology is a joyful science". Could humour overcome the heaviness of some of our theologies? Could it survive an excessively serious theology?

> And God saw that everything he had created was good (*Genesis*).
> And God saw that everything he had created was... (*XXI century*).

2. Humour is a way of speaking about humanity (and thus about ourselves). Humour is a universal human phenomenon. There is no aspect of human existence that is not tempted by the "gleam in the eye of the accomplice" which is humour, generous and creative, offering relaxation and freedom.

Why do we feel the urge to laugh precisely in the midst of the most solemn and sacred moments? And who has not felt that most primitive human reaction, the smile, when a grave and sombre celebration is ruined by the irony and mockery of unexpected events? This humour, sometimes felt but not revealed, is one way of reaffirming the validity of that which is common and ordinary, of the human and earthly.

> Laughter, in the most serious of times, not only releases tensions, it is also a way the human has of reasserting his own dignity in circumstances in which he may seem the most undignified because he is then the most dependent on forces over which he has no control. [7]

Could it not be that we laugh because in the depth of our consciousness we are convinced that God is also laughing?

> The human being recognized himself in nature (Karl Marx).
>   Poor nature!

3. Humour contains a liberating element which consists, according to Sigmund Freud, of

> its refusal to be hurt by the arrows of reality or to be compelled to suffer. It insists that it is in fact impervious to wounds dealt by the outside world. [8]

This "liberating element" of humour ferments the creativity to criticize the violence of the present and sigh for a different tomorrow. It is therefore in itself a protest against oppression. As a divine grace that anticipates liberation, humour is a powerful protest and also a powerful consoler. The history of humour conserves its grace; human beings can listen to it again and again because they need relief and strength to continue living. Leonardo Boff suggests that the appearance of humour creates "a feeling of relief from the burden of the limitations of life. The spirit feels liberated for a few moments... That is why human beings can smile and adopt a position of humour when faced with the system that seeks to contain and domesticate them."[9]

> The rivers aren't growing, the country is sinking.

4. Humour is indispensable for communion in the church. Humour rises spontaneously from those who love and feel loved.

> The non-serious world may be mutual love, communication. The joke is a social good; it carries on the smile, which is the doorstep to the human. To smile is sometimes to show that one is not so serious as appears, it is to palliate censure, to ensure a spiritual communion that the over-serious man

knows nothing of. To smile is sometimes to deflect the other from the closed world of self-interest so as to lure him into communion with the non-serious. All the more reason why laughter should consolidate the union of laughers; laughter has a social role like humour — that blend of the serious and the non-serious. [10]

Many churches give the impression that they believe laughter is incompatible with their vocation. They manifest their ecclesial and pastoral being as rigid and sad, as if they alone bore the burden of the salvation of the entire world. We need to learn to laugh at ourselves. It is most probable that our God-talk (theo-logy) is not all that accurate.

In our church, we are worried about ecology.
Really? That's great!
Yes, it seems that the pastor's salary is not sustainable and his sermons are recycled.

5. Humour inspires the utopian disposition. Genuine and religious humour is rooted in faith, hope and love; its joviality is founded in these theological virtues. Without a utopia, says Joan Manuel Serrat, life would be a rehearsal for death.

It is laughter that rocks the walls of hollow tombs. The force of it can roll back stones from those tombs, and the conviction of it assures the resurrection. Such religious humour may be one of the most noble capabilities that humankind has...

Humour teaches man that no conditioning altogether conditions him, and that everything that offers him resistance can also support him, as water supports fish... The man who smiles in face of his death already lives his immortality... [humour] draws men together and tells them that after the void of the leap their feet will find solid ground again so that they can continue on their way. [11]

6. We turn to humour because it has enormous value for education. Humour has a sense of what is relative and capable of untying the knot of the absolute. Perhaps this is why Rudolf Bultmann once wrote that "orthodoxy has no humour".

This questioning and self-critical character of humour makes it a valuable resource for education. In what follows we will apply it to the theme of social ecology, using as a starting point the comic strip "Mafalda" written and illustrated by the Argentine humourist known as Quino.

Experience has shown that with the following study materials, the readers' eyes move first to the comic strip. Its humour and its drawings captivate the attention, make us laugh, but also make us think and, above all, motivate us to continue. After a time, when we return to the study guide, the same thing will happen because "a history full of humour conserves its humour permanently".[12]

In conclusion, we affirm that social ecology is one of the most timely paradigms for Latin American reflection and praxis. While accepting this paradigm could mean revising, reformulating and even abandoning some of our truths, it would probably also mean the broadening and deepening of many of our questions. And if this paradigm moves us to a greater faithfulness to the God of life, it is welcome.

Two Bible studies

The two studies which follow are part of a broader work arising out of the conviction that much of what is written about ecology in the Latin American context does not respond adequately to the needs of most of our ecclesial communities. These studies are not recipes, but guides for reflection following the method of "observe, interpret, apply", tools for beginning a participative and popular socio-ecological praxis.

THE LIMITS OF ENVIRONMENTAL SENTIMENTALISM (JOB 14:7-14)

Quino

—"Let it rain, let it rain, the old lady is in the cave..."
—"Who could have imagined this social derivation?"

Looking at the comic strip

1. Look at the first two panels. What environmental elements do we see here?

2. How does Mafalda react when it starts to rain? Do you like the rain? Why? Have you ever done what Mafalda is doing?

3. Why does it rain? What produces rain? What role does rain play in the environment? What would happen to our country or region if it didn't

rain for an entire year? How would this affect the environment? And people?

Note: Mafalda enjoys the environment and is singing a children's song that continues like this: "...the birds sing, the moon rises, yes!, no!, let the rain fall!" This song celebrates the goodness of the environment. Such sentiments are important, but just as important is the social reality that we find around every corner. To enjoy the environment and want to protect it without relating this to more serious social problems characterizes a sterile and politically unproductive environmental sentimentalism, sometimes described as "pure ecology".

4. Look at the third and fourth panels. What has changed? What remains the same?

5. What feelings are reflected in Mafalda's face and in her words? Have you ever felt that way?

6. Natural phenomena such as rain, wind and flooding do not affect everyone in the same way. Why not? What does this have to say about the limitations of looking at the environmental crisis from a purely sentimental standpoint (pure ecology)?

Note: The dramatic condition of natural systems is related to serious social problems. Of the almost 500 million inhabitants of Latin America, more than 185 million live in poverty and over half of these are indigent. The massive exploitation of natural resources in the region has not helped their situation. Every year 700,000 Latin American children die during their first year of life; of the survivors, 15 percent will not finish grade school. Forty-five percent of the young people are unemployed or underemployed. To say that poverty is a front-line environmental problem is not to say that the poor are the problem but that they are the ones who suffer the most from social-environmental deterioration. [13]

7. Share your thoughts about the following phrase: "Even the rivers, when their flow is enriched, wash away the poor."

8. Think about some aspect of environmental deterioration in our neighbourhood or community. Analyze how it affects the poor among us, remembering to inter-relate the environmental crisis with the social and economic crisis.

Reading the scripture text

Note: Job 14:7-14 comes out of a dramatic experience of the innocent human suffering of the poor. [14] From our perspective we consider the text to be a critique of pure ecology or environmental sentimentalism —

preoccupation solely with the preservation of this or that species while forgetting the dramatic situation of poverty.

1. Read verses 7-9. What are these verses referring to? What words and elements refer to the environment?

2. What feelings does the environment's "cycle of rebirth" cause in you?

3. Like the comic strip, the text moves us beyond admiration for nature. Read verses 10-14. What are the social implications of this text?

Note: Job's words about the fleetingness of human life are not a philosophical reflection but a cry from out of the experience of his own miserable life. This is where he discovers with pain that he shares his adversity with many others. His questioning of God is not his alone; it takes shape in the pain of the poor of the world. A deeper understanding of this comes from reading Job's words in chapter 24:1-14.

4. Meditate on verse 13. What questions or reactions does this pathetic pain elicit? Have you heard similar cries? In what kind of situation?

5. In verse 14 the question of life and death remains, again not as a philosophical meditation but as the reality of one who knows he is close to death. But there is a note of hope. What is this hope?

6. How can we integrate our feelings and admiration for the environment and nature with the painful "environment of poverty"?

7. What practical things can we do in our community? For answering this question, which points us to action, it is helpful to think about the three subsystems of every environment:

— natural subsystem (rivers, trees, mountains, animals)
— constructed subsystem (streets, bridges, houses)
— human subsystem (people)

THE THREE MOMENTS OF AN ECOLOGICAL SPIRITUALITY (PSALM 104:1-24)

Quino

— "Well, Mafalda, what do you think?"
— "My Lord! This is so beautiful that humanity is going to have a hard time ruining it!"

Looking at the comic strip

1. Without reading the words, observe the details of the landscape, the faces of the characters. In your minds, add colour and smell to the comic strip. After a few minutes, share your impressions and feelings and the colours and aromas you imagined.

2. Have you ever been somewhere similar to this? What did you feel and see there? Share your "ecological memories".

3. Look at Mafalda's eyes, mouth, hands, body language in the first panel. What does this suggest about the first moment of an ecological spirituality?

4. What does the size and height of the characters in the second panel indicate? What does this mean in the context of an ecological spirituality?

5. Mafalda's first two words in the second panel suggest the second moment of an ecological spirituality. What is it? Why is it expressed as an exclamation?

Note: The expression "My Lord!" is not only speaking *about* God (theo-logy) but also speaking *to* God. This is the intimate relationship between spirituality as a devotional experience (contemplation, prayer, thanksgiving, adoration) and theology as discourse (speaking about God). Gustavo Gutiérrez points out that it is impossible to separate these two aspects. "Authentic theological reflection has its basis in contemplation and in practice. Every great spirituality has at its beginnings a level of experience."[15]

6. As a result of ecological contemplation, how would we speak of God? What images of God would our testimony of faith express? Can you think of some images of God that characterize testimony or theological discourse that is indifferent to nature?

7. The rest of Mafalda's words indicate the third moment of an ecological spirituality, without which contemplation and theological discourse would lack authenticity. How would you define this third moment? Why is it so important today?

8. To help reaffirm these three moments of an ecological spirituality, fill out the following chart on a large piece of paper or chalkboard by making a list of concrete things we can do under each heading to move in this direction.

First moment	*Second moment*	*Third moment*
Eco-contemplation	Eco-theology	Eco-commitment

Reading the scripture text

1. One person may read the entire passage aloud while the others follow, silently taking note of all the elements of creation mentioned in the Psalm. In our minds, let us add sound and music to the text.

2. The Psalm specifically encompasses the first two moments of an ecological spirituality: contemplation and theology. Observe closely verses 1-4, the acclamation that introduces the poem. What is the Psalmist's tone? How does he refer to God? What images of God does he use in his poem?

3. For discussion of the rest of the Psalm, divide into three groups, one for verses 5-9 (memories of creation), another for verses 10-18 (elements of creation) and a third for verses 19-23 (time). The following questions may serve as a guide for each group's discussion:

— List the elements and species of nature that are mentioned.
— What words or phrases jump out in these verses? Why?
— What is the relationship between the creator and his creation?
— What functions or objectives are fulfilled by the different aspects of creation or species mentioned?
— What harm has been done to these elements or species today? What has caused this? What effect does this have on life today and for the future?
— Think of hymns or choruses that reflect the attitude of contemplation and the theology found in this Psalm.

4. After each group shares its conclusions with the rest of the participants, read together verse 24. After hearing the Psalmist's exclamation of awe and reverence, conclude the session by expressing gratitude and praise to the creator in prayer.

NOTES

[1] J. Ramos Regidor, in *La Praxis por la Vida,* E. Gudynas y G. Evia, Montevideo, CIPFE, CLAES, NORDAN, 1991, p.6.

[2] See F. Hinkelammert, *Las armas ideológicas de la muerte,* 2nd ed., San José, DEI, 1981; *Capitalismo: violencia y anti-vida,* San José, DEI and EDUCA, 1978.

[3] Regidor, *op. cit.,* p.12

[4] Cándido Grzybowski, in *Tempo e presenca,* XIV, no. 265, Sept.-Oct. 1992, p.35.

[5] Gudynas and Evia, *La Praxis por la Vida,* pp.24-25.

[6] *Ibid.,* p.6

[7] Andrew Greeley, "Humour and Ecclesiastical Ministry", in *Theology of Joy (Concilium* no.95), ed. J.-B. Metz and J.-P. Jossua, New York, Herder, 1974, p.138.

[8] Cited by Marc Tannenbaum, "Humour in the Talmud", *ibid.*, p.141.

[9] Leonardo Boff, *Gracia y Liberación del Hombre*, Madrid, Cristianidad, 1978, pp.234f.

[10] J. Château, cited by Gérard Bessière, "Humour — A Theological Attitude", in *Concilium* no. 95, pp.85f.

[11] Greeley, *ibid.*, p.139; Bessière, *ibid.*, pp.90, 92.

[12] Boff, *op. cit.*, p.234f.

[13] Gudynas and Evia, *op. cit.*, p.35.

[14] Cf. G. Gutiérrez, *Hablar de Dios, desde el Sufrimiento del Inocente*, Salamanca, Sígueme, 1986.

[15] Gustavo Gutiérrez, *We Drink from Our Own Wells*, tr. Matthew J. O'Connell, Maryknoll, NY, Orbis, 1994, p.136.

Orthodoxy and the Ecological Crisis

Milton B. Efthimiou

When I first received the message on the environment of His All Holiness, the late Ecumenical Patriarch Dimitrios, to the entire Christian world, it was a jolt to me. Yet I welcomed it, because it forced me to acknowledge that the environment is indeed the responsibility of Christianity, and that at the very root of Christian theology, there is a biblical and, as far as the Orthodox are concerned, patristic ecological ethic and principle. Reading that document forced me into a further study of the relationship between Christianity and ecology.

The document begins: "Thine own of thine own we offer unto thee." These words from the liturgy capture the heart of the Orthodox vision and understanding of our relationship to both creation and the creator. Creation, ourselves included, is of God. We do not own creation but are the free agents through whom creation is offered to the creator. Whenever I utter these words in the divine liturgy of St Chrysostom or of St Basil, I think of the creation in relation to the creator as these fourth-century saints wanted us to; or, to put it in twentieth-century terms, to bring the spiritual, ethical, material resources of the church to bear on ecological problems. This is what Christian ecology is all about.

One might ask what Christianity adds to ecology? From a scientific point of view, Christianity adds virtually nothing! To phrase it differently, being Christian does not necessarily make a person a better ecologist. So why bring biblical Christianity or patristic Orthodoxy into the ecological picture? Let me take an example from Orthodox worship, which in my view is one of the most profound ways of understanding creation. In every vespers service in Orthodoxy throughout the world Psalm 103 is sung: "Bless the Lord, all his works. In all places of his dominion, bless the Lord, O my soul." This Psalm tells us of the sanctification of all creation. On 6 January every year, we bless the waters in church, which we then take to all homes, to fields of nature and to everything that lives within nature. We bless creation in this way with holy water.

The theological way of explaining this is that all natural elements show how the church recognizes, in the words of the message of Patriarch Dimitrios, "the transformation of all aspects of creation through the salvation and glorification of humanity and thus of all creation".

The most striking part of this blessing of waters, which also exists in the blessing of the water in baptism, is the following statement of hope: "Therefore, O King, who lovest mankind, do thou thyself be present now as then through the descent of the Holy Spirit, and sanctify this water... Grant to all those who touch it, who anoint themselves with it or drink from it, sanctification, blessing, cleansing, and health." Orthodox theology teaches us that hope is a virtue only when it is centred on God's will. Orthodox worship is a celebration of this "hope" in the will of God, whose spiritual power flows down to our level and gives us hope using all aspects of our senses: sight, sound, taste, smell and touch. That is why Byzantine icons take elements of the natural world — animals, plants, countryside, mountains, rivers — to show the transfiguration of God's creation and material world and our place in this world relative to our salvation.

For the Orthodox world, the most stirring aspect of Patriarch Dimitrios' message is the section dealing with the eucharist. The eucharistic assembly (to use a familiar phrase of Metropolitan John of Pergamon) is the most sublime way of addressing our harmonious universe or "cosmos", which is endowed with its own integrity, its own integral, dynamic balance, transformed by God the Holy Spirit through redemption and worship. To put it simply, material from creation in the form of bread and wine is offered to God with the acknowledgment that all of creation is God's and that we are returning to God that which is his. We are thus called upon to examine God's creation with due care and safeguard its integrity while making use of it. The very partaking of the body and blood of Christ means, as the patriarch's message says, that God "meets us in the very substance of our relationship with creation and truly enters into the very being of our biological existence".

Time is running out. Christian theology is reminding scientists, governments and religions of the world that we must be sober and realistic and acknowledge that the degradation of the earth reveals a moral dimension. The indiscriminate application of advances in science and technology, gradual depletion of the ozone layer, industrial waste, burning of fossil fuels, unrestricted deforestation, use of herbicides, coolants and propellants — all of these are a result of human sinfulness.

Unfortunately, the word "sin" no longer moves us. Yet environmental degradation is the result of our collective sinfulness, no different from the sinfulness of addiction to drugs, pornography or alcoholism. It is instructive at this point to paraphrase St Paul: "The things that I do not want to do environmentally, those things I do. And the things that I want to do environmentally, those things I never do, or seldom do." This is how the ecological crisis reveals its moral character. The difficulty is to get the churches in our communities throughout the world to reverse the lack of respect for life evident in the patterns of environmental pollution. This has to be counterbalanced by the interest of production and concern for the dignity of workers.

Look at the automobile. Who can live without it today? And yet, in the US, the automobile accounts for one-eighth of all the natural resources consumed. But the automobile is not the root cause of the sin. It is a symptom. It is related to the things we want to do, to be free to do. So the issue is not just one of giving up the automobile, but of challenging the entire system based on the lie of consumerism that there can be freedom without ecological responsibility. We cannot do without technology; yet, we have not learned to live with it, and that is what is helping to destroy the planet. Until we face this moral crisis and name the sins involved, we are not going to understand that we must curtail our freedom to use the almost unlimited possibilities our technology gives us.

Fr Andrew Rossi has suggested that we have to practise "voluntary self-divestiture". We have to divest ourselves of some of our possibilities for the sake of the earth and for the sake of our souls. This phrase "voluntary self-divestiture" is a reminder of the great saints and ascetics of early Christianity, who followed just such a path, not because they were denying life, but rather, through asceticism, to affirm life. One can see this in the writings of St Basil the Great, St Athanasios, St John of the Ladder, Isaac the Syrian, St Augustine, Gregory the Great, St Mary of Egypt, St Katherine, Sts Lydia and Phecia. To put it differently, ecological sin not only has to do with the degradation of the earth through deforestation and industrial waste and burning fossil fuels. The saints of the church teach us that nature is polluted and destroyed because of our basic human weakness, our basic human nature, which is not separate from the earth's nature since we are all part of God's creation. The lives of the saints teach us that God's creation is destroyed by the avarice, greed, gluttony, pride and all the negative passions of humans.

These are the real destroyers of nature. This is why there is an ecological crisis — because of our sins. The Greek fathers had a simple word which tells it all: *philautia*, self-love. We all suffer from the primary sin of self-love, the fathers tell us. It is the mother of passions. How do we stop it? Someone has remarked that we can only do so through "eco-asceticism". The only way to root out self-love is voluntary self-denial, a permanent change of behaviour in order to free ourselves from enslavement to those things and technologies that devour God's good green earth because of the socio-economic system of *philautia*.

Many Christians who profess a firm belief, without reservation, that God created everything and who may even oppose any teaching of evolution unfortunately seem not to see how their Christianity may have an impact on creation. They live and act in ways that may be moral and ethical, but they do not apply these principles to the earth and the environment. The words of Archbishop Iakovos, primate of the Greek Orthodox Church of North and South America, in a recent encyclical on the environment should serve as a mandate for us all: "We must not forget that life was given to us for the building up of good works, not for destruction and dissolution."

To continue to profess the gospel of Christ, to read and live the lives of the saints and fathers of the church, to act in a profoundly ethical manner while at the same time supporting the system that is destroying the planet — this is the ultimate contradiction for Christians. Orthodox theologian Gennadios Limouris puts this in a theological perspective relating creation, the kingdom of God and eschatology (the doctrine of last things). Limouris suggests that in a comprehensive vision of history, a perspective of time running from beginning (*arche*) to end (*telos*) and guided by the sovereign will of God towards the accomplishment of his ultimate purpose, the term "creation" implies an active creator, who demands something from human beings because of their unique position in the created order.

What is implied by both Archbishop Iakovos and Fr Limouris is that God's kingdom is not only a future event but is especially a daily ongoing experience and process.

And so we know what we must do! We know the Christian witness that we must have, a witness that recognizes the creator, a witness that develops a sensitivity to the suffering of all creation. We must hear and understand the words of a centuries-old exhortation in the Great Euchologion, or prayer missal:

> The earth is without words, yet groans and cries: "Why, all people, do you pollute me with so many evils? The Lord spares you but chastises me completely: so, understand and supplicate to God in repentance..."

Creation in Ecumenical Theology

Wesley Granberg-Michaelson

Only in the past decade has theological attention to creation emerged as a widely acknowledged point of orientation in ecumenical circles.[1] While this new focus is a welcome change from earlier neglect and suspicion and suggests new paradigms for approaching all of theology in an ecumenical context, it still poses more questions and challenges than answers.

Some perspectives on "nature" emerging in earlier ecumenical discussions demonstrate the obstacles posed to any serious treatment of creation as a fundamental theological point of reference. An explicit example is found in one of the preparatory papers for the WCC's world conference on Church and Society (Geneva 1966):

> The biblical story... secularizes nature. It places creation — the physical world — in the context of covenant relation and does not try to understand it apart from that relation. The history of God with his people has a setting, and this setting is called nature. But the movement of history, not the structure of the setting, is central to reality. Physical creation even participates in this history; its timeless and cyclical character, as far as it exists, is unimportant. *The physical world, in other words, does not have its meaning in itself.*[2]

Such a stance reflected well the theological disposition of that time. The "movement of history" was the starting point. "Nature" was secularized, and this was applauded. Creation here is nothing more than the backdrop or stage for the main drama of history. This was consistent with both neo-orthodox theology, which had a strong influence on earlier ecumenical thought, and the orientation of those who stressed the urgency of social and political revolution as the new starting-point for any ecumenical theology.

Movements of liberation in history were extracted from the biblical story and projected forward into the modern setting as the dominant paradigm. Creation was reduced to nature. Nearly everyone in the ecumenical movement seemed comfortable with statements like this one from the WCC's third assembly (New Delhi 1961): "The Christian should welcome scientific discoveries as new steps in man's dominion over nature."[3]

A new opening

The WCC study of a Just, Participatory and Sustainable Society (JPSS), initiated by the Nairobi assembly (1975), provided a new opening for looking at questions about the undergirding state of the earth within ecumenical discussions. This was largely stimulated by an important consultation organized by the WCC's sub-unit on Church and Society in Bucharest in 1974. A gathering of scientists, economists and theologians — including some of the key figures who had initiated the "limits to growth" debate — considered the prospects for human development and the role of science and technology. The Bucharest meeting introduced the concept of "sustainability" — the idea that the world's future requires a vision of development that can be sustained in the long run, both environmentally and economically. The evident limits to non-renewable resources presented a radical challenge to the common faith in progress and continuous growth, whether from traditional capitalist models or from socialist hopes for a restructuring of economic relationships. But concern over such "limits" to the earth's resources came into tension with the demands from poorer countries for development and economic justice.

The JPSS study did not resolve this tension, but it did open an ecumenical window to the need for respecting creation in its own right and acknowledging its limits as part of any vision of justice for a common global future. The JPSS effort came to an abrupt and premature end in 1979.[4] But the paradigm of "sustainability" took on a life of its own, even after discussion of it in the WCC faded. By the 1980s "sustainable development" had become the framework for the influential World Commission on Environment and Development (the Brundtland Commission) and for the discussions which finally led to the 1992 "Earth Summit" in Rio (the United Nations Conference on Environment and Development — UNCED).

The WCC's 1979 world conference on "Faith, Science and the Future" focused more directly on the relationship between technology and nature. It featured discussion of some of the undergirding theological issues, even while the debate continued between the North and South over limits to growth and just access to resources and technology. At the same time, worldwide secular attention to the seriousness of environmental issues, which began to grow in the 1970s, was forcing the issues of theology of creation more directly into the WCC's agenda.

The time was ripe for a new opening in ecumenical work that would address, both theologically and programmatically, the earth. It was becoming clear that the created world is not just the stage on which the larger drama of history is played, but has a key role in that drama itself. This was recognized clearly in the famous call of the WCC's sixth assembly (Vancouver 1983) for "a conciliar process of mutual commitment to justice, peace and the integrity of creation" (JPIC).

"Integrity of creation" was a new phrase in the ecumenical lexicon, and it cried out for definition. However, its very ambiguity proved to be one of its strengths, for it invited a new phase of ecumenical discussion. The sub-unit on Church and Society provided one forum for such dialogue. Particularly evident in the work of the sub-unit in the mid-1980s, following Vancouver, was the influence of process theologians like John Cobb and Charles Birch, who had long been articulate ecumenical voices speaking to the crisis of creation.

Various attempts were made to explore the theological challenges posed by the ecological crisis, and to ask what it means to affirm the integrity of creation. A small meeting in 1987 of scientists and theologians issued a report on "Reintegrating the Creation". Another consultation in Annecy, France, offered a clear definition of integrity of creation, and stressed that the theme of liberation applied to all of life, not only to humanity.[5]

But the most significant development came when the WCC's programme on Justice, Peace and Integrity of Creation called a major consultation on the integrity of creation theme, bringing together a wide diversity of perspectives and WCC programmes. Held in Granvollen, Norway, in early 1988, this initiative made it clear that the JPIC emphasis, among its other aims and accomplishments, was enabling new and widespread attention to the threats to the global environment and the challenges presented in reframing a theology of creation.

Central to the JPIC process was an insistence on the inter-relationship between the integrity of creation and issues of justice and peace. Some at Granvollen, including indigenous peoples, women and representatives from the Pacific, argued that the sequence of JPIC should in fact be reversed and the process should begin with the integrity of creation, which is foundational for justice and peace. That discussion would continue right into the JPIC world convocation (Seoul 1990). Meanwhile, some churches and groups, including the United Church of Christ in the USA, established new programme initiatives named "Integrity of Creation, Justice, Peace".

The report from Granvollen was divided into two parts, one exploring theological and biblical affirmations, the other beginning with stories and experiences of various groups of people. Orthodox participants offered an important contribution to the first part, and the Granvollen report helped to make the wider ecumenical community aware of the vitality of Orthodox theological perspectives in this area. While divisions over basic questions of theological method were apparent during the consultation, these did not prevent an agreement over the central questions. Its report concluded:

> The drive to have "mastery" over creation has resulted in the senseless exploitation of natural resources, the alienation of the land from people and the destruction of indigenous cultures... Creation came into being by the will and love of the Triune God, and as such it possesses an inner cohesion and goodness. Though human eyes may not always discern it, every creature and the whole creation in chorus bear witness to the glorious unity and harmony with which creation is endowed. And when our human eyes are opened and our tongues unloosed, we too learn how to praise and participate in the life, love, power and freedom that is God's continuing gift and grace.[6]

Granvollen, then, ensured the space for a growing ecumenical discussion of the integrity of creation in the two following years leading to the JPIC world convocation. Various regional JPIC meetings suggested further points of emphasis. Yet the ecumenical tension between justice and creation was by no means resolved. In fact, two programmes of the WCC, Urban Rural Mission (URM) and the Commission on the Churches' Participation in Development (CCPD), organized a "justice forum" immediately prior to the JPIC convocation precisely to declare that justice must be the priority and the starting point in the JPIC process.

The world convocation adopted ten affirmations and four "covenants". One affirmation declared the creation to be "beloved by God"; another, dealing with land, developed the biblical assertion that "the earth is the Lord's". Debate on these affirmations during the convocation gave a picture of ecumenical discussion at that point. Several participants stressed the intrinsic value and interconnectedness of all the creation, sustained through the presence of God's Spirit. Although no arguments were heard advancing the paradigm of divinely mandated and ruthless human domination over nature which would justify careless exploitation, there were clear divergences over the uniqueness of the human role within the creation and the meaning of humanity's creation in the "image of God". This did not give a licence for ruthless destruction; but what does this mean in terms of humanity's place and value over against the rest of the created order?

The covenants adopted by Seoul meant to call the churches to concrete commitments in the areas of justice, peace, creation and racism. The focus for integrity of creation was the threat of global warming and climate change. This began a long-term WCC programme addressing the practical, international policy-making issues as well as the theological questions involved.

The JPIC world convocation brought the challenge of global ecological issues into a clear place within the ecumenical agenda. Yet, as we have seen, the theological issues were far from resolved; moreover, the interlinkage between justice, peace and integrity of creation was still more of a slogan than a reality shaping WCC programmes and priorities.

The WCC's seventh assembly (Canberra 1991) provided further impetus for continuing this focus on creation and deepening theological understandings. The assembly theme, "Come, Holy Spirit — Renew the Whole Creation", and in particular the first subtheme, "Giver of Life — Sustain Your Creation!", opened these new avenues.

The sub-unit on Church and Society co-ordinated a pre-assembly consultation on the first subtheme in Kuala Lumpur, Malaysia, in 1990. That consultation made several important assertions. First, it stressed that concern for creation and the desire for justice cannot finally be seen as competitive, either theologically or in practice. It underscored the interdependence between them. Second, the Kuala Lumpur report further affirmed the intrinsic value and majesty of creation. It also outlined those voices which needed to be brought into a deeper dialogue around these insights, including scientists, theologians from various confessions, indigenous people, women and ethicists. And Kuala Lumpur drew attention once again to the meaning of sustainability. But perhaps most important, the report developed the relationship of the Spirit to creation, as set forth by the assembly theme and subtheme:

> The Spirit is God's uncreated energy alive throughout creation. All creation lives and moves and has its being in this divine life. This Spirit is in, with and under "all things" (*ta panta*). The Spirit strives to bring them to their full perfection (redemption). Because of the presence and pervasiveness of the Spirit throughout creation, we not only reject a view in which the cosmos does not share in the sacred and in which humans are not part of nature; we also repudiate hard lines drawn between animate and inanimate, and human

and non-human. All alike, and all together in the bundle of life, "groan in travail" (Rom. 8) awaiting the full redemption of all things through Jesus Christ "in the power of the Spirit".[7]

The assembly report urged a major ecumenical study project to develop further this theological emphasis, as well as practical steps, including a WCC initiative in relationship to the UNCED the next year. This latter suggestion was taken up following the assembly, as the WCC entered into discussions concerning a possible "Earth Charter", modelled after the Universal Declaration of Human Rights.

At the Earth Summit itself (June 1992), a major ecumenical gathering convened by the WCC issued a "Letter to the Churches" which underscored the urgency of the situation posed by the deterioration of the earth's capacity to sustain life. The message of the consultation was presented both in a booklet ("Searching for the New Heavens and the New Earth") and a video ("The Earth Summit — What Next?"). And this occasion served to deepen commitments by member churches and ecumenical organizations to address in their own contexts the challenges of building a sustainable future.[8]

Work after the Earth Summit was carried forward within the WCC's new Unit III on Justice, Peace and Creation. The Council's programmatic reorganization, which was implemented at the beginning of 1992, placed the former sub-unit on Church and Society together with the former CCPD as well as the Programme to Combat Racism, the Commission of the Churches on International Affairs and the sub-units on women and youth in that unit; and a staff team on "Economy, Ecology and Sustainable Society" attempted to reflect programmatically the interlinkage among these issues.

Two points of emphasis emerged. First, a consultation was sponsored, in co-operation with the Ecumenical Institute at Bossey and the Visser 't Hooft Memorial Fund, to explore more concretely how ecological issues change economic paradigms. Several economists, ecologists and theologians worked together on this occasion, which in some ways revived the focus on defining the sustainable society.[9]

Attention to the threat of global warming, which had been highlighted at the JPIC world convocation, also increased following the Earth Summit. Delegations from the WCC had been monitoring the international negotiations leading up to the climate change treaty signed at UNCED. Now the task became alerting churches to the issue, encouraging responses at local levels and advocating stronger international steps as the convention from the Earth Summit moved towards implementation.

A year-long process, including various regional meetings, led to the publication of a major study paper by the WCC for its member churches. It explained the issue, presented the international challenges it poses, set forth the theological and ethical questions which are raised and pointed to steps which churches can undertake in response.[10] The paper and a public statement on the subject were approved by the WCC central committee meeting in Johannesburg at the beginning of 1994.

In its conclusion, the paper returned to central theological issues, and declared:

> Many biblical passages praise God for maintaining and constantly renewing the order of creation... (Ps. 76:16-17). As human beings, we have to respect this order if we are to live on Earth. When the limits set by God are transgressed, the fragile balance can easily be broken. Climate change drives this lesson home. It makes the vulnerability of human existence plain and suggests that when humans think of themselves as masters of creation they have taken the course of self-destruction.[11]

An evolving discussion

What then has changed, especially in the last decade as the WCC has attempted to affirm, both theologically and practically, the integrity of creation? The following points stand out:

1. *Churches in the South as well as in the North are addressing the threats to creation as part of their mission and witness in their societies.* One of the problems that arose early and often in international and ecumenical discussions of environmental questions was a tendency to see this as an agenda of wealthy Northern industrialized societies and their churches. This has changed dramatically in the past decade. While contexts and starting points radically differ, ecumenical discussion today on the integrity of creation generally begins from the foundation that this is a truly global and ecumenical issue.

2. *The integration between ecology and economy, and the inter-dependence between the protection of creation and the demand for justice, is now widely accepted.* The ecumenical tension between these, and even the spirit of bureaucratic competition that attempted to reinforce a rivalry between them, has largely been overcome. Of course, in specific contexts, it often seems that choices are demanded between ecology and economic justice — between preserving trees and cooking food. But the ecumenical framework stressed by the JPIC process, which insists that in the end, the flourishing of creation and the building of justice are one, is now generally accepted ecumenically.

3. *Defending the integrity of creation highlights the critical relationship between cultures and Christian faith*. This recognition first became evident when the voices of indigenous peoples began to be heard more clearly. Increasingly, other voices as well have stressed that the threats to creation result from a conflict of cultures. Thus, the relationship of cultures and the gospel, which came into sharp focus at the Canberra assembly, and is usually seen as a missiological issue, also becomes a critical part of ongoing ecumenical exploration concerning the theology of creation.

4. *The relationship of the Spirit and creation has become a central theme in this process*. Canberra also underscored this relationship. Much of the ecumenical discussion in recent years has explored the presence of the Spirit within and upholding all creation. This has enabled interchange, for example, between Orthodox, feminist and indigenous peoples' theological perspectives in attempting to discover a relationship with creation that respects its intrinsic value and reflects biblical understandings.

5. *The paradigm of mastery over the earth has been replaced by a search for new models of inter-relationship*. There now is an ecumenical consensus that has moved decisively beyond the views which secularized nature as an object for domination and justified a careless and destructive "subduing" of the earth. Models that stress the "community of life" and look to the restoration of political, economic and ecological relationships have emerged in new ecumenical developments in both theology and ethics concerning the creation. Yet, more questions than answers are raised in the course of this search, and these form the agenda for ongoing ecumenical initiatives in this area.

Open questions

What are some of the issues which should engage the next stage of ecumenical encounters focused on the creation, the fate of the earth and the response of the church?

1. *How do we understand humanity's place within the creation?* In ecumenical discussions, this issue is far from settled. At the WCC's fifth world conference on Faith and Order, held in Santiago de Compostela, Spain, in August 1993, one of the section reports underscored this need, and called specifically for a new ecumenical study into "Christian anthropology" in light of the questions emerging from developments in the theology of creation.

2. *How holy is creation?* The discussion of the Spirit and creation begun by Canberra leads not just to affirming creation's "integrity", or its

intrinsic value apart from its utility to humanity, but raises the issue of whether and how creation carries the qualities of the sacred. Christian faith, historically, has always insisted on the distinction between worshipping the creator (which is required) and worshipping the creation (which is forbidden). But stress on the immanence of God's Spirit with the creation requires a more careful discussion of this issue.

3. *Is creation's natural, biological order altered by sin?* Much traditional theology assumed that the entry of sin into the world brought predation, decay and physical death to the natural world. Yet anyone who has kept an organic garden knows that, biologically, life comes out of death. Should not this be understood as part of the goodness, or rightness, of the creation, declared in Genesis? And does the power of sin point to an alienation in the relationships between humanity, the created order and God?

4. *Is God's transcendence irrelevant?* Most recent theological reflection on ecology and creation has rightly stressed the holistic, interdependent and relational nature of all reality. What has been discovered about ecology becomes a paradigm for theology. Some of the most creative work, ecumenically, in this direction reflects on the relational character of the Trinity as a basis for approaching our whole view of life and reality. But in response to this stress on holistic paradigms, some ask how we are to understand anew God's transcendence, or if such categories are still valid. This becomes linked, of course, to how judgment and hope are seen in relationship to the creation.

5. *What about orienting theology around place instead of time?* Some theological reflections from indigenous peoples (George Tinker, for example) and some Asian and feminist theologians (Kwok Pui-lan, for example) have stressed that traditional Western theology follows an agenda of time, asking when God's action in history was initiated and will be completed. But some non-Western cultures move instead around the questions of place. Where is God's reign discovered in relationship to the ground, the mountains, the water and the sky? Further, some North American writers, such as Wendell Berry, argue that rootedness in a place is critical to the formation of a culture and a spiritual life, which makes the connection between creation and God concrete in our lives and communities.

6. *Does ecological theology, reflecting on creation, provide a new paradigm for doing ecumenical theology?* There are striking parallels between ecological paradigms and ecumenical ones. All things aɪ interdependent, organically related. Diversity is the life of the whole and

that which actually enables unity. Connectedness is a given. Our "sin" denies or destroys the reality of this belonging to a whole. Is it not the case that present efforts to deepen the theology of creation also open up new paradigms for ecumenical theology, undergirding fresh understandings of unity and koinonia?

In the end, ecumenical theology does more to provide a method than to assure an outcome. In searching for a theology of creation that responds to global realities, the World Council of Churches has contributed to theological dialogue around the world through expanding the framework and the partners in the process. The range of theological views have been expanded chronologically, looking to "pre-modern" theologies as well as post-modern ones. Confessionally, crucial voices such as the Orthodox have been invited in a central place in this discussion.

Geographically, the WCC has helped to take discussions of theology of creation out of a strictly European and North American framework, making space for the insights which are rapidly emerging from the Pacific, Africa, Asia and Latin America. Culturally, an ecumenical framework has stressed not only the interaction of different cultural voices, but the inner connection between cultures and the understanding of creation. Liturgically, the foundational role of worship has been highlighted in ecumenical approaches which, in the face of the degradation of the elements of life, uphold sacramentally the gift of creation.

Future work, expressed especially through the WCC's new "Theology of Life" programme, will serve the churches well if it continues to bring these strengths of the ecumenical process to its study and work for the integrity of creation and a sustainable future.

NOTES

[1] A helpful summary of the history of ecumenical exploration of creation is offered by Lukas Vischer, "The Theme of Humanity and Creation in the Ecumenical Movement", in *Sustainable Growth — A Contradiction in Terms? Economy, Ecology and Ethics After the Earth Summit*, Geneva, Visser 't Hooft Endowment Fund for Leadership Development (available through the WCC), 1993. On the involvement of the Lutheran churches, see especially Per Lønning, *Creation — An Ecumenical Challenge?*, Macon, GA, Mercer University Press, 1989. From a Reformed perspective, the preparatory papers for the 1989 general assembly of the World Alliance of Reformed Churches give particular attention to creation and covenant within the overall framework of the WCC's programme emphasis on justice, peace and integrity of creation. For special attention to the theme within Orthodoxy, see *Justice, Peace and the Integrity of Creation: Insights from Orthodoxy*, ed. Gennadios Limouris, Geneva, WCC, 1990.

² Harvey Cox, ed., *The Church Amid Revolution*, cited by Douglas John Hall in the entry on "Creation" in *Dictionary of the Ecumenical Movement,* eds N. Lossky et al., Geneva, WCC, 1991, p.247.

³ From the report of the assembly section on "Service", in W.A. Visser 't Hooft, ed., *The New Delhi Report*, London, SCM Press, 1962, p.96.

⁴ For a fuller discussion of the JPSS programme, its ending and its contribution to the WCC's later JPIC emphasis, see my article "An Ethics for Sustainability", *The Ecumenical Review*, Vol. XLII, no. 1, Jan. 1991, pp.120-30.

⁵ The report from the former consultation appeared as one in a series of pamphlets issued by the WCC sub-unit on Church and Society in 1987. Presentations from participants in the Annecy consultation were collected together with some other contributions in *Liberating Life*, eds Charles Birch, William Eakin and Jay B. MacDaniel, Maryknoll, NY, Orbis, 1990.

⁶ Quoted in Hall, *loc. cit.*, p.249.

⁷ The report of the Kuala Lumpur consultation was published as a pamphlet by the sub-unit on Church and Society in 1990 and distributed to all members of the assembly participating in the work on this subtheme.

⁸ For a full interpretation of ecumenical involvement at the Earth Summit, see Wesley Granberg-Michaelson, *Redeeming the Creation*, Geneva, WCC, 1992.

⁹ The consultation report, cited in footnote 1, is *Sustainable Growth — A Contradiction in Terms?*

¹⁰ *Accelerated Climate Change — Sign of Peril, Test of Faith*, Geneva, WCC Programme Unit on Justice, Peace and Creation, 1994.

¹¹ *Ibid.*, p.32.

Ecology and the Recycling
of Christianity

Kwok Pui-lan

In Asian religious art the circle is as prevalent as the crucifix in Western Europe. Tibetan Buddhist monks make the sand *mandala* to enhance their visualization of the sacred. The serene Buddha or the *bodhisattvas* are portrayed in images of circles and concentric circles to symbolize inner peace, grace and perfection. Hindu mythology and religious art vividly portray the powerful symbol of reincarnation to address human suffering and finitude. People living close to the land have always described the movement of the moon and stars in a cyclical way.

The image of the circle is also important for women in both biological and symbolic ways. Women's bodies follow periodical cycles with significant hormonal and physiological changes. More attuned than men to the cycles of the seasons, women from time immemorial have performed rituals when the moon waxes and wanes. Today, women cast the circle in spirituality groups, learn to dance Sarah's or Hagar's circle to express their solidarity and create circles of sisterhood for fellowship.

Since the Enlightenment, Western Christianity has understood time and history in a linear and progressive way. The Prometheus myth was reinforced by developments in science and technology. But Christians with an ecological awareness have begun to question the presuppositions of the Enlightenment and the promises of technology. They have redis-covered "recycling" as a significant ecological and spiritual theme. When asked whether she is a Christian or not, Anne Primavesi, author of *From Apocalypse to Genesis: Ecology, Feminism and Christianity*, answers that she is a "recycled Christian".

Asian people, women all over the world and conscientious Christians suddenly find a common language when they talk about the sacred and the natural process: circles, cycles and recycling.

Ecology and women's concerns

Our present ecological crisis is a result of the breaking down of the great chain that connects human beings, all sentient things and nature. The disruption of the eco-balance due to disregard of interconnectedness has a devastating effect on the most vulnerable links of this chain: women and children in the Third World. Deforestation, acid rain, soil erosion and the indiscriminate use of fertilizers and pesticides lead to the breaking down of the local sustenance economy on which most women and children are dependent. An increasing number of women migrate to the cities to work as cheap labour in factories, and some of them end up selling their bodies in the flourishing sex industry. Others who cannot find jobs at home seek employment in the Gulf states and other newly industrialized countries. Many of these migrant workers are exploited and some are sexually abused.

Third World women do not benefit from development models based on industrial and technological growth. In fact, they have paid a heavy human price for so-called "national development" or "economic miracles". Women's productive labour and sexuality are exploited, and women's lives are becoming more subject to technological surveillance and state and corporate control.

Third World women are also blamed for causing the population explosion, leading to the disequilibrium between human beings and natural resources. Pharmaceutical formulas and new contraceptive devices are tested on Third World women and sterilization has been forced on great numbers of them. Technological advances such as the ultrasound test have had the unintended effect of selective abortion of the female fetus. Recent demographic studies have revealed that there are 100 million women missing in the world, 60 percent of them in Asia.

Technological control, a Western-oriented model of development and patriarchy form an "unholy trinity" dominating the lives of marginalized women. Participants in the 1992 meeting of the Ecumenical Association of Third World Theologians in Nairobi condemned patriarchal structures which dehumanize women, the denial of women's rights and economic and political freedom and all forms of violence done to the female sex. Such oppression is often condoned or reinforced by patriarchal religions, androcentric language and expressions and male interpretation of the classics and scriptures. Feminist philosopher Mary Daly has argued that women must speak of "gyn/ecology", an environment that is healthy for women's well-being and growth.

The recycling of Christianity

The ecological crisis and the degradation of women challenge us to reflect on whether Christianity has promoted inter-relatedness, mutuality and eco-justice. Many eco-conscious Christians are aware that an anthropocentric, hierarchical and patriarchal religious system is part of the problem, not part of the solution. Some of our traditional Christian beliefs need to go through a recycling process so that they can be reappropriated for the contemporary world. The idea of "recycling" is not new in our tradition: its meaning is anticipated by the religious themes of conversion, metanoia and even resurrection.

From a hierarchical to an ecological model. Feminist theologians have long pointed out that a dualistic, hierarchical understanding of God and the world is the root problem of Western Christianity. A hierarchy of being puts God infinitely above human beings and human beings above nature; a dualistic worldview separates the mind from the body, the male from the female and humans from the non-human world. The worth of an individual or a natural object thus depends on its position in the hierarchy, instead of on its intrinsic value and dignity. An ecological model does not project God as away from the world and above human beings. God, human beings, nature are interdependent and inter-related, just like the three interconnected arrows of the familiar symbol for recycling. A dualistic perception of the world must give way to a correlative and holistic understanding, just as each point on the circle is related to the centre and to the other points. An ecological model values diversity in the biosphere and respects multiplicity in terms of race, gender and sexual orientation.

From anthropocentrism to bio-centrism. Western Christianity places human beings at the centre of the universe. The whole creation was created for the benefit of human beings, who are to dominate over the fish, the birds and every living thing on the earth. Creation was condemned and cursed as a result of human sinfulness. But by the grace of God human beings are offered the possibility of salvation. They in turn can save the planet by assuming responsibility as sons and daughters of God.

By contrast, creation can also be understood by telling the story of the earth and the biosphere. Thomas Berry points out that planet earth came into being about 10,000 million years ago, and life on the planet 7000 million years later. Plants appeared about 600 million years ago, and animals arrived a little later. Human consciousness only came about 2 million years ago. The biosphere existed long before us, and its complexity has just begun to be understood by biologists in the twentieth century. It is arrogant on our part to think that the earth exists solely for our disposal, and that the salvation of the vast and expansive galaxy depends on just 5000 million human beings.

Western anthropocentrism thinks of God in terms of the image of human beings: God is king, father, judge and warrior. God is the Lord of history, intervening in human events. On the contrary, Oriental people and indigenous people who are tied to the soil imagine the divine, the Tao, as silent and non-intrusive. They speak of the earth with respect and reverence as the mother who is sustaining and life-affirming. A shift from anthropocentrism to bio-centrism necessitates a change in our way of thinking and speaking about God.

From passive spirituality to passionate spirituality. The quest for an adequate spirituality has become increasingly urgent in our eco-crisis. In the past, spirituality has been seen as synonymous with asceticism, spiritual discipline, meditation, prayer and otherworldly pursuits. According to a dualistic worldview, the spirit is against the body, the emotion and the appetite. We now need to speak of a holistic, bio-philic and embodied spirituality. Instead of being passive and emotionless, this new spirituality must be passionate, erotic and full of fire. It must move us to live with our full capacity, to seek justice in our relationships and to walk humbly with God and mother earth. It must evoke wonder and awe in us when we see the falling star, the autumn leaves and the morning dew.

This passionate spirituality must enable us to work for peace. Peace is not the absence of war or conflict, but harmony, well-being and blissfulness because of just relationships. Peace is not passively waiting for politicians and strategists to work out a solution for us, but passionately active in our local communities to empower the powerless, strengthen the weak and restore what has gone wrong.

A new solidarity in the 1990s

The challenge for the churches in the 1990s is to broaden our vision and deepen our commitment to work for the integrity of creation, justice and peace. When the ecumenical movement first took shape, the vision was to promote church unity to carry out the church's witness and mission. In the 1970s, people of other faiths were included through religious dialogue as a step towards building a wider human community. In our present age, the ecumenical movement must move from an *ecclesial solidarity* to an *ecological solidarity*.

The word "solidarity" originated in the French legal tradition, and referred to the natural bond of people of the same background. Later, this term was used by the Christian workers movement, and was understood by Marx as the self-organization of the oppressed. Its usage in Europe has implied a strong tradition of justice. However, people of Asia understand "solidarity" rather differently. In Chinese it means gathering together into one and connecting to each other. In Korean, it connotes binding one another into a circle. Its usage in Oriental languages awakens the ecological awareness of the interconnectedness of all things.

Ecological solidarity is closely related to the Ecumenical Decade of the Churches in Solidarity with Women (1988-98). The World Council of Churches has urged the churches to pay attention to women's full participation in church and community life, to struggle against racism, sexism and classism and to give visibility to women's perspectives and actions in the struggle for justice, peace and the integrity of creation. For many decades women of the Third World have been active participants in the struggle for justice, human rights, freedom and the integrity of creation. In the first world, women are among the most vocal leaders and visionaries of the peace movements and the Green movement.

Ecological solidarity means assuming mutual responsibility instead of seeking scapegoats and creating new victims. Indigenous peoples have been saying for centuries that the taking of their land robbed them not only of the means of existence, but of the meaning of life. Our world will not be safer if the testing of nuclear explosives, the dumping of radioactive wastes and the storing of nuclear weapons are done far away from Europe and North America in the Pacific. Our cities will not be less dangerous if the toxic waste is dumped in the Osage nation in Oklahoma or in the Rosebud Sioux reservation in South Dakota. Our lives will not be enriched if we ask the next generation to pay our debts and to be responsible for the mess we have created. We are part of each other, and the breaking down of one ecosystem affects all the others.

Ecological solidarity is our covenant with the land, the ocean, the forest, the rivers and the mountains. Without the hills, where else can we lift up our eyes to ask for help (Ps. 121:1)? Without the trees of the field, who will clap their hands when we go out in joy and are led back in peace (Isa. 55:12)? If we poison the Red Sea, even God might not be able to perform mighty miracles. Our covenant with nature is not based on fear and anxiety because nature is seriously polluted and its resources are limited. We need to renew our covenant with the planet earth out of joy, celebration and gratitude because we are part of nature and the natural process.

Theology of Life
and Ecumenical Ethics

Larry Rasmussen

Ada Maria Isasi-Diaz and Yolanda Tarango helpfully sketch theology's task:

> It is unacceptable to speak of Theology (with a capital T) as if there were only one true way to deal with questions of ultimate meaning. Theology is... acceptable only as a heuristic device that provides a "space" in which different theologies can meet to discuss their commonalities and differences in order to deepen their understanding. This conversation is an important one for the different theologies to engage in because the struggles to which they relate are interconnected. [1]

This paper treats theology as the "space" Isasi-Diaz and Tarango call for. It cannot and does not wish to substitute for the vital reflection of faith emanating directly from churches and movements engaged in inter-local, intra-local and international struggles. It does not claim or aspire to be a theological package which need only be "applied" or "contextualized" in order to serve different locales. Theologies that are not local are not real, just as an ethic that is not somebody's is nobody's. The theology here, instead, gathers recent ecumenical themes and with them offers an articulated space for the "Theology of Life" initiative which the World Council of Churches has embarked upon as part of its follow-up of the Justice, Peace and Integrity of Creation (JPIC) process. With discussion and improvement, it might outline a coherent framework for varied theologies of life as these find voice through the interconnected struggles that have shaped our lives in recent and tumultuous decades.

The formative biblical strands
The theological-ethical lines of the Hebrew Bible take their cues from the character and presence of God. This God, unlike many others in the god-rich world of the ancient Near East, was not recognized as simply a power or force in the universe which transcended human powers and

suffused all nature with its energy. Rather, this sacred power was a moral force that rejected the inevitability of oppression and injustice and commanded and made possible transformation of the world on the terms of community. Community and social justice were the focus of biblical faith at the very outset.

Hebrew conviction about this godly power included a very strong ethical component: we are morally responsible before God for the condition of the world. In the ancient world, where forces outside and beyond the control of human beings bore down from all sides, this was an extraordinary affirmation of human agency and freedom. It was the claim, set down near the beginnings of the recorded human adventure itself, that co-participation with God in creation is the human vocation! Few claims about God could have contrasted more sharply with cultures and religious traditions which pictured life as subject to great uncontrollable powers. These reigning powers — sometimes embodied in human forms and offices, sometimes in the forces of nature, sometimes in spirits and gods and goddesses — needed to be appeased, submitted to, prayed to, feared. For the vast majority, life was essentially fated.

That the God of the Hebrews was power for transformation towards a moral order in which humans played an important role was grounded in the people's own transformation. The God who "knew" the suffering of slaves and heard their cries was the God whose power was experienced as the power for peoplehood and freedom. This God created a people from a ragtag band who were no people. This God hewed a way where there was none.

This same God, these ex-slaves came to believe, held this new people responsible for the shape and condition of the community and world that was theirs. Their vocation as a "redeemed" and "saved" people was to give concrete social form to the ways of the God who rescued and redeemed them, and they were to do so in ways which made this God's own ways of justice and mercy their own.

In short, the governing power of the universe was not experienced or understood in the first instance as the principle of order and necessity — that might sum up fate and pharaoh quite well! — but the principle of freedom and responsible moral agency.

What began with Moses and the first recorded slave rebellion soon becomes, in the biblical account, a paradigm of liberation and transformation as a way of life. "A way of life" is, in fact, the heart of the Hebrew and Jewish endeavour (and early Christian as well). This way is always an ethic inferred from the character and presence of the righteous and compassionate one who showed them mercy. Yet the specific point at the moment is the conviction that with this God, ordinary people — indeed, the apparently powerless — can subvert deeply entrenched powers and help effect a new world. In Michael Lerner's words, Judaism was "not just a religion about how wonderful the physical world is but a religion that insisted there is nothing inevitable about the hierarchies of the social world". [2]

Jesus and his movement maintained the outrageously hopeful Jewish conviction that with this God new creation can happen at the waiting hands of a small number of very common, even hesitant, but emboldened and Spirit-filled people. Drawing chiefly on the early Christian readings of the Genesis creation stories, Elaine Pagels has shown that until the time of Augustine and Constantine the gospel itself is understood in terms of extraordinary freedom and agency for creating new community (in this case amidst a dying culture and epoch, a "passing age"). [3]

At the same time, Judaism was also what Lerner calls "a religion about how wonderful the physical world is". The liberating God was the creator of the universe itself. Thus the Hebrew Bible again and again celebrates the immense grandeur of creation, gives thanks for the breath of life that animates all creation — it is nothing less than the ongoing presence of the same Spirit which brooded over the waters of first creation — and marvels at the detail of a gracious God's good creation, knowing that Wisdom herself has been present from the beginning. A universal moral order is to be discerned in creation, it is claimed. Humans, while occupying a special place of power and responsibility within the orderings of life, ought properly to stand in awe of this universe, respect and learn from it, and humbly remember that like all earth creatures from *adamah* (earth, soil, ground), they too will return there. [4]

The salient matter, however, is that these biblical themes weave a single strand: the power that created the universe and sustains it from day to day is the same power that "champions the powerless and creates the demand for a moral universe infused with justice and compassion". [5] Psalm 77 is a striking example of this double theme becoming a single one, moving almost unconsciously between the ways of God as creator and as redeemer/liberator. Yet the psalmist does not begin in praise, but in despondency, hardly able to speak. Racked by the world's troubles and fearful that the Ancient of Days has forgotten to be gracious and has exchanged compassion for searing anger, the psalmist reaches deep to remember the character of this God of Exodus and to confess in awe, fear, and gratitude, despite feeling all the weight of the world's woes.

Lerner summarizes well this "double helix" genetic ribbon of the faith: "Celebration of the grandeur of creation goes hand in hand with transformation of the social world."[6] To illustrate, he cites sabbath. Sabbath is both a day to give thanks for life and the blessing of creation and a day to remember liberation from slavery and our vocation of doxological witness to God as creator and redeemer.[7]

"God as creator and redeemer" invites theological and moral reflection on the contested relationship of creation and redemption in a theological ethic of life. Again, important clues are found in Hebrew scriptures.

Israel is redeemed from Egypt. Egypt is portrayed as the historical embodiment of the forces of chaos, that is, the powers of death, the anti-creational forces of the cosmos. And Israel is redeemed for a vocation — to embody redeemed creation as community. Israel is redeemed *for* life, even abundant life.

But there is no return to Eden or any normative Golden Age. Even the Promised Land, though rich with creation's bounty, is not pictured as the lost Garden of the Tree of Life. This is significant as implied commentary on the relation of redemption to creation, just as the choice to place Genesis before Exodus in the canon is significant. God's creative purpose for the whole universe (Gen. 1-11) is set out first in sacred scripture, and even the acknowledged "fulcrum text" of the election of Abraham (Gen. 12:1-3) immediately ties this election to "all the families of the earth".

Why no Eden, no Golden Age, no utopia, no portrayal of a fixed, normative created order? Why in fact are Adam and Eve themselves virtually absent from the rest of the Hebrew Bible? Is it because creation is not only not static, but not complete? The very commands of God in Genesis — to be fruitful and multiply (given to fish, birds and human earth creatures), to till and keep (to humans), to join in ongoing creation and joyful sabbath (extended to all creatures) — would seem to say that "good" here does not entail complete development or perfection. Divine creating is living, dynamic, continuing, unfinished. Old Testament scholar Terence Fretheim even says that "for the creation to stay just exactly as God originally created it would be a failure of the divine design". God's creating activity is not "exhausted in the first week of the world!"[8] All creation participates dynamically in it from one generation to the next.

Redemption serves creation. Redemption means reclaiming broken or despoiled or incomplete creation for life. It is not extra-creational or extra-human, much less extra-terrestrial! Redemption is Spirited actions, often very ordinary everyday ones, against the anti-creational forces that degrade and destroy. Yes, the ultimate goal is "a new heaven and a new earth". But even the most apocalyptic writings see this, like John of Patmos, as a radical transformation of the created order and not its utter obliteration in favour of realms literally out of this world.

Negatively, redemption means freeing Israel (and all creation) from all that oppresses or victimizes. Its reach is from inner spirit to socio-political and economic spheres to cosmic realms. Positively, redemption means realizing the life potential of all things.

Israel's own vocation is to become, in Fretheim's words, "a created co-reclaimer of God's intentions for the creation".[9] That vocation is as a "witness to the nations", however, and as such signals for all peoples their vocation as co-participants and "created co-reclaimers" of God's creating in the direction of and for the purposes of abundant life. Why does God redeem? For one reason only: because life and blessing are not yet gifts for all, or are precious gifts endangered.

We add that our own era has witnessed what we did not think possible: that human activities could overwhelm creation with chaos, life with death. We had not imagined, and do not yet comprehend, that we have in actual fact taken up a new vocation as co-*un*-creators, and on a scale that outstrips the potential of all previous generations.

To summarize: whatever else theology of life and ecumenical ethics might mean, they root here in the strong biblical sense of moral responsibility before the God who is the power in and of creation and the transcending power who beckons the redeeming transformation of creation in the steady direction of compassion and justice. From this God we receive the gift of life. Before and with this God, we are responsible for it.

But of course the theology of life does not end here. Indeed, neither does the Bible! The Bible's own moral trajectory remains incomplete, a matter of which the biblical communities were painfully aware and of which the prophets and Jesus constantly reminded them. The "good news" for some was sometimes bad news for others or no news at all. Good news for Abraham and Sarah was bad news for Hagar and Ishmael. Good news for freed slaves became bad news for peoples they took as slaves. The social patriarchy that runs throughout Scripture, even against its own theme of liberation and shared power, continues as bad news for women. Sexual ethics and Greek renditions of gender, nature, body and mind in Hellenistic Judaism itself — and thus in formative Christian beginnings — continue as bad news for many to this day. Jewish biblical scholar Tikva Frymer-Kensky's conclusion is thus profoundly "biblical" when she says that "it is now our task to weave the rest of the Bible's religious faith..., in particular those [areas] that deal with the incorporation of all aspects of physicality, into our religious view of the universe".[10]

That is our task and more. The purpose of this opening section is only to say that while the biblical "moral project" of life clearly remains incomplete, an ecumenical theology and ethic of life should pursue it within the space marked by two interwoven themes: the healing, mending and transforming of the world (tikkun olam) and the celebration of the gift of life itself as the gracious creation of a suffering and caring God in an awesome universe. The Bible's own theology of life turns on these themes.

The contribution of science

The next contribution, offered by science, jumps from ancient sacred texts to recent discoveries.

A theology and ecumenical ethic of life poised at the cusp of a new millennium on an overburdened planet would do well to set before the eyes of faith the extraordinary unity we share with one another and all things, living and non-living. The unity is vividly supplied by two pictures science offers.

The first is the perspective presented by photographs of planet earth from space. The small blue, brown, green and white marbled planet, riding a tiny orbit in a vast universe, vividly says that we are all inhabitants of a single round space, occupants of one home, members of one finite, enclosed life-system. There may be life elsewhere in one of some 100,000,000,000 galaxies with billions and billions of stars each, but if so, we don't know of it. So far as we know, this fertile planet is the only Noah's Ark of life in the universe. Its thin envelope of life, then, is its distinctive feature.

The stirring image from space is more important as an image, even a religious image, than as an analysis. The latter is drawn from other satellite studies as well as innumerable ground-level ones. These show that for the first time in history human beings are slowly closing down the basic life systems of the planet and are actually changing their biophysical make-up in unprecedented, comparatively rapid and degrading ways. This includes the enveloping atmosphere itself. "The stark sign of our time is a planet in peril at our hands," says the blunt language of the WCC's Canberra assembly.[11]

The thirty years since the WCC's watershed world conference on Church and Society (Geneva 1966), have accelerated what Hannah Arendt identified shortly before that meeting as the distinctive and highly problematic mark of the twentieth century: we no longer "observe or take material from or imitate processes of nature [only] but seem actually to act into it". Furthermore, we seem "to have carried irreversibility and human unpredictability into the natural realm, where no remedy can be found to undo what has been done" or where undoing itself involves further destruction. This new capacity to act has a new level of consequences. Soon it not only begins "to overpower and destroy" humans themselves but also "the conditions under which life was given" to us. [12] This is the negative reality of occupying one space, one home, one round, finite, enclosed system, one saturated planet.

But whether viewed negatively or positively, *oikos* as "the household of life" is certainly the right word and symbol for our reality! Never has "oikoumene" been so important a notion or carried so rich a burden and message. "Ecumenical" does indeed mean the whole inhabited world — humankind and otherkind together in a precarious and undeniable unity of life and death. And "ecumenics" means realizing right relationship among the diverse members of the household so as to foster the flourishing of life for all. "Economics" means the "law" (*nomos*) of the household (*oikos*). It means arranging those societal systems which provide for the material well-being of all the planet's members and abiding by the rules of the ecosystems upon which each and every economic system is utterly dependent. "Ecology" is knowledge of the "house rules", or the "logic" (*logos*) of the oikos. It is knowledge of the inter-relationship of organisms and their environment and of the mutual requirements for life together. On the grandest scale, it means living in accord with earth's basic requirements as a total biospherical system, including human society as the single most decisive element of that system. It means, in other words, acknowledging and respecting the integrity of creation and thus restraining human appetites in order to abide within nature's needs for its own regeneration and renewal. *Oikonomos* is usually translated "steward". But that is a weak way to signal broad human responsibility for the world we affect, a task entrusted us by no less than the creating, redeeming, sanctifying God.

For a life-centred ecumenical ethic, all this means just what Sallie McFague says: "The moral issue of our day — and the vocation to which we are called — is whether we and other species will live and how well we will live." [13] Posed differently as a question: Is koinonia possible for the oikoumene on terms within hailing distance of shalom? Can koinonia encompass the fullness of life as the well-being of society and nature together?

The real and frightening unity of a common dynamic and destiny on a small planet is only one of the crucial reports offered by recent science. The other, potentially as important, is quite different at first glance. It is the common creation story now available from scientists and theologians alike.

We, and all else, are variations on exactly the same thing — stardust. The atoms in our bodies, and all atoms everywhere, were born in the supernova explosions of early stars. Everything is thus radically "kin" from the very beginning. When you look at the Southern Cross, Orion or the Big Dipper, the gnat on your arm, the flower near your path or the food on your plate, you are gazing at a neighbour who shares with you what is most basic of all — common matter together, as old and venerable as time and space themselves. In fact, if you look at more recent complex forms of life — plants and animals — you observe molecules which are very much the same. The most basic functions of cells are exactly the same in all life-forms. DNA and RNA processes and cell division processes are identical across life forms. (The DNA molecule specifies the characteristics of all living organisms, from bacteria through human beings.) "The wonderful lesson to come out of biology in the last five years," Victoria Foe explains, "is the same genes, the same parts, turn up again and again, from one species to another... The important lesson to realize is that we're all made of the same fabric, we're part of the same web."[14] The reason is remarkable: all life forms apparently share the same ancestor. We (all life forms) emerged from an ancient single-celled being.[15]

What could be a more radical and visible ecumenical unity than this! All that is (*ta panta*) has a common origin and is related in its most basic being.

Everything is also radically diverse and unique. Regrettably, we have poor eyesight and a cramped imagination, so we see and understand little of what surrounds us. Annie Dillard tells of biologists finding in one square foot of topsoil only one inch deep "an average of 1,356 living creatures... including 865 mites, 265 springtails, 22 millipedes, 19 adult beetles, and various numbers of 12 other forms..."[16] This does not include what may be up to two thousand million bacteria and millions of fungi, protozoa, algae and innumerable other creatures which make the topsoil the one inch of *adamah* it is![17]

Or, looking in another direction, we soon lose the capacity to take in what we can see or even imagine. We can take in a mountain or a portion of a forest or the horizon of a desert, the horse, the hut, the corn and the weather. But beyond that we can hardly even imagine our own galaxy, the Milky Way. This, our home port, is 100,000 light years in diameter and has somewhere between ten billion and one hundred billion stars (our census is crude). Nor can we quite imagine what fifteen billion years is (the age of the universe thus far).

The upshot is that the enduring unity that has been ours (humankind's and all else's) from the very beginning has evolved as highly complex networks characterized by staggering differentiation (how many varieties of mushrooms or coniferous trees are there?) and even implausible individuation (how many zebras have the same pattern of stripes?). Genetics itself teaches the uniqueness of the individual. Life — no, life and non-life, organic and inorganic matter together and continuous — is a radical unity marked by inter-related and interdependent fecundity and variety whose detail and wonder escapes our shrivelled sight and imagination. When we do catch a glimpse, we are moved to psalms. But that is, alas, too rare a response. Most of the time we just assume that life is, and will go on.

The diversity and individuation we have described has its own expression within the human species. Our lives are concrete, particular and different. We are who we are in different places with different cultural, linguistic, religious, political, economic and gender traditions. We differ one from the next; no two among the five billion of us is a clone of the other. And if we could peer backwards or forwards a few thousand years, we might find it difficult even to recognize our genetic forebears and posterity as persons with whom we could share an afternoon's conversation about almost anything. Life, even life within the same "kind", is a many-splendoured thing.

This, then, is science's second contribution: the stunning portrayal of a common creation in which we are radically united with all things living and non-living, here and into endless reaches of space, and at the same time radically diverse and individuated, both by life-forms and within life-forms. And all of it is not only profoundly inter-related and inseparably interdependent but highly fine-tuned so as to evolve together. We are all — the living and not living, organic and inorganic — the outcome of the same primal explosion and same evolutionary history. All internally related from the very beginning, we are the varied forms of stardust in the hands of the creator God. This reality is the most basic text and context of life — and a theology of life.

One may hope that the sense of our home as this *oikos* in this *cosmos* will stimulate the same sense of creation's grandeur and eucharist (thanksgiving) to God for the gift of life which the biblical communities knew. But we should do even better, because this is in fact a description of immensity and intricacy which far surpasses anything known by the biblical communities. The weight of the nucleus of an atom of life (1,000,000,000,000,000,000,000,000 times less than a gram), the incomprehensible "genius" of DNA, the vastness of a cosmos we hardly have measures for — all this eluded even the most awestruck psalmist or the most imaginative prophet with their bold visions of creation redeemed. Little wonder that Thomas Berry calls the universe itself the primal expression of the divine and the primary revelational event. Little wonder he urges us all towards a mystique of the cosmos and the earth and says that "the universe, by definition, is a single gorgeous celebratory event".[18] Neither theology nor ethics has truly fathomed what science presents us as bearers of meaning and power and as cosmic story-tellers in an infinitely magnificent evolution, an evolution which is, however, gravely threatened by our presence, at least on the only *oikos* we know and the only one that is fine-tuned for our survival. We must pray aloud in deep humility before life's creator and sustainer and bow before all else (such as green plants) upon which we depend for every breath we take and every morsel that passes between our teeth.

Let us post a criterion in passing. Any "God-talk" in the necessarily particular theologies of life of different traditions and locales which has a notion of God that does not include the entire fifteen billion-year history of the cosmos and does not relate to all its entities, living and non-living, ancient forms and very recent ones (such as humans), speaks of a God too small.[19] Any theology of life which does not assert both radical unity and radical differentiation as reality and necessity together also fails.

Yet the universe as "a single gorgeous celebratory event" is not all that life says to us. There is also utter wretchedness and awful oppression. Indeed, it is not at all clear from either scientific evidence or common experience that life will triumph over death, at least in forms hospitable to us and numerous other of God's beloved creatures. In fact, it is the threats to life, rather than the celebration of it, that stimulated the ecumenical theology and culture of life initiative in the first place. So amidst deep and deepening gratitude for life, the turn is to healing and tending and transforming, with God, the fragile creation of which we are immensely privileged to be part. Anything less consigns millions to the most common and worst forms of hell we know. The contributions of science thus move with urgency into the concerns of life-centred ecumenical ethics and the quest for cultures of life.

Life-centred ethics

In an essay on "Latin America and the Need for a Life-Liberating Theology", Ingemar Hedström writes:

> In light of [the] ravaging of people and land in Central America, we realize that the preferential option for the poor, characteristic of Latin American liberation theology, must be articulated as a preferential option for life. To exercise this option is to defend and promote the fundamental right to life of all creatures on earth. The right to life in all its fullness involves partaking of the material base of creation, that is, of the material goods that permit life. All people, and not the powerful alone, must be availed of such goods; all people, not the powerful alone, must do so in a way that reserves rather than despoils the earth and other forms of life. In order to exercise this right in a just and sustainable way, we must rediscover our primal roots in the earth, as creatures of the earth. [20]

Ravaging of people and land. Hedström begins his essay with a citation from J. Combe and N. Geward: "All the great civilizations of the world began with the felling of the first tree... the majority of them disappeared with the felling of the last."

A life-centred ecumenical ethic begins with "the material base of creation, that is, of the material goods that permit life". The initial reason is confessional. Christianity, despite its checkered history under the influence of earth-denying and body-denying spiritualities, is radically a religion of incarnation. God is mediated in and through embodiment. God is sacramentally present as life in "the material goods that permit life". God is in, with and under the finite and creaturely. The second person of the Trinity is utter commitment to and testimony of the "physicality" of God in covenant with the earth, just as the first person expresses the unutterable mystery of God and the third person God's radical immanence and transcendence in the Spirit. [21] "The end of God's ways," Dietrich Bonhoeffer liked to quote from F.C. Oetinger, "is bodiliness."

The confessional statement is also a moral one. It means ethical priority for basic creaturely needs, lest "people and land" continue to be "ravaged" and God's good creation ever and again violated. We can discuss this dimension of a life ethic with commentary on two topics: community (koinonia) and power.

"We commit ourselves anew to living as a community which cares for creation," said the WCC Canberra assembly. [22] But what does a caring community require?

For life, creatures need space. Without adequate hospitable habitat, we do not live. This is not only the case for humans, with our needs for food, water, shelter, work and festivity. All life-forms need particular space and habitat carefully fitted for them. This is the great element of "democracy" in life and its requisite equality: we all need a space for the basics of life itself. [23] Without that which good space provides — productive land, a hospitable atmosphere and healthy water, the numberless forms of life that provide for one another in intricate and astounding ecosystems — none of the other goods we cherish, including artistic and spiritual ones, is even possible. If justice means the fullest possible flourishing of creation under the conditions of various limits and constraints, then nothing is more basic to justice than adequate space for life's basics. It is the first requirement of community and thus the foundation of koinonia.

This leads Sallie McFague to the provocative remark that "geography... may well be the subject of the twenty-first century", since it raises questions like: Where is the best land and who has access to it? What good space is available on this planet and who controls it? Who cares for it? Who will inherit it and what will they receive?[24]

We do not inhabit abstract "space". We live in highly particular spaces and places, in particular and dynamic economic, social, ethnic, political, cultural and religious communities and hierarchies. So the question of "space" is specific, a matter of the tangled worlds we inhabit, worlds often in deep conflict over space and place. Issues of justice, peace and the integrity of creation come home as mundane issues within human populations as well as between human populations and other populations. Here, too, the ethical priority is basic creational needs. For this reason, "the ecological sin is the refusal of the haves to share space and land with the have-nots". [25] Whether we name this *the* sin, as McFague does, or some other viable candidate, the point is much the same: no life-centred ethic can bypass either human requirements in their differences (what is needed for a particular people at a particular time for a viable habitat and way of life) or the requirements of non-human populations (what other species in their differences need for their own viable habitat). All discussions of koinonia should begin here.

One phenomenon of recent times is that viable community is breaking down almost everywhere, and we are amidst a long season of unavoidable and dangerous social experimentation in which the need is to preserve and build up sustainable local community while at the same time developing regional and global institutions of widespread participation. Churches have indispensable roles to play in this, both in the creation of koinonia within their own membership and in joining with movements of broader membership. This is the case whether the subject is an economics of sustainability, equity and solidarity, or reconciliation of groups at deep odds with one another and the mediation of conflict, or the slow upbuilding of civil society and basic moral formation for viable community.

A life-centred ecumenical ethic finally turns on the issue of power. It does so in many ways.

The first is the recognition that the distinctive mark of our epoch is the quantum leap in human power to affect all of life in fundamental and unprecedented ways. Some of this is because of new capacities. Some stems from sheer cumulative effect (5 thousand million people going about their lives, rather than the 1.6 thousand million at the turn of this century). Some of it is the heavy and wildly disproportionate impact of certain populations (essentially the affluent nations and allied élites). But the outcome is that any ethic which does not track the effects of power in all relationships, intra-human and between human and otherkind, is blinded to the key moral reality of the age. Sustainable society and community cannot happen apart from power and its transformations.

There is another reason why a viable theological ethic of life turns on the matter of power. It lies at the heart of faith. It may come as a surprise to some, but Christians rarely talk about anything but power (despite their occasional reluctance about the word). Power claims are intrinsic to Christian ways of leaning into the world. The theme shakes itself loose in hymnody ("Holy, holy, holy, Lord God *Almighty*..., perfect in *power*, in love and purity"), in classic confessions ("We believe in God, the Father *Almighty*..."), in the most familiar prayer of all ("For thine is the kingdom, the *power* and the glory"), in preaching ("Our God is *able*..."), and in the first believers' convictions ("For the kingdom of God depends not on talk but on *power*" — 1 Cor. 4:20). None of this should be a surprise, since the scriptures themselves consistently portray God as power. God is the power to create, destroy, plant and pluck up, renew, redeem, restore, heal, save. Indeed, in the rituals and records of all peoples, divinity is itself associated with nothing so much as power. The *raison d'être* of the sacred itself is nothing less than marking, evoking and channelling extraordinary power. For believers of many faiths, God is identified as the unsurpassed power who offers unsurpassed power for life. For basic reasons of faith, then, power belongs at the centre of an ecumenical life ethic. [26]

There are other related reasons to insist on attention to power. Power is elemental to being itself. Power is what lets us and everything else, including all those creatures in Annie Dillard's topsoil, to "stand out" from nothingness. Power is the flow of energy apart from which nothing that is, exists. Nothing good ever happens apart from power, just as nothing evil does, and for the very same reason: nothing happens apart from power. Nothing can.

This can and should be said theologically, in the way Orthodox Christians have for nearly two millennia: God is the uncreated energy of the created, energy-suffused universe. That means: God is a power-sharing God. That means: all power is from God. That means: power in its most elemental sense is simply "power to", the power of agency, human and non-human agency alike, in the vast web of this miracle we call life. And all of it, as the Orthodox also say, is the expression of God's own life. All of it, atom-to-atom, molecule-to-molecule, cell-to-cell, breath-to-breath, day in and day out. This is power at its most basic, power as cosmic energy and its flow, sometimes identified by religious peoples as the Spirit which animates all life. An adequate ethic asks what these elementary life-giving and life-sustaining flows mean for the way we live.

Two further dimensions of power belong to our discussion. The first is an analysis of the basic symbols, images, metaphors and models in our lives, and their internal connections to social arrangements and practices. This is true for all reigning symbols, images, and metaphors and models (in the media, in the marketplace, in our homes, in the public political sector). But I will illustrate with religious ones. We know from sociology and psychology of religion that we rather consistently image power "on earth as it is in heaven". That is, if you tell us your image of God (as opposed to your stated propositions about God) you will also tell us what is your image of power. Yet we too rarely do power analysis of critical, reigning Christian symbols. Instead, claims about the power of some symbol (the cross, for example) are substituted for analysis of the specific dynamic and outcome of that symbol's reality in and for the women and men and children in a given community and for our treatment of nature. Claims about the symbol are offered instead of a description of the way it actually functions as part of community power dynamics. We communicate images of God in various ways, but without telling how they are related to the social arrangements of power that shape the context, form and meaning of our lives together. Differently said, we don't ask how concrete material practices and social interactions are internally connected to our God-talk and our ethics-talk. Thus we are not enabled to see what powers are at work in our lives and how they are at work.

The analysis of symbols, images, metaphors and models leads to power analysis of the social arrangements themselves. This may take place along lines of race, gender, class, culture, ethnicity, sexual preference or almost any way in which human interaction is patterned. Are the power relationships in these patterns those of "power over", "power against", "power with and among", "power within", "power on behalf of", or what? Is the power at work reputational power, coalitional power, communicational power, structural power, charismatic power or some other form? It is overt or covert, masked or apparent? In short, what kind of power is operating by what dynamics and as constitutive of what kind of community relationships for what good or ill purposes?

Whatever particular theologies and ethics of life we articulate, then, the criteria should include viable habitat for all creatures, a place in nature and society which addresses basic creaturely needs and permits flourishing and power to pursue life's possibilities among ourselves in ways that aid and abet the same for others. Such criteria will mean church-advocated actions which are sometimes deconstructive (liberation from oppressive arrangements), sometimes reconstructive (creating more just and sustainable community arrangements) and sometimes prospective (sending signals of the kind of future which may not be possible in the present but is within the reach of hope).

All that remains is to reiterate Hedström's contention that a Christian life-centred ethic exercises "the preferential option for all life" and to spell out briefly its moral norms.

The option for all life may sound hopelessly "airy". But it is neither vague nor meaningless when understood in view of the passion and resurrection of Jesus at the heart of the Christian story. There it is revealed as quite specific: God's own way for the well-being of all creation means joining the suffering of creation as a power there for life. Compassion (suffering with) is the passion of life itself, wherever suffering is a reality. It is the only way to life from the inside out. Power that does not go to the places where life, human and non-human alike, is most obviously ruptured, jeopardized or ruined is no power for healing at all. The only power that can heal and tend and transform creation is power drawn to the flawed and broken places, there by the grace and power of

God to call forth powers the weak never knew they had, or to repudiate as destructive the powers of the strong who exploit. This is not suffering as itself a goal or good, both of which are serious pathologies. Nor is it a call to meritorious self-sacrifice. It is suffering in the manner of Jesus — joining God, through incarnational accompaniment of and involvement in creation's suffering, so as to turn us all towards life rather than death. In this manner the way of the cross is also the way of resurrection. When the church embodies this way as its own, it is the sign of new creation.

If this kind of compassion is the central disposition of a life-centred ethic for our time, the moral norms which serve the ethic are the following:

— *Sustainability*, as the ongoing capacity of natural and social systems to thrive together, both for current generations and future ones.

— *Participation*, as the inclusion of all involved voices in society's decisions, and in obtaining and enjoying the benefits of society as well as sharing its burdens.

— *Sufficiency*, as the commitment to meet the basic material needs of all life possible.

— *Solidarity*, as the obligation to stand with others, with a view especially to the most vulnerable of every community.

Conclusion

I do not believe a theology of life and ecumenical ethic is either desirable or possible except in the way Isasi-Diaz and Tarango say — articulated theological space inviting participation from lived life itself in all its variety. Dale Irwin is surely correct "that the ecumenical movement itself is, and always has been, a multi-faceted affair encompassing different historical and theological agendas which have never been reducible to one, and which resist being synthesized into a single coherent framework".[26] This is only a confirmation of what was said by the Second Vatican Council in its Decree on Ecumenism, *Unitatis Redintegratio*: "The heritage handed down by the apostles was received differently and in different forms, so that from the very beginnings of the church its development varied from region to region and also because of differing mentalities and ways of life" (para. 14). This does not mean that we cannot speak meaningfully of a conciliar movement or even of conciliar unity. It means that praxis in the ecumenical movement is always dynamic. It breaks old boundaries, reaches different crossroads, achieves new unities which bear new imperatives and discovers faith both as a steady guide and a permanent openness to God and the world.

It also means there will be no single theology of life or ecumenical ethic, cast in the form of a single consciousness with agreed-upon language and voice. It means that while we may achieve some common formulations, they themselves are best when they represent converging points of agreement that permit a diversity of local idioms and meanings. If there is one story we embrace, it is already in the manner of the four (different) gospels or in the manner of the earliest churches, scattered as they were on three continents around the Mediterranean and involving multiple cultures, languages, peoples and ways of life from the very onset of gospel proclamation.

What I have tried to do in this paper, then, is to create a meaningful space within which more particular theologies of life and life-centred ecumenical ethics might meaningfully be discussed. "A meaningful space" does not mean a "neutral" one or one without substantive judgments and interpretations. This paper has offered theological and ethical substance from biblical, scientific, theological and ethical sources which both have ecumenical rootage and give some direction for discussion, and which in any case encourage rather than inhibit ecumenical voices and perspectives.

NOTES

[1] Ada Maria Isasi-Diaz and Yolanda Tarango, *Hispanic Women: Prophetic Voice in the Church*, San Francisco, Harper & Row, 1988, pp.2-3.

[2] Michael Lerner, "Jewish Liberation Theology", in Michael Zweig, ed., *Religion and Economic Justice*, Philadelphia, Temple University Press, 1991, p.131.

[3] Elaine Pagels, *Adam, Eve, and the Serpent*, New York, Random House, 1988.

[4] Cf. the title of Christopher Stone's recent book on environmental ethics, *The Gnat is Older than Man* (Princeton University Press, 1993), based on a passage from the Talmud: "The world was made for man, though he was the latecomer among its creatures. This was design. He was to find all things ready for him. God was the host who prepared dainty dishes, set the table, and then led his guest to his seat. At the same time man's late appearance on earth is to convey an admonition of humility. Let him beware of being proud, lest he invite the retort that the gnat is older than he."

[5] Lerner, *loc. cit.*, p.131.

[6] *Ibid.*

[7] *Ibid.*

[8] Terence Fretheim, "The Reclamation of Creation", *Interpretation*, XLV, 1991, p.358. I draw heavily from Fretheim for this discussion of the relation of creation and redemption.

[9] *Ibid.*, p.365.

[10] Tikva Frymer-Kensky, *In the Wake of the Goddesses: Women, Culture, and the Biblical Transformation of Pagan Myth*, New York, Free Press, 1992, p.220.

[11] "Giver of Life — Sustain Your Creation!", in *Signs of the Spirit*, official report of the WCC's seventh assembly, ed. Michael Kinnamon, Geneva, WCC Publications, 1991, p.55.

[12] Hannah Arendt, *The Human Condition*, Chicago, University of Chicago Press, 1958, p.238. The original context of Arendt's comments is a discussion of the role of forgiveness in human affairs, including political and policy affairs. She is saying that our actions on the biosphere are not as susceptible to "forgiveness" as are human's actions upon one another. The consequences are not as easily "forgiven", courses are not as easily altered, nor new beginnings with a different set of consequences undertaken.

[13] Sallie McFague, *The Body of God: An Ecological Theology*, Minneapolis, Fortress, 1993, p.9.

[14] "Drawing Big Lessons From Fly Embryology", *The New York Times*, 10 August 1993, p.C12.

[15] Cf. Charles Birch and John Cobb, *The Liberation of Life: From the Cell to the Community*, Denton, Texas, Environmental Ethics Books, 1990, p.45: "The evolution of a living cell from organic molecules may have happened more than once on the earth. But probably only one original cell gave rise to all the rest of life on earth. This seems to be the only possible explanation of the basic similarity of the cells of all living organisms... Life is like a great branching tree with one central stem."

[16] Annie Dillard, *Pilgrim at Tinker Creek: A Mystical Excursion into the Natural World*, New York, Bantam, 1974, p.96, cited by McFague, *op. cit.*, p.38.

[17] McFague, *ibid.*

[18] Thomas Berry, *The Dream of the Earth*, San Francisco, Sierra Club Books, 1988, p.5.

[19] This is Sallie McFague's effort to "sober" what she calls "our natural anthropocentrism"; *op. cit.*, p.104.

[20] Ingemar Hedström, "Latin America and the Need for a Life-Liberating Theology", in *Liberating Life: Contemporary Approaches to Ecological Theology*, ed. Charles Birch et al., Maryknoll, NY, Orbis, 1990, p.120.

[21] These are the suggestive terms of McFague, *op. cit.*, pp.161f. Paul Tillich argued that Spirit itself is the most adequate way to speak of God in our time. Spirit unites power (Tillich's way of speaking of the depths of the divine) with *meaning* (the Logos) in such a way that they mean "life" or the "spirit." "The statement that God is Spirit means that life as spirit is the inclusive symbol for the divine life", cf. *Systematic Theology*, Chicago, University of Chicago Press, 1951, I, p.250, and the whole of Vol. III on the Holy Spirit. The WCC has, leading up to and after the Canberra assembly, given focus to the Spirit, but I suspect we have only begun to understand it as the meeting place for all our discussion and work, including with people of other faiths.

[22] Kinnamon, ed., *op. cit.*, p.55.

[23] James Nash and others argue correctly that the moral and legal notion of "rights" must be extended from "human rights" to the even more inclusive notion of "biotic rights". See Nash, *Loving Nature: Ecological Integrity and Christian Responsibility*, Nashville, Abingdon, 1991, esp. pp.162-91; and "Human Rights and the Environment: New Challenge for Ethics", in *Theology and Public Policy*, Vol. IV, no. 2, Fall 1992, pp.42-57.

[24] McFague, *op. cit.*, p.101.

[25] *Ibid.*, p.117.

[26] Cf. Larry L. Rasmussen, "Power Analysis: A Neglected Agenda in Christian Ethics", in *The Annual of the Society of Christian Ethics*, Washington, Georgetown University Press, 1991.

[26] Dale Irwin, "Hearing Many Voices: Dialogue and Diversity in the Ecumenical Movement", doctoral dissertation, Union Theological Seminary, New York, 1988, pp.4-5.

The Earth Is the Lord's

Samuel Rayan, S.J.

The earth is the Lord's

Everything the earth contains belongs to God: its fullness and all its rich resources. This is the jubilant proclamation of Psalm 24. This faith-confession recurs throughout the Bible (cf. Ex. 9:29; 19:5; Lev. 25:23; Deut. 10:14; 1 Sam. 2:8; Pss. 2:8; 8:6-9; 47:8; 65:6-14; 50:10-12; 89:12; 95:4-5; Acts 14:15; 17:24-26.)

The land is mine, says the Lord (Lev. 25:23). So are the gold and the silver of the land. So too are its wine and its grain, its wool and its flax (Hos. 2:10-11). As a fundamental doctrine, this truth was surely familiar to every Israelite; and when Jesus said, "Give to Caesar what is Caesar's and to God what is God's", his listeners grasped his meaning swiftly. They knew that no more could belong to Caesar than the image and the title about which alone — as distinct from the coin that bore them — Jesus had posed a pointed question. Let Caesar take what is his and quit.

The earth is the Lord's. Much more is implied here than legal-juridical titles and rights. The earth is constituted by being God's own. That relationship is the whole of its reality. God called the earth into being, firmed its foundations and set it upon its pillars. God is calling and creating it now; now God is loving it into existence and bringing it forth from the depths of divine tenderness. The coming into being of the earth here and now is a burning, flaming locus of live and surpriseful encounter with God.

The earth is something, somebody, that God loves and overwhelms with gifts. God fashions it and names it. The name "earth" is mentioned more than fifteen times in the opening chapter of the Bible. In that book of the acts of God, the earth and earthlings are at the centre of all of God's concerns. Think of the infinite care with which God watched over the evolution of the earth and accompanied the endless process of its unfolding into myriad forms of life and movement and colour and shape and scent. The earth is central to God's purposes. It is significantly placed at the heart of the prayer Jesus bequeathed to his disciples. Great and beautiful things should happen on the earth, should happen *to* the earth. The kingdom of God should happen to it. Thus transformed, the "new earth" sums up in the closing chapters of the Bible the outcome of a long history of God's saving action and passionate concern.

That action begins with God's creative summons to the earth, and earth's response to God with a prompt and clear "Here I am". The earth is God's beloved daughter. When she is small, God stands her at a distance and, mother-like, bids her learn to walk and beckons her to come closer, which she does through that fascinating and adventurous pilgrimage we call evolution — a pilgrimage in three stages: the material, the biological and the cultural, each with its marvels of free fantasy and exquisite achievement. Millions of years God bends over the earth adorning her with lights and flowers, celebrating her with bird songs and cascading life and loveliness. God graces her in the end with the clarity and the warmth of the human, the highest point of her own incandescence and the flower of her relentless quest for untrammelled existence. The creation chapters in Genesis have an air of festivity. They reflect a birthday celebration with candles and flowers and the giving of gifts. And God saw that it was good. And God was happy.

The earth is God's cherished bride, not only in her ultimate newness as she will be "coming down, out of heaven from God prepared... for her husband" (Rev. 21:2), but from the very beginning. From the beginning God has been crowning her with splendour far more magnificent than the splendour of Solomon (Matt. 6:28-30). God robes her in green and red and gold, lays her pavements in carnelians and her foundations in sapphires, makes her battlements of rubies and her walls of carbuncles; and all her gates are precious stones (Isa. 54:5-12; Rev. 21:18-21). God establishes the earth in justice, which is also the foundation of God's own throne and reign (Isa. 54:13; Ps. 89:15). God warms and renews and refreshes his earth-bride, daily and seasonally. God waters the land and cares for it, enriching it with natural resources; God drenches the furrow, levels the ridges, softens the soil with showers and blesses it with crops. God turns the deserts into pasture land and clothes the hills with gladness. The meadows he covers with flocks, the valleys he decks with grain, and the year he crowns with goodness — abundance of life everywhere and shouting and singing and resounding joy. Thus God deals with his precious earth (Ps. 65:7-14).

With a word of creative love God makes his earth-bride inexhaustibly, surprisefully fecund. And God said, "Let the earth bring forth" (Gen. 1:24). And the earth brought forth in joy every kind of plant and tree and cattle and reptile and wild animal. Then God's breath and bits of earth united to give birth to human beings, to women and men fashioned in God's own image and likeness, and in the likeness and image of the earth, which in its turn is an image of the heart and womb of God, where it was first conceived and nurtured. And the Spirit of God hovered over waters; and the power of God overshadowed Mary, and therefore the child born of her was called holy (Gen. 1:2; Luke 1:35). The earth is God-betrothed. God has covenanted her to himself. This is God's pledge: as long as the earth lasts, seedtime and harvest, cold and heat, summer and winter, day and night shall not cease to be. The covenant covers Noah and his posterity and every living creature of the earth (Gen. 8:21-22; 9:8-17). The pact is that never again will the earth be cursed because of the evil deeds of humans; "never again shall all flesh be cut off... and never again shall there be a flood to destroy the earth" (Gen. 9:11). God's rainbow set in the clouds is the sign and sacrament of the covenant between God and the earth (Gen. 9:13-17). It is on the basis of this engagement that God will be at peace with the heavens, and the heavens will respond to the earth, and the earth will respond to the grain and wine and oil (Hos. 2:21-22).

The earth is the Lord's, for it is the Lord's self-manifestation. It is something God is saying and doing, an ongoing revelation, an unfolding word of God in which something of God's thought and heart are disclosed and much of God's attitude to us is conveyed: the way God holds us dear and precious, the way God relates to us in life-bearing gifts. For whatever can be known about God, God has made clear; since the creation of the world, invisible realities like God's power and divinity have become visible and recognizable in the things God has made (Rom. 1:19-20). God has never remained hidden without a clue; God has never left himself without witnesses. From the heavens God sends down rain and rich harvests; our spirits he fills with food and delight (Acts 14:17; 17:24-26). These are God's accredited witnesses — the primal testimony God gives to himself. The earth, then, is a revealed word of God, always alive and fresh, never frozen into human words which age and die and need in every generation to be hermeneutically resuscitated. The earth and everything in it are loving and saving words addressed to us and addressing each other. God says it all with rainbows and flowers, with rice and wheat, and the glory of sunsets, the charm of children, the beauty of brides, the innovativeness of youth and the prayers of trees, the mystery of silent things and the joy of friendship.

Human language is incapable of expressing properly who God is and what God wishes to communicate. Since our language is inadequate even to convey what our own hearts feel and know deeply, we speak in signs, and it is in signs that we can be spoken to. In addressing us God uses spatial signs like land and water and bread and temporal signs like "the seasons, the weeks, the days, the life-cycles of fauna and flora, the flow of the tides, the life-span of men and women with its birth and death and new life".[1] The earth is a sacrament which conveys to us God's heart and life, God's generosity, power and tenderness, God's fidelity and total dependability. The earth is "a mighty symbol of God's great action of sharing his love".[2]

The cherished language of symbols is silence. The earth speaks in the eloquent silence of hills and trees. "Silence, my soul," said Tagore, "these trees are prayers." A language the earth loves to speak is the silence of the night and the silence of the womb, the silence of seeds as they sprout and the silence of buds smiling into blossoms. The earth speaks, and God speaks too, in the silence of loving looks, of tears shed and unshed and of hands gently laid on shoulders bent beneath a load of sorrows. The earth speaks in the quiet language of many colours, and of graceful movements of gazelle, lark and fish, and of running water. In this, too, earth is the sacrament of God whom the Bhagavad Gita celebrates as the "silence of hidden realities" (*Gita* x.38). But the earth communicates also in the idiom of the roar of the sea, the warble of birds and brooks, the murmur of the breeze. The heavens in their blue silences and their thunderclouds declare the glory of God. No speech, no words, no voice heard, but the call goes on throughout the universe (Ps. 19:3-4). And "deep calls to deep at the thunder of your cataracts" (Ps. 42:7). It is because the earth and all it holds are such silent-eloquent symbols of the divine that Jesus can, in his parables, touch them with a word and open them up to reveal in their depths the mystery of the reign of God and of the Passover. The kingdom of God is like a mustard seed, like a treasure hidden in a field. The grain of wheat must fall to the ground and die in order to rise to a harvest of life (Matt. 13:31-44; John 12:24).

The earth is the Lord's table, laid with care for God's daughters and sons, "a feast of rich food and well-aged wines" (Isa. 25:6), a table God lays with flowers every morning. The earth is itself a cup of joy God fills for God's family, a large round of bread God bakes, a big bowl of rice God cooks each morning over the fire of God's heart. Bread for breaking and cup for sharing and passing round, so that all women and men and things may live and have life in abundance, and become God's family, and say together, our Father in heaven, our mother in the earth, meaningful be your name in the food you give and the rice we share day by day. Over this bread and cup, over these bowls of rice and water, you bend with a blessing and a word of consecration: Take and eat, all of you, take and drink, this is myself given for you, this is my life poured out for you so that your life may be full and your joy may be complete. This is the earth of the covenant. The rainbow and the rain and everything beautiful and awesome and alive shall be remembrances of the earth I have covenanted to myself for ever. The word of the Lord. And we have had our invitation to this feast of the Lord, this dear little earth of our God.

The earth is the Lord's. She is God's body, God's bodiliness, the love-reality that is God become seeable and touchable and historically processive. That the world is the body of Brahman is a favourite theme of the eleventh-century Hindu mystic and theologian Ramanuja. In this earthiness of the divine, in its movements and moods and evolutions and rhythms, we may encounter God and touch and feel and follow. The earth's seasons, are they not seasons of the heart of God loving, conceiving, brooding, warming, life-giving and exploding into glory? We have no way to take the touch of God but the touch of the earth, though God has his own ineffable ways of touching our depths, to which we ourselves have little or no access, since (in the words of Francis Thompson),

> its keys are the cincture-hung of God,
> its doors are trepidant to his nod,
> its floors by him alone are trod.

The earth is the Lord's, in that it is an articulation and embodiment of God's freedom and joy. In one of India's theological traditions, the earth is Brahman's *leela*, God's play, God's playfulness. In another, it is the dance of Shiva. In neither is the earth the child of compulsion and necessity. It is born of spontaneity characteristic of freedom and joy. It is the manifest form of *ananda*, bliss, which designates the divine. Gustavo Gutiérrez observes that the concluding chapters of Job present creation as God's delight, as radical grace, as the exuberance of God's joy. Much in creation is art, not consumer goods. Not everything is destined for human control and human utility.[3] Many things are there for our contemplation and especially for the beauty and wonder of the world. This is why the earth itself is not totally determined. The autonomy and spontaneity and the consequent variety which mark the course of evolution as well as the appearance and habits of living things reflect the freedom from which they fountain forth. No two mango trees or oaks are exactly alike. No leaf or flower copies another. Every tree has its own style of being tree, its own identity and "personality".

God's earth is a loving earth, patient, nurturing, self-giving. Her freedom is her ability to love and give herself for the life of others. How richly and endlessly she gives herself to us and to God, in how many beautiful ways and forms! The food and drink which sustain us, the sounds and signs which mediate our communications, and the skyscapes and seascapes that frame our life are the earth's gifts, tokens of her devotedness and concern. A fire burns in her heart, a flame no floods can quench; for love is stronger than death, for God has set the earth as a seal upon his heart, as a seal upon his arm (S. of S. 8:6-7). Surely, it is love that makes the earth so rich and inexhaustible in creative imagination.

The earth is the Lord's, and she rejoices in being his. She exults before the face of the Lord, she claps her hands with her trees and her rivers, she offers her flowers and wafts her incense, and the dance of her worship never ends. In God's presence her mountains skip like rams, and her hills frolic like lambs (Ps. 114:4-8; 98:7-9). The heavens brim over with gladness as the fields exult and all the forest trees sway and sing (Ps. 96:11-12). Ours is a celebrant earth. Her fire and hail and mist and snow, her teaks and cedars and all her animals, wild and tame, praise their Lord (Ps. 148).

Thus and in many other ways, the earth is the Lord's. It is God's creation and self-expression, God's word and image, symbol of his presence and power, beauty, love and strength, imagination and joy. The earth is where God abides and comes to meet us. The earth is sacred. The trees are sacred. Water is sacred. We are sacred. Such are the implications of the first article of the Christian creed. Such has always been the faith tradition of tribal peoples the world over, whose culture has informed the major part of human history and whose wisdom laid the foundations on which we build. When Black Elk, a holy man of the Oglala Sioux, speaks of "the beauty and the strangeness of the earth", he is inviting us to love and reverence, as is Gerard Manley Hopkins, for whom

The world is charged with the grandeur of God...
There lives the dearest freshness deep down things...
Because the Holy Spirit over the bent
World broods with warm breast and with ah! bright wings.

The earth is ours

We have heard Psalm 24 celebrating the earth as the Lord's. We listen now to Psalm 115 celebrating heaven as belonging to the Lord and the earth as given by God to human beings. According to the Bible and the teaching of many early Christian thinkers, as well as the traditions of the tribal centuries of human history, the earth and its resources are God's gift for the whole of God's human family of this planet. They are meant to serve the needs and the creative possibilities of all God's children. The earth is a song of glory and love God gives for all of us to learn to sing after God, our common home, the table around which we are together, the bread we share, our holy communion, a place of creative engagement. This shared earth is both the basis and the sacrament of gentle human community. The earth is our mother, the abiding source of life for all living things. Breathing, eating, drinking, we are ever nurtured at her breasts and in her womb.

The earth is interior to human existence. Multiple relationship to the earth in the shape of work, food, knowledge, contemplation and gift-giving is constitutive of the human. Our self-understanding and all our mental and physical activities and movements are bound up with, even determined by, these relationships. We *are* earth, bits of it which have come to develop a mysterious interiority, the capacity for reflective thought and for freedom and love. The earth is our bodily self, our common body inseparably and for ever. This body, all human persons have in common with all living things and with the entire cosmos. Hence the sense of equality and shared dignity within a cosmic sisterhood/brotherhood which gave birth to the well-known canticle of Francis of Assisi:

Most High, all powerful, all good Lord...,
All praise is yours... through all that you have made:
And first my lord Brother Sun who brings the day...
How beautiful is he, how radiant in all his splendour!
Of you, Most High, he bears the likeness.

All praise be yours... through Sister Moon and the stars.
In the heavens you have made them, bright and precious and fair.
All praise be yours... through Brother Wind and Air,
And fair and stormy, all the weather's moods...
And praise be yours... through Sister Water,
So useful, lowly, precious and pure.

All praise be yours... through Brother Fire
Through whom you brighten up the night.
How beautiful is he, how gay, full of power and strength.

All praise be yours... through Sister Earth our Mother
Who feeds us in her sovereignty and produces
Various fruits with coloured flowers and herbs...

The relation between the earth and us is to be one of respect and love. To the Aboriginal peoples of Australia and to tribal peoples everywhere and to all Asians the earth is earth mother, mother earth.

This rock and all these rocks are alive with her spirit.
They protect us, all of us. They are her... temple.[4]

How does one relate to one's mother, and how does one repay a mother's gifts? In McLaren's film *A Chairy Tale*, the chair refuses to let a man occupy it as long as he is absorbed in his reading and pays no "personal" attention to the chair. It is only when he lifts his eyes off his book, lays the book aside and begins to care for the chair that the chair receives him gladly. "And they sat happily together ever after." The author is not seeking to make a point in psychology. It is a theological point he is trying to score. A spiritual message is what he wants to convey. The earth and the things it holds are not to be taken for granted, nor treated as dead, nor merely "used" as if they had no identity and truth of their own. They have; therefore they deserve to be recognized, acknowledged, respected. It is on that condition that they and we are glad, sister-like, to serve one another. Against every disrespect shown the earth would rebel — to our confusion if not to our undoing. Authentic Christian, human feeling and teaching are witnessed to by Francis's canticle, Hopkins's poem, tribal traditions and confessions like the following, witness of an ancient theologian:

I honour all matter and venerate it. Through it, filled, as it were, with a divine power and grace, my salvation has come to me. Was not the thrice happy and thrice blessed wood of the cross matter? Was not the sacred and holy mountain of Calvary matter? What of the life-giving rock, the holy sepulchre, the source of our resurrection: was it not matter? Is not the blessed table matter which gives us the bread of life? Are not the gold and silver matter, out of which crosses and altarpieces, and chalices, are made? And before all these things, is not the body and blood of our Lord matter? Do not despise matter, for it is not despicable.[5]

Read "earth" for "matter": the meaning will suffer no damage. Witness of a modern scientist-believer:

Now the earth can certainly clasp me in her great arms.
She can swell me with her life, or draw me back into her dust.

> She can deck herself with every charm, with every honour, with every mystery.
>> She can intoxicate me with her perfume of tangibility and unity.
>> She can cast me to my knees in expectation of what is maturing in her breast...
> She has become for me, over and above herself, the body of him who is, and of him who is coming. [6]

A third witness is the Sioux Indian chief Luther Standing Bear:

> The Lakota was a true naturist — lover of nature. He loved the earth and all things on the earth, the attachment growing with age. The old people came literally to love the soil, and they sat or reclined on the ground with a feeling of being close to a mothering power. It was good for the skin to touch the earth, and the old people liked to remove their moccasins and walk with bare feet on the sacred earth... To sit or lie upon the ground is to be able to think more deeply and feel more keenly, see more clearly into the mysteries of life and come closer in kinship to other lives about him... For the animal and bird world there existed a brotherly feeling... [7]

A last testimony is a voice of more recent times:

> Matter matters. It matters both to God and to people. God made matter, gave it to people for dominion and used it in revelation and redemption... Therefore any liturgical celebration must take matter seriously... The church should actively witness to times of planting and reaping in the fields; it should bless the handiwork of its people who live with technology; it should celebrate outside whenever possible... It should put matter into motion; it should move around in it and dance with it, touch it, taste it, listen to the sounds of life, play with its colours... It should celebrate the goodness of the world as it comes from the Creator Redeemer. [8]

The earth, then, is a theological category. A profound "theological respect" for it is called for. All that we have said above about the earth's belonging to God gathers to a head and comes to complete truth in Jesus Christ. In him the earth does indeed become the face of God and the place of saving encounter. In Jesus' resurrection, the earth, which has seen and borne in its bosom so much death and dying, finally transcends death and attains abounding and endless life. In Jesus the earth has become supremely honoured, seated as it is at the right hand of God. In Jesus the earth becomes the ultimate expression of compassion and of freedom. In Jesus the earth now is the finest word God speaks to us; and the best bread God breaks with us for the life of the world. "Each recurring season manifests some new aspect of the mystery of Christ living in the world." [9] The *kenosis* and the *plerosis* of the earth's seasons reflect the paschal mystery and echo the call to die daily to selfishness and greed and rise to the glory of God's sons and daughters and to the fellowship of God's household. The earth is liturgical reality. We celebrate the earth and in her we celebrate her God, our God.

Something to cherish

The earth is precious: to God and to us. The preciousness of the earth is a central witness of the Bible and of all tribal traditions. God was the first to appreciate the worth and the wonder of the earth. "God called the dry land Earth, and the waters that were gathered together he called Seas. And God saw that it was good" (Gen. 1:10). "The earth brought forth vegetation: plants... and trees... God saw that it was good" (Gen. 1:12). "God made the two great lights... and the stars. God set them in the dome of the sky to give light upon the earth... God saw that it was good" (Gen. 1:16-18). "God created... every living creature that moves..., with which the waters swarm, and every winged bird... God saw that it was good" (Gen 1:20-21). "God said: 'Let the earth bring forth living creatures...' God made the wild animals... and everything that creeps... God saw that it was good" (Gen. 1:24-25). "God saw everything that he had made, and indeed it was very good" (Gen. 1:31).

The earth is precious: to God and to us. It is precious in itself. It is unique, the only one of its kind. And it is beautiful beyond words. An anonymous lover of the earth invites us to its contemplation:

> If the earth were only a few feet in diameter, floating a few feet above a field somewhere, people would come from everywhere to marvel at it. People would walk around it, marvelling at its big pools of water, its little pools and the water flowing between the pools. People would marvel at the bumps on it, and the holes in it, and they would marvel at the very thin layer of gas surrounding it and the water suspended in the gas. The people would marvel at all the creatures walking around the surface of the ball, and at the creatures in the water. The people would declare it precious because it was the only one, and they would protect it so that it would not be hurt. The ball would be the greatest wonder known, and people would come to behold it, to be healed, to gain knowledge, to know beauty and to wonder how it could be. People would love it, and defend it with their lives, because they would somehow know that their lives, their own roundness, could be nothing without it.

In 1854 Chief Seattle bore witness to the tribal inheritance of the divine capacity for wonder:

> Every part of this earth is sacred to my people. Every shining pine needle, every sandy shore, every mist in the dark woods, every clearing and every

humming insect is holy in the memory and experience of my people... Our dead never forget this beautiful earth, for it is the mother of the Red Man. We are part of the earth and it is a part of us. The perfumed flowers are our sisters..., the ashes of our fathers are sacred. Their graves are holy ground, and so these hills, these trees, this portion of the earth is consecrated to us... The air is precious to the Red Man, for all things share the same breath; the air shares its [the land's] spirit with all the life it supports. Our God is the same God. This earth is precious to him.

Therefore the earth may not be slighted, abused, wasted, conquered, plundered, privatized, destroyed. It deserves to be treated with reverence and tenderness. It has to be bequeathed healthy and whole and beautiful to generations to come, to be source and support of life to them, to be for them too the sacrament of God and foundational grace as it is to us.

The earth is a symbol that sums up all the gifts of life and love which God shares with humankind and all living beings. It is not so much a thing or object as a relational reality, vibrant and alive, dynamically mediating life and love from heart to heart. It is communion like bread and rice, and a celebration of togetherness. Hence the necessity to avoid and prevent the grabbing and monopolizing of the earth and its resources by individuals and groups. They must remain common to humankind, and to the whole people, in each place. Any further allotment of basic resources can be valid only if its purpose is to ensure the earth's freedom to meet the needs and serve the possibilities of all God's people. Exclusive private ownership which holds the earth captive and prevents it from promptly reaching out to its hungry children with the milk of life is unacceptable.

Early Christian thinkers, therefore, considered concentration of land in a few hands unjust and contrary to the earth's God-given nature and purpose. The earth must always retain its character of communion: communion with God and holy communion among ourselves. It must always remain a eucharistic mystery: the bread of God, the body of God given for the life of the world. The stand taken by many early Christian thinkers may be summed up as follows:

1. Human equality was the basis on which the church fathers built their doctrine of land ownership. Equality springs from (a) our common origin in the heart of God (and, we may add, in the heart and womb of the earth); (b) our common nature, all of us having the same basic needs and identical power to love; and (c) our common destiny, all being called to life in God and life with one another. All of us are here by equal permission of the creator. With equal rights, then, we all breathe the air, walk the earth and use the land and other productive elements necessary

for dignified human existence. We share the same history; we shall share the same earth. Our right to the use of the common earth is a right vested in each human being entering the world. It is limited only by the equal rights of all others. Basic human equality forbids concentration and privatization of God's earth.

2. The earth is God's provision for his entire family on this planet. It is what the fathers call *ta koina*, common goods destined for the benefit of everyone. It is not *ta idia*, the fruit of somebody's labour. The fathers speak of a common sky, common light, common universe. For them earth, air, light, water are "causes of life", of which nobody may be deprived, for which nobody may be forced radically to depend on somebody else.

3. Therefore private ownership which excludes others, concentration of land and accumulation of wealth which leaves others dispossessed and impoverished involves fraud, robbery, plunder and radical injustice. In the midst of the poor the wealthy are thieves. Inheritance is accumulation and transmission of stolen goods. Their restoration to the community is a demand of justice.

4. What the fathers condemn is the institution of private ownership and not merely its abuse. They identify all private property with avarice, violence, deprivation, spoliation, thievery. According to them, private property is the root cause of discords, conflicts and wars. It is not God's law, but human law, the law of the emperor; it contradicts the purposes of God written into the fabric of the earth.

5. Early Christian writers reject private ownership as idolatry. Private ownership involves avarice, which Paul identifies with idolatry. Its claim to exclusive rights disputes the absolute rights God alone has over the earth and its richness. Idolatry is avoided only if the true meaning of wealth is honoured, and the true meaning of wealth is sufficiency for all and community of all, and brotherhood and sisterhood. Earth and wealth are medium of friendship and shared life.

6. Sufficiency and community were what the early church strove after, as is clear from Acts 2 and 4 and from the praxis of equality in the breaking of bread (1 Cor. 10 and 11). Religious orders renouncing private property and holding goods in common emerged in the church at a time when the church's original self-understanding as a community of friends was being smothered by the emergence of ruling classes and the church itself was being remoulded in the image of Roman social realities. These movements were attempts to retain some memory of the primordial communitarian vision and to realize afresh the Deuteronomic injunction

that there shall be no poor among God's people (Deut. 15:4). The ideal of common ownership has always been upheld in the church as evangelical. It is perhaps a measure of our theological and spiritual ambiguity that what is evangelical is officially held to be good for a few but not for the many, not for the village, the city, the state, the world. The earth demands that we return to our roots and blossom from there into the new community of the dream of God and of the earth. [10]

Areas of concern

In our relation to the earth today, three factors cause concern and contradict the biblical and Christian view of the earth and its mystery: the commercialization of the earth, the global imbalance in land-population proportion and the ecological crisis.

1. In no authentic humanism or genuine religious perspective will the earth be viewed and treated as a "thing" we possess and dispose of. The earth is too closely bound up with life and worship and the experience of God's goodness and greatness to be regarded as merchandise. We could take lessons from ancient tribal traditions. The Pacific peoples have been reminding us that it is the land which possesses us, not we it. "I see you come into the sacred place of my tribe to get the strength of the Earth Mother... We say the earth is our mother — we cannot own her; she owns us." [11] Land is not possession; land is human beings. Hilaire Belloc defined the human person as "a land animal". The earth should never be a market commodity put up for sale and haggled over — any more than our own bodies and selves, or the self and body of our mother, or the sacraments of God. The earth is sacred. In the speech of Chief Seattle cited earlier, he says:

> The great chief in Washington sends word that he wishes to buy our land... How can you buy or sell the sky, the warmth of the land? The idea is strange to us. If we do not own the freshness of the air and the sparkle of the water, how can you buy them?... We are part of the earth, and the earth is part of us.

Such is the spiritual depth and cultural refinement of America's homeland people. All immigrants would do well to hear and heed. It is the homeland people's experience that "the white man does not understand... The earth is not his brother, but his enemy... He does not care... He treats his mother the earth and his brother the sky as things to be bought, plundered, sold like sheep or bright beads."

When white delegates came for signature for a treaty alienating Indian lands, a chief of the Blackfeet Tribe refused:

Our land is more valuable than your money... As long as the sun shines and the waters flow, this land will be here to give life to men and animals. We cannot sell the lives of men and animals; therefore we cannot sell this land. It was put here for us by the Great Spirit, and we cannot sell it because it does not belong to us. You can count your money and burn it within a nod of a buffalo's head, but only the Great Spirit can count the grains of sand and the blades of grass of these plains. As a present to you we will give you anything we have that you can take with you; but the land never. [12]

In this worldview, shared by all primal societies, the earth is God's family, our sister and mother, our partner in life and worship, co-pilgrim with us. Its reduction to the state of commodity is a fundamental aberration. Akin to this was Israel's outlook in the tribal period of its history. Remarkable vestiges of these early convictions remain enshrined in the final redaction of the Bible. For instance, the permanent alienation of land is forbidden, as it might lead to landlordism and the dispossession of many. "The land shall not be sold in perpetuity, the land is mine," says God (Lev. 25:23). If the reasoning is valid, the conclusion should be: the land shall not be sold or bought at all. Sold land always remained redeemable, the buyer having no right to retain it when his money was returned by the original owner or his relatives (Lev. 25; Deut. 15). The degradation and profanation of the earth to a condition of merchandise began with the advent of class societies. It was perfected in ancient Rome, and its laws, passed into feudal societies, became the ethos of capitalism and spread over the world during the centuries of colonial subversion of ancient cultures. The earth needs to liberate itself from the crudeness and violence of commercial culture, and win back its dignity as the sacrament of God and source of our shared life.

2. A second major factor which contradicts the Christian vision of the earth is the present imbalance in the distribution of population over the surface of the globe. Tissa Balasuriya, who raises the point as a theological question, sees in this unequal distribution "one of the main defects and injustices of the world system". [13] European expansion from 1500 to 1950 has resulted in the European occupation of most of the habitable parts of the earth.

West Europeans occupied North, Central and South America, Australia, New Zealand and parts of Africa. They made colonies of the whole of Asia except China, Japan and Thailand. The Russians, an East European people, expanded their empire to the Pacific and the borders of China. [14]

Europeans appropriated to themselves "most of the vast open spaces of the earth", building a world system aimed at perpetuating their domination for the benefit of the Euro-American peoples. Thus today we have a "white-racist world system".[15]

To illustrate the imbalance: the population of India, China and Japan, comprising forty percent of the human race, is confined to ten percent of the earth's surface, while Canada, Australia and New Zealand, with one percent of the world population among them, occupy thirteen percent of land space. Brazil, only slightly smaller than China, sustains a mere tenth of China's population. Bolivia is three times the size of Japan, but has only five million persons, compared to Japan's one hundred and fifteen million. Bangladesh, which is only half the area of New Zealand, supports a population twenty-five times that of New Zealand. In North America, the ratio of land to agricultural worker is 78.4 to 1, while in Asia and the Pacific the ratio is 0.98 to 1; and in China and other centralized economies, the ratio is still lower, 0.51 to 1.[16]

This induced and unjust imbalance has racist dimensions as well:

> The whole world system is based on a sort of apartheid... The different racial groupings are allotted separate (and unequal) "preserves" in which they have to live. The yellow peoples have China, Japan and the adjacent islands. The blacks have Africa. The brown people are allotted India, Pakistan and South East Asia. The rest of the world... is largely reserved for whites. When black, yellow or brown peoples have been free to migrate, it has generally been as slaves or as cheap labour for the whites.[17]

This continues to be so even today. Australia advertises to get whites to settle there and will readily take 250,000 whites from Zimbabwe, but only grudgingly admits 25,000 Asians, and that on condition that they have skills, education and financial backing. "No land-rich country will admit that racism is its basic objection to world population resettlement." But the facts are there for all to see. "All the underpopulated countries — USA, USSR, Canada, Brazil, Argentina, Australia, New Zealand — have immigration laws that discriminate against Asians."[18]

This global imbalance and the immigration policies of the under-populated countries are "among the most pernicious obstacles to human development and justice". Hence a planned and peaceful reallocation of land to peoples is a basic necessity. It should be on the world agenda. "It is one way in which the creative growth of humanity can be related to the use and transformation of the earth." It will decrease pollution and waste; for "Third World people have long traditions of care for the earth, unlike the present occupants of North America and Australia". And yet "hardly any international body that deals with the problems of world development considers this aspect of the question seriously... The present distribution of land is taken as an untouchable Absolute."[19] But to do so is to overlook fundamental realities like the earth's vocation and yearning to home and nurture adequately and justly every one of God's and its children.

3. The third factor which ill accords with a Christian, even with a human, perspective on earth and nature is the ecological crisis. It is not only a question of Christian or other viewpoints and theologies; it is a question of human survival on this tiny planet. The earth system is being polluted and destroyed through wasteful, profligate and predatory practices by modern profit-oriented scientific-technological culture, be it industrial, agricultural, or communicational. The earth's standing, meaning and history as the home of life are under threat of death. Signs of the crisis are many. Precious resources are diverted to destructive and poisonous purposes like arms race, stockpiling of nuclear weapons, "Star Wars" and similar insanities which can wreck and ruin, which have wrecked and ruined, the earth and life partially, totally, irreparably. Nuclear, radioactive and other fatally toxic wastes are being dumped in the oceans or on islands and continents of the poor and the powerless. These, together with polluting effluences and emissions from factories, and the acid rains they spawn, are causing large-scale disease and death to plants, birds, beasts, fish, lakes, rivers and human beings. The atmosphere of most cities, thick with toxic fumes, has become a major menace to health and life. Three-Mile Island, the Bikini Atoll, Bhopal and Chernobyl (to name a few) are symbols of human sacrifice demanded by the modern Moloch of our economic and political system. They are ominous warnings of what is in store for the earth and for us if we continue hurtling down the course we have wrongly chosen.

Chemical fertilizers and pesticides poison and weaken the soil, paving the way to greater use of them and greater disaster for health of the earth and living things. Water is overused or wasted, and underground water sources are being drained dry. Accumulation of carbon dioxide in the atmosphere and the felling of tropical trees by the thousands to pamper a throwaway consumerist culture leads to a rise in the earth's temperature, drastic changes in climatic conditions and depletion of the ozone layer. These are already threatening to reduce the earth's luxuriant forests and fertile fields into deserts.

In this cultural system the destruction of environment goes hand in hand with forms of social pollution represented, for instance, by growing unemployment, dependence of vast human masses on a few centres of power for basic human needs like food and water, the exploitation and

degradation of the poor, especially women and children, within a broad
and deep commercialization of life, intense human suffering from a sense
of loneliness and meaninglessness as people are increasingly cut off from
quiet communion with nature, as their mutual relationships become
deadened and mechanized, as their native and necessary feel for poetry
and mystery are eroded by shallow pragmatism or sheer greed. The
greatest pollution is the dominance which the machine has come to
exercise over the earth and human beings, though we know that human
beings and not machines are the source of fresh life and creative
imagination. The worship of destructive technology signals the death,
slow or swift, of the human race and of the earth.

The psalm "A Requiem for the Earth" is a poignant and powerful
protest against the madness that rapes and ruins the earth, the mother and
home of all the life we know.

> Earth,
>> not yet dead, but about to die,
>> peace be on you.
> Here is a song I scribble in my heart
>> for your funeral
>> — and mine.
>
> When in the shadow of death's poisonous flower, tomorrow
>> your body will lie cold and numb,
>> there will be none left — not I, either,
>> to pay you homage, or let a tear drop on your ashen face.
> So I scribble this for you,
>> earth, about to die.
>
> You gave birth to children innumerable, insociable.
>> You watched them eat each other; you wept in secret.
> Then they started eating you; and you, all-enduring one,
>> you made no move to protest or prevent.
> They who had drunk at your breasts and grown plump
>> felt a new thirst — their last thirst —
>> to suck the blood of your sacred heart.
> They stripped you of the green in which
>> the sun had clothed his beloved bride.
> Into your flesh they sank their nails and drank
>> the blood that gushed from your wounds...
>
> Raped, ostracized, with shaven head, bent
>> beneath the burden of your own children's sin and shame
>> you wander, alone, in space...
> earth, not yet dead, but about to die, peace be on you...[20]

Look at the flowers, the birds

Spiritual and theological writers have, in recent years, been summoning us to conversion and demanding that we pause to rethink and re-feel our attitudes towards the earth and towards its fullness, now in process of depletion. Our irresponsible approach to nature has to go. The traditional "orthodox Christian arrogance" towards God's inarticulate creation must be shed. Tissa Balasuriya is right in maintaining that "to want to dominate the earth without respect for its own laws, needs, rhythms and limits is clear proof of a lack of love — of God, the author of nature".[21] The God who said "master the earth" also said "care for the earth" (Gen. 1:28; 2:15).

It is essential for us to rid ourselves of all sneaking contempt for matter and to develop a respectful concern for what God loves into existence and uses redemptively. A poetic approach to nature must balance and correct the reductionist scientific-technological approach. It would be well for us to follow in the steps of Jesus and look at the flowers and contemplate the birds and encounter the mystery, recognize with St Francis the equality of all creatures, and the sisterhood which integrates all women and men, sun and moon, water and fire, into a single rainbow reality. A feel for the mystery of life in all its forms and for the mystery of the earth as the bearer of life. This mystery is bound up with the ultimate mystery, the womb of all reality.[22]

The call now is to pass beyond traditional other-worldly and inner-worldly asceticism, and know the need of a new pro-worldly asceticism which unfolds into a glad "conviviality" of earth, people and God,[23] conviviality which recognizes the earth as humankind's common table laid by God for God's terrestrial family and friends. Around that table we gather, not in competitive scramble but in joyful fellowship, nurturing and sheltering one another. Such conviviality calls for a critical examination and rejection of unjust social institutions which maintain "unbalanced distribution of land and life-essential resources"; and which contribute "to the destruction of the delicate inter-relationship of the ecological system".[24]

> If the earth were only a few feet in diameter...
>   people would come from everywhere to marvel at it...
>   people would walk around it... people would love it,
>   and defend it with their lives, because they would
>   somehow know...
>   their own roundness could be nothing without it.
> If the earth were only a few feet in diameter.

NOTES

1 Scott McCarthy, *Creation Liturgy: An Earth-Centred Theology of Worship*, San Jose, Calif., Resource Publications, 1987, p.vii.

2 *Ibid.*, p.73.

3 Gustavo Gutiérrez, *On Job*, Maryknoll, NY, Orbis, 1987, pp.67-75.

4 Oodgeroo and Kabul Oodgeroo Noonuccal, *The Rainbow Serpent*, Canberra, Australian Government Publishing Service, 1988.

5 John Damascene, cited in James M. Carmody and Thomas E. Clarke, eds, *Word and Redeemer*, Glen Rock, NJ, Paulist Press, 1966.

6 Pierre Teilhard de Chardin, *The Divine Milieu*, New York, Harper and Row, 1960, p.138.

7 Teresa C. McLuhan, *Touch the Earth: A Self-Portrait of Indian Existence*, New York, Simon and Schuster, 1976, p.6.

8 McCarthy, *op. cit.*, pp.93-94.

9 *Ibid.*, p.vii.

10 Charles Avila, *Ownership: Early Christian Teaching*, Maryknoll, NY, Orbis, 1983, pp.131-55.

11 Noonuccal, *op. cit.*

12 McLuhan, *op. cit.*, p.53.

13 Tissa Balasuriya, *Planetary Theology*, New York, Orbis Books, 1984, p.92.

14 *Ibid.*, p.21.

15 *Ibid.*, pp.24f.

16 *Ibid.*, pp.25,30f.

17 *Ibid.*, pp.28f.

18 *Ibid.*, pp.94,26.

19 *Ibid.*, pp.26,28,92.

20 O.N.V. Kurup, "Requiem for the Earth", in *Kavita 1160*, Trivandrum, India, Kavita Samiti, 1985.

21 *Op. cit.*, p.153.

22 Cf. Lawrence Cunningham, ed., *Brother Francis*, Huntington, IN, Pyramid Publications, 1977, pp.112,120; Warren G. Hansen, *St Francis of Assisi: Patron of the Environment*, Chicago, Franciscan Herald Press, 1971, p.51; McCarthy, *op. cit.*, pp.76,83.

23 Andre Dumas, "The Ecological Crisis and the Doctrine of Creation", *Catholic Mind*, LXX, 1296, New York, America Press, 1975, pp.25f.

24 Mary Evelyn Jegen and Bruno V. Manno, eds, *The Earth is the Lord's*, New York, Paulist Press, 1978, p.128.

Giver of Life —
"Sustain Your Creation"

M. Adebisi Sowunmi

The world is in the throes of both ecological and economic crises which are already assuming catastrophic dimensions for humankind and for the rest of the environment. The manifestations of these crises include air, water and soil pollution through toxic chemical and radioactive waste, soil erosion and salinization, desertification, deforestation, the extinction of plant and animal species, global warming and loss of human life and spirituality. The lattermost is a destruction of the human essence, resulting in alienation from one's culture, which creates loss of self-esteem and human dignity, lack of motivation and a sense of hopelessness. Many of the victims of this human spiritual destruction are destined to become alcoholics, drug addicts and criminals.

Many governments, the United Nations and its agencies and environmentalist groups have recognized the gravity of this situation, and general awareness is growing of the urgent need to halt, or at least drastically slow down, the current rate of environmental degradation. Numerous conferences, seminars and workshops have been held, and copious data have been assembled on issues related to one or the other crisis. Conventions and agreements have been ratified. Yet the situation has hardly improved; indeed it seems in some ways to be deteriorating. Why? I submit that one basic cause is the scandalous lack of willingness or outright refusal by a majority of the guilty rich and transnational corporations, because of greed, selfishness and the desire to make excessive profits, to undertake the radical changes in life-style and in the economic system that are required. The time has come for all those who wish to contribute to the renewal and conservation of the environment to initiate or intensify practical measures to achieve this goal through a change of direction in the relationship with the rest of the created world.

In what follows I shall draw on three perspectives based on my personal experience as a scientist, as a Christian (though not a theologian) who has reflected on the biblical accounts of creation and as an indigenous person (in this context, indigenous people are defined as the initial or original inhabitants of a land who have lived closely with the land).

Insights from science

Perspectives from science show us that the earth was designed to be sustainable, how delicately balanced the natural systems are and that the enormity of the destruction brought about by humanity is out of proportion to its population size and age on earth.

The earth is the only planet in our solar system that can support life as we know it, for four main reasons:

— The presence of bodies of water in liquid form; liquid water is essential, for all life processes in cells occur in colloidal aqueous solution.
— The maintenance of an atmospheric temperature range that permits water to occur in liquid form. The average global atmospheric temperature of the earth is +15°C. This warmth is due to the atmosphere that surrounds the earth, which includes the gases carbon dioxide, nitrous oxide and methane, known as natural greenhouse effect gases because they absorb radiant heat, thus warming the atmosphere. The other three terrestrial planets in our solar system do not support life — Venus is too hot and very rich in carbon dioxide, the atmosphere of Mars is mostly carbon dioxide (96.5 percent), and Mercury is airless.
— The atmospheric composition of gases, especially the life-supporting oxygen and carbon dioxide for photosynthesis.
— The built-in mechanism of self-regulation known as homeostasis, by means of which the components of each ecosystem maintain a dynamic equilibrium.

Although about 70 percent of the earth's surface is made up of water, less than 1 percent is terrestrial fresh water, on which all terrestrial life depends. It is therefore all the more serious when this comparatively small amount of water is polluted.

Planet earth is very small compared with the rest of the universe, which comprises some hundred thousand million galaxies, each in turn containing some hundred thousand million stars. Our own sun is "just an ordinary, average-sized, yellow star".[1] The earth is but one of the nine planets orbiting the sun.

The human population of the earth is about six thousand million. But if the age of modern humankind on earth is compared to the estimated age of the earth itself and of life, the figures are quite sobering. The estimated age of the earth is 4700 million years, while the fossils of the oldest known living organisms, recovered from a rock formation in northwestern Australia, date back about 3500 million years. Modern humans are believed to have evolved not earlier than 100,000 years ago. Thus long before modern humans came on the scene, the earth was in existence and populated by a diversity of plant and animal species that had evolved over time.

It is shocking and frightening how much destruction of life and of the environment humankind has effected in just about 200 years. A few examples illustrate the alarming scope and rate of this destruction or degradation of creation:

— in Latin America, the clearing of rain forests for cattle ranching has eliminated about two million hectares of forests;[2]
— as many as 100 hectares of tropical forests are being destroyed per minute; Africa has lost 52 percent of its original rain forest, Asia 42 percent, and Latin America 37 percent;[3]
— in the last thirty years, African elephants have been massacred at the alarming rate of 100,000 per year;
— due to global warming (brought about by human-related release of gases and compounds), sea levels are said to be rising at the rate of 20 cm. per decade; there have been erratic and devastating climatic conditions — such as hurricanes in Europe — which might have been caused by global warming;
— material resources are wasted through wars; the Gulf War of 1991 is said to have cost the US-led coalition more than US$100,000 million; worse still is the situation of poor countries in Africa which expend their far scarcer resources on civil wars;
— not only are plants and animals destroyed by humankind, but also fellow human beings, physically, psychologically and spiritually; for example, deforestation results in the displacement and gradual extinction of indigenous peoples, for whom the forest was life since they derived all their sustenance from it. The native population in Brazil, said to have been more than six million in the sixteenth century, is today a mere 200,000. Due to unjust and inhuman national and international economic systems, the poor are becoming more impoverished. Forced to live below the subsistence level, some resort to crime and violence while others waste away as drug addicts and alcoholics.

Biblical references to creation

Our present predicament is due, in large part, to misconceptions about or sinful disregard of God and his creation.

— God is the creator and owner of this world (cf. Gen. 1:1; Ps. 24:1; Isa. 48:12-13; Job 38-40);
— God is the giver and sustainer of all life (cf. Ps. 104:29b,30);
— in creation God established order out of chaos (Gen. 1:1-31; Isa. 45:18; the rendition of this latter verse in *The Living Bible* is particularly graphic and incisive: "For Jehovah created the heavens and earth and put everything in place, and he made the world to be lived in, not to be an empty chaos");
— God's purpose in creation was for his own pleasure (Rev. 4:11) and for the harmonious co-existence of all his creatures whom, in his love and grace, he had designed to move about freely and be happy and secure (Ps. 104:10-23);
— God has provided abundant and diverse resources to satisfy the natural needs of humankind and of all other creatures (Ps. 104:10-18,21,27-28);
— God created a very rich diversity (as many as thirty million) of plant and animal species (Ps. 104:24), a vivid testimony to his unsurpassable wisdom (Ps. 19:1-6);
— every human being is made in the image of God (Gen. 1:27) and is therefore of equal worth and value before him;
— God created humans to be partners with him in caring for creation (Gen. 1:28; Ps. 8:6);
— everything God created was perfect and formed a cohesive or integrated, interconnected whole (Gen. 1; Ps. 104:5);
— the Spirit of God is actively involved not only in the initial act of creation but also in the reproduction of life, in the continual sustaining and renewing of the earth (Ps. 104:30);
— God created the world out of nothing (Gen. 1:1).

Thus both science and the Bible clearly show that God created a perfect earth, with awe-inspiring grandeur and an amazing array of biological species; and he made provisions of abundant resources to satisfy the needs of humankind and of all other creatures.

Insights from indigenous cultures

Indigenous peoples all over the world — Pacific Islanders, Africans, American Indians, Aboriginal Australians — have similar beliefs and philosophies regarding the land and their relationships to the land and the rest of the environment. For example:
— the land is "mother" — the source of nourishment, survival and indeed life. It should be reverenced. In some communities the land cannot be owned since the people are owned by it;

— creation is regarded as interconnected, humankind being an integral part of it. Some believe that any serious misdemeanour disrupts the harmony of creation, resulting in ecological disasters;
— indigenous people have an excellent knowledge of their environment, not over-exploiting its wide range of resources. Several are known to use more than a hundred different plant species for dietary, medicinal and other domestic purposes. A sign of their harmonious existence with the environment and judicious exploitation of it is that they can remain for generations, over thousands of years, in the same area;
— hunting was solely for food and other basic needs, not for sport or fun;
— agriculturists practised mixed cropping, which was similar to the natural ecosystems in having a diversity of species;
— people collected from the environment only as much as they needed;
— communal spirit and kinship bonds were very strong; negative individualism, selfishness and greed were very much discouraged; indeed, among the Aboriginal people the idea of private property of any sort was unknown.

Thus these cultures promoted harmony between humankind and the environment and a healthy concept of how to relate to it. Hitherto what has been known about these cultures has come largely from academic studies in ethno-archaeology and anthropology, usually by foreign scholars who often regarded the people as "primitive". This attitude must change. The rest of the world and the "modernized" descendants of these cultural groups need to learn what they can appropriate from them towards establishing an economic order for the sustainability of creation.

Colonizing powers imposed on these people their own cultures, which they in their arrogance and ignorance considered to be superior and "civilized". The fact that the so-called superior cultures have been the ones largely responsible for the degradation of the environment as well as the economic crises of the impoverished ex-colonies is a clear indication of the failure of their ideologies and life-styles.

Some causes of the economic and ecological crises

Considering the two interlinked crises against the backdrop of the brief analyses made above, one may conclude that the underlying cause is essentially the replacement or domination of the "culture of life" of the indigenous, non-industrialized peoples by a "culture of death" characteristic of the rich and powerful in industrializing and industrialized countries. The latter culture is at variance with God's purpose in creation. The Holy Spirit is not allowed to operate in the lives of those who control

and sustain the political and economic systems of those countries. In this idolatrous "culture of death",
— economic, political and military powers are worshipped and valued above human life;
— the environment (including humankind) is exploited only to satisfy the selfishness and greed of the exploiters;
— God's Lordship over all the world is in effect denied;
— there is a callous, greedy, unjust and selfish exploitation of the impoverished by the rich — either as individuals or as nations. According to a World Bank report of 1987, the net outflow from Latin American, African and Asian countries was US$30,000 million. Much of the fish caught in Third World waters goes to feed pets and livestock in the North rather than people in those countries.[4] Japan imports 70 percent of its current timber demands, 97 percent of this from Southeast Asia, and Japanese consumers throw away 20,000 million pairs of wooden chopsticks each year. Australia destroyed 20 million sheep in a three-year period because of the glut in the wool market, yet the sheep were overbred when the market was buoyant.

Leaders in both rich and poor countries on the whole lack the political will, commitment and patriotism to improve the conditions of living there; in some cases disproportionately huge sums are spent on militarization.

A radically new global political and economic order, informed by Christian ethics and Christians perspectives on creation and by values from indigenous cultures — both of which promote sustainability and justice for all creation — is urgently needed. The oppressed must be fully involved in formulating this, and their views must be given prominence. Furthermore, a fundamental change is required in the life-style, mentality and attitude of the rich and powerful in both industrialized and industrializing countries, so as to enhance the renewal and sustainability of creation.

How are recommendations such as these to be practically realized? Are we prepared to be personally involved? If not, we should stop pretending to be interested in the renewal of creation. But if we are sincere, we should be receptive to the Holy Spirit and be ready to be part of the answer to our own prayer, "Giver of life — sustain your creation!"

NOTES

[1] Stephen Hawking, *A Brief History of Time*, London, Bantam, 1990, p.37.

[2] *Global Economy Handbook*, 1990.

[3] "Rainforests", Friends of the Earth press release, July 1987.

[4] *Business Times*, Malaysia, 2 August 1984.

Ecology and Ethiopian Orthodox Theology

Tsehai Berhane-Selassie

Ethiopian Orthodox Christians interpret and practise Christianity from the perspective of how they see their environment, their lives and their relationship to God and the Bible.[1] Their relationship with their environment stretches the tenets of Christianity to include their experiences of the physical world around them in a particularly African manner. As was the case in the definitions proposed by many ancient philosophers, "Man" is the centre of the universe; ecology in the understanding of Ethiopian Orthodox Christianity starts and ends by placing human beings at the centre.

In this paper we shall seek to illustrate some of the processes of adapting Christianity to African culture and ecological experience with particular reference to how Ethiopians interpret the story of creation and how they then apply these interpretations to express and define their ecology. Using the biblical story of creation as a starting point, we shall see how Ethiopian Orthodox Christians fill the space around them with spirits and how they relate to life on earth and define their environment and their country in terms of their concepts of sin and God's covenant of mercy.

Our discussion draws on popular knowledge among Ethiopian Orthodox Christians, rather than official precepts of the church, since it is at this level that Christianity can be said to have made a strong mark on an African people who have adapted it to suit their culture. The history of the church, the social position of the priesthood and laity, the spread of church sites, its characteristic rites and rituals and cultural expressions and modes of behaviour disclose some of the ways in which Ethiopians have been affected by Christianity and practised it from their own African perspective. This is not necessarily the same as the formal Orthodox definitions; it incorporates other belief systems, including the basic African polytheism.

An historical overview

Christianity was brought to Northern Ethiopia in the first quarter of the fourth century by Syrian monks who travelled to what was then the kingdom of Axum. The southern limits of that kingdom are unclear, but by the eighth century, Christian monks had arrived about 2000 km. further south around Mount Zeqwala, near the present-day capital, Addis Ababa, in the central highlands. By the eleventh century, it had penetrated about 500 km. further south to the highland massifs of southern Ethiopia.

The topography of the country presented formidable barriers to communication. About two-thirds of Ethiopia is mountainous, with very little plateau. The valleys are deep, and many low-lying areas contained malaria, fever and hostile wildlife. For the most part, the highlanders practise mixed farming, while the lowlanders are pastoralists. Since the lowlands formed the preferred trade routes to the Red Sea and the Nile Valley, people in these areas were influenced by Islam to varying degrees. Trade-oriented lowlanders have at times competed with the generally Christian highlanders over the control of the trade routes. However, people in the two ecological zones are economically interdependent, if only because of the pastoralist and agriculturalist modes of production; and through the centuries the two religions have found means of coexistence.

The evangelical history of the Ethiopian Orthodox Church was intermittent, taking, as we have seen, almost seven centuries to reach the southern regions. In addition, its sphere of influence was seriously challenged at various stages by followers of non-Christian forces, most seriously by Islam in the fifteenth and sixteenth centuries. Further challenges came with the introduction of Western Christianity — Catholicism in the sixteenth and seventeenth centuries, Protestantism in the last decades of the nineteenth century. Nevertheless, the church still commands broad and pervasive influence on the customs of various linguistic groups at different cultural levels. Even among the followers of other Christian churches, the precepts of its formal theology prevail, though in a diffuse and limited manner. At the same time, the church's beliefs and practices are deeply imprinted with the life-styles and world-views of almost all people in the highlands, especially with regard to the human-ecology relationship.

For centuries, the spiritual head of the Ethiopian Orthodox Church was a Copt (Egyptian). Bishops, locally known as *abun*, were appointed from among the monks of Egypt and sent to live out their lives in

Ethiopia. In 1956 the Ethiopian church separated from the Egyptian, set up its own patriarchate and became autocephalous or self-governing.

Beliefs and practices

The practices of Ethiopian Orthodox Christianity are largely based on the Old Testament. Strict rules prescribe fasting, abstinence from food, rituals of prayer and observance of holy days on which land is not to be farmed or food prepared. All churches keep *tabots* representing the ark of the covenant — tablets with the Ten Commandments or the letters Alpha and Omega written on them. Some are elaborately made and decorated with gold and silver, others are simply made of wood. Indeed, the ark which God commanded Moses to build is said to exist in the ancient church at Axum.[2]

The layout of churches emulates a map of the Holy Land, even in such details as the "Bethlehem" where the bread of sacrament is baked. In fact, eleven monolithic churches at Lalibela are designed to represent the whole landscape of the Holy Land, complete with the River Jordan. According to tradition, these churches were built between the eighth and thirteenth centuries by human hands during the day and by angels at night. With pilgrimages to the Holy Land itself difficult, pilgrimages to ancient churches and monasteries are an important part of Ethiopian piety, and the multitude of monasteries, convents and churches imprint the country with a distinctive version of Christianity.

Until the 1974 revolution, priesthood in the Ethiopian Orthodox Church was tied to access to land.[3] A considerable amount of land, popularly believed to be one-third of the traditional Christian areas, was allocated for those who served the church. As a consequence, the church has a tradition of a large number of priests. Only married men may be priests, but unmarried monks and lay priests (*dabtara*) also serve the church. Between 1974 and 1991, the socialist government's land redistribution programme took away much of the land that belonged to those who served the churches. Many priests left the church to seek other means of livelihood, and trees and other land features that had been preserved were destroyed.

The position of women in the church is very subordinate. They cannot be deacons, priests or *dabtara* although they participate in what could be seen as equivalent to choirs in Western churches. In traditional areas, men and women still stand on different sides of the church, separated by curtains. Popular thought sees women as impure; and menstruating women are considered polluting. Along with new mothers, they are not allowed into the church until purified by a priest.

Because of this exclusion — and given the low rate of literacy among the population as a whole — women scholars in the church are very rare. Women do often consult with the *dabtara* for advice, divination and medicine, and are more free and flexible in relating to people and ideas from other religious systems. Women have thus been instrumental in incorporating worldviews that define human-ecology relationships, including veneration of natural features in the environment.

Although the church's structure and practices have created a rigid hierarchy and distance between laity and priesthood, its formal theology, like that of all Christian churches, emphasizes the equality of people before God. While Eve in the Old Testament was seen as the devil's instrument in bringing about sin, women are to be respected, because the Virgin Mary in the New Testament carried the Saviour of the world.[4] In popular thought, this is translated into special respect for virgins because they might bear bishops or other important people in the future.

Human beings are part of God's creation, even though they are special to him because they are made in his image. Popularly, very little else is linked between the rest of nature and the biblical story of creation; and although constant reference is made to "God's creatures", this term has the narrow connotation of non-local or alien people. An exception is the respect due to birds, based on the apocryphal story that after the fall birds fed Adam because they saw him hungry. Attitudes towards ecology and environment are not as clearly delineated in theology as they are in popular thinking and practice. Theological discourse and exegesis in these areas is not well-known, which has also contributed to the accommodation of ideas that may be alien to the main tenets of the Orthodox theology.[5]

In addition to Christianity, Islam, Judaism as practised by the Falasha and various forms of polytheism also prevail in the country. All four have influenced each other, and the relationship between Orthodox Christians and their ecology is deeply intertwined with religious beliefs of various types. Most Orthodox Christians move easily among different practices of the religious systems under various conditions. Orthodox women (more than men) seek advice and solace from Muslim savants and other soothsayers and may also engage in polytheistic practices.

In general this has resulted in a holistic concept of space accommodating human beings, spirits, wildlife and other environmental features such as open water, the air and forests. In traditional rural areas, human beings may even define their communal belonging in terms of the land where the placenta was buried at their birth. Where married people reside in the land of the husband's lineage, this symbolizes access to communally owned land. Growing up in a neighbourhood also means attachment to locations of neighbourhood continuity, welfare and sense of belonging, symbolized by central trees, fields and other natural features.

Violent historical events over the last two decades have been changing these practices if not the belief system: the socialist revolution of 1974, the disappearance of the Falasha, who were airlifted to Israel in the 1980s and the emergence in the 1990s of some forms of Islamic and Protestant fundamentalism among a small sector of the population. Still, a large part of the population — perhaps 31 million out of 51 million, are followers of this ancient Orthodox church, and its churches are the most widespread.

In Addis Ababa alone, there are two hundred churches dedicated to the various names of God, angels, saints (both Ethiopian and early church), holy places and important symbols of Christianity. No one knows quite how many churches there are throughout the country. Some are in caves or underground monolithic buildings, and more are still being uncovered by believers, archaeologists and historians. Churches are thus still an important aspect of ecological definition. It is interesting in this respect that, with devillagization and the return of rural people to their old scattered hamlets, the classification of space is being seen in terms of earlier holistic conceptions, including the emphasis on the locations of the churches.

Human space and the world of spirits

Like many African people, Ethiopian Orthodox Christians believe that the world is shared equally by spirits and human beings. Ethiopians classify the physical environment as "human" and "non-human" space, and they also classify spirits into what I would call "human" and "non-human" beings.

In popular thinking this division emanates from the relationship between God and Eve and God and the devil at the time of creation. Temporal space, human life and spirits are viewed holistically as encompassing both spiritual and practical life. This popular Orthodox Christianity sees no contradiction between the main tenets of the biblical creation stories and the world of spirits. According to one popular narrative, soon after creation Adam and Eve were given thirty children by God, who visited the couple and their children quite frequently. One day Eve decided that it was embarrassing to have God count her children all the time; and the next time he came to visit, she hid fifteen of them. When God asked if these were the only children she had, she said Yes. So God said: "All right, then, let the others remain invisible." They became the ancestors of the spirits which still live alongside human beings.

Since the spirits are descended from Adam and Eve, they are what I refer to as "human" spirits. Depending on the occasion, human attributes, characters, religious and ethnic affiliations are imputed to them. Just like human beings, some are good, others are evil. Some are Christians who observe Orthodox fasts and holy days, others are Muslims, still others Catholics. At the time of the Italian invasion of Ethiopia in 1935, stories spread that some of these spirits had revealed themselves as *ferenje*, "white Europeans".

Spirits have their own abode. Depending on their supposed attitude towards human beings, some of these places are to be venerated while others are to be avoided. Some spirits living in low-lying areas, especially along valleys, are believed to cause fever, inexplicable diseases and possession. According to the formal principles of Orthodox Christianity, people are discouraged from communicating with these spirits or frequenting their environments on their own, lest these spirits possess them and cause disease or insanity. As *zar* (possessing spirits), they can also mislead human beings into worshipping forces other than God. *Zar* may possess a lone individual going to river banks, open and isolated fields or rubbish dumps.

Similar spirit cults exist throughout the country, and their followers include Muslims and members of other religions. The *zar* cult, practised mostly by women and other vulnerable members of society, is also found in Sudan and many parts of North Africa. Members of the cult form support systems around women who have become possessed, giving them material and financial contributions and helping them to cope with the harsh realities of life in poverty. According to anthropologist I.M. Lewis, the popularity of the cult rises and wanes with the general economic conditions of society.[6] In addition, the categorization and allocation of space for the spirits is an important aspect of acknowledging them at all times.

So far as Orthodox Christians venture to explain the cult of spirits, all discomfort in God's world emanates from these spirits, the siblings of human beings, who have their own space although they are invisible because Eve decided to hide her children from God. Respect for certain sites in the environment around the abode of human beings is traditionally dictated by the supposed presence or absence of spirits that have descended from her. To a large extent, belief in their presence dictates how human beings relate to the environment.

A few spirits live in highland areas, occupying the tops or branches of evergreen trees. Indigenous trees which are considered to be the abode of malign spirits are called *adbar* (which refers metaphorically to an important person or location). The spirit inhabitants must be acknowledged, and respect for the *adbar* trees, some of which are said to be hundreds of years old, is an extreme expression of this attitude. People of all religions offer sacrifices and hold rituals under them.

The rituals held under *adbar* trees represent the need for stability. The *adbar* is seen as representing the "spirit" or the underlying dynamic force of a community that lives in a place. *Adbar*, signifying a source of stability, communality and guidance, is considered a potent force and is found in all villages. All who pass by are expected to stop and share in the feast. In urban areas, people use their own doorsteps or any opening meant for common use by neighbours for *adbar*. A bride leaving her parental home is blessed with the words: "May the *adbar* follow or accept you." Dreams are also often seen as emanating from the *adbar*.

The concept of spirits who live in temporal space accommodates both Christian saints and other deities. The most popular veneration of the Virgin Mary is held under huge sycamores centrally located in villages or neighbourhoods. In many parts of the south and centre and some parts of the north, a female deity called Atete and the Virgin Mary are celebrated under the same tree by the same people. Indeed, Atete, celebrated mostly by women as a personal protector, is often confused with the Virgin Mary, the favourite Christian saint of Orthodox women.

More or less throughout the whole country, families celebrate the birthday of the Virgin Mary, which falls on the first day of the month of Genbot (April/May) according to the Ethiopian Orthodox calendar. Women initiate the rituals and whole neighbourhoods partake of the food they prepare. A rational analysis of the timing of this ritual would place it in the context of the climate and the agricultural season. In much of Ethiopia, Genbot is a dry month, just before the rains. Little or nothing is harvested, and food is often short. As a result the month is characterized by fever and general ailments. Interestingly, the ritual involves throwing food in all directions and uttering prayers to placate the spirit and solicit her blessing. The celebrations for both Atete and the Virgin follow similar rituals, the only difference being the use of beads to represent the personal presence of Atete and the feasting by the women who gather to help the celebrant. The strong emphasis on food and the wish for abundance are both essentially the concerns of women, who are basically responsible for the welfare of families.

Spirits are sometimes supposed to live in forests. For example, on the steep slopes of a narrow ridge in the Eja part of Gurage country is a forest that is preserved because both Orthodox Christians and Muslims in the area believe it to be the abode of a "thunder spirit". The lush vegetation on the sides of the hill presents a sharp contrast to the surrounding ridges and mountain slopes: it is the only locality not affected by gully erosion.

A similar respect for the forest continues among the Orthodox Christians of Dizi, in western Ethiopia. The Dizi practise slash-and-burn agriculture, designating space for spirits in the forests, swamps and clearings. By a careful system of fallowing they manage to combine forestry and cultivation of cereal. While I was conducting research in 1992-93, the Dizi people seriously challenged the resettlement pro-gramme which was bringing people from the north to engage in intensive continued agriculture. They spoke of the anger of the local spirits over the destruction of their forest, which was resulting in shortages and drought. They reported that the local spirits were demanding first harvest of barley and milk.

Perceptions about spirits also come into play in determining the space for human dwellings. In general people do not build houses close to artificial ponds that collect water during the rains, lakes or rivers. Such surface water is normally found on lower ground, and some people would rationalize the decision to build houses on higher ground as a way of avoiding flooding during the rains. But very often this would be explained by the need to avoid the spirits which dwell in the water and are believed to cause eye diseases, fever and even possession.

Some lake-dwelling spirits are seen as benign and beneficial. Lake Hora, one of the crater lakes in Bishoftu, is a site of annual pilgrimage for people seeking children.[7] Infertile women and men perform a special ritual that includes sacrificing a bull and sprinkling themselves with lake water, using fresh grass and reeds. The local inhabitants are highly sensitive to the traditions of worshipping Atete, and it is thus perhaps understandable that Christianity in the area is highly interactive with the fertility cult of Atete.

A similar ritual is observed at the site of a thousand-year-old monas-tery by a crater lake in the centre of the extinct volcano at the top of Mt Zeqwala.[8] According to the Christians, St Gabre Menfes Qedus (after whom the monastery church is named), who evangelized in the area in the eighth century, chased Satan all the way from northern Ethiopia and drowned him in this lake. Twice a year both the saint and various spirits, including Atete, are venerated at the same time by the same people. No one sees any contradiction here. Both those who venerate the saint and the spirit share the reeds, the moss and other vegetation in the woods around the church for various aspects of their worship. Indeed the lake on Mount Zeqwala represents everything that goes into perceiving the environment according to the basic polytheistic African belief systems that co-exist with Orthodox Christianity.

"Educated" modern people often believe that people are worshipping the trees, the water or specific localities designated for the spirits. Many old indigenous trees were thus destroyed by "revolutionary" cadres after 1974, and people were forced to build their villages at ecologically inappropriate sites. Zealous fundamentalist Protestant Christians are still known to go around destroying such trees. Many indigenous trees, which had been preserved because of the infusion of Christianity with traditional religion, were also cut down for fuel.

Both the revolutionary cadres and the fundamentalists fail to see the social and ecological implications of the practice. By contrast, traditional Orthodox priests handle the attention paid to spirits in a way that is ecologically friendly. Relating to spirits is not restricted to non-literate lay people who venerate spirits under the *adbar* tree. The Orthodox lay priests, the *dabtara*, claim to know how to control the spirits, in order to use them if necessary, but mostly to exorcise them from the human beings they possess. Perceiving the human being as central to God's creation, Orthodox theology seems to tolerate precepts which preserve the rest of nature too, if necessary accommodating spiritual beings as well.

After the violent changes in the country ordinary Ethiopians are now re-creating their traditional relationship with the environment. In the last several years, rural people in some parts of the country have started to plant seedlings to grow the indigenous trees. Many people worried by continuing poverty, both men and women, explain the planting of trees on the old sites in terms of placating the *adbar* again.

Human beings and "non-human" spirits

Ethiopian Orthodox Christians relate to what I would call a "non-human" spirit, Satan, in a totally different way. According to popular narrative, Satan is a fallen angel who rebelled against God by convincing Eve to eat the forbidden fruit and then trying to cheat the angels into believing he was actually the creator. Under God's orders, the angels, led by the archangel Michael, defeated Satan and put him in hell, where he took charge of all human souls for 5500 years, until Christ died and went to hell to rescue them.

Satan was then put in chains for eternity. However, his children still roam the earth as invisible beings, and along with Satan himself they can be "called up" by the *dabtara*. They are the source of all pageantry and the glorious structures put in place by earthly kings. They are believed to know the future and to make people rich and grant them stature in society. Women are often the mediators between the *dabtara* and those who seek their services.

Satan and his children are "called up" under the greatest secrecy because formally and in public both society and the church frown upon the activity, which people seem to resort to especially in times of stress.

The pageantry and ritual for "calling up" Satan resembles the ceremonies of Ethiopian rulers and dignitaries under the old monarchy. Indeed, it was widely believed that the monarchs, "descendants of Solomon and David", made use of the *dabtara* to dialogue with this non-human spirit. Earthly power, novelties and sudden plenty are associated with Satan. Stories abound of sacks of sugar, cereals and other good things left behind by the devil for his worshippers.

In addition to maintaining secrecy in "calling up" the devil, it was necessary to avoid talking to him. Parts of the ritual were seen as contravening the important tenets of Christianity; and drawing attention to them emphasized the un-Christian nature of the practice. A *dabtara* found "calling up" the devil would be stripped of his priesthood; and both he and his clients would be shunned by society, at least publicly. It is strongly believed that the devil demands human sacrifice in these sessions, and that those who get power and wealth through such a procedure will never come to a good end. Thus, although his existence is acknowledged, the "non-human" spirit is feared, and those who associate with him are condemned.

Space for Satan is allocated, like the *zar*, in water. He is also believed to be in the air. The *dabtara* are said to "call up" Satan from both environments. Rivers in very deep gorges, such as the Abay (Blue Nile), and lakes, such as the deepest of the crater lakes in Bishoftu, are feared as Satan's dwelling places. Only *dabtara* or their companions who wish to use Satan frequent these sites, especially at night.

* * *

To recapitulate, accommodating the biblical story of creation to the widespread African belief in spirits is an important characteristic of popular Ethiopian Orthodox Christianity. By not defining nature explicitly in biblical terms the church has allowed for traditional beliefs, especially where their influences have been strong socially. It has tolerated systems of social support for vulnerable members of society, especially women (as in the *zar*), and strategies of preservation of huge indigenous trees, which can be seen as important landmarks and symbols of neighbourhood stability (as in the *adbar*). Sectors of the church hierarchy, such as the *dabtara*, relate to the invisible descendants of the first human beings created by God; and by turning a blind eye to the activities of the *dabtara*, the church has even become a participant in entertaining thoughts and ideas of sharing the environment with invisible forces such as the spirits which cause disease and other discomforts.

Popular theology in the Ethiopian Orthodox Church emphasizes the tenets of Christianity by restricting the idea of sharing space with those spirits I have called "human-spirits" and frowning upon relations to "non-human" ones, especially Satan, who demands equal attention with if not denial of God. Human beings on earth can relate to other "non-human" spirits in non-physical space, such as the angels and God Almighty, but only through the rituals and prayers of the Ethiopian Orthodox Church. Heaven and hell, both non-physical spaces, are different from earthly spaces.[9] No one, therefore, should relate to Satan chained down in hell, nor claim to have control over the angels and saints of God up in heaven.

In the deeply contrasting topography of Ethiopia, with difficult and unpredictable ecological conditions and an underdeveloped health care system, spirits are seen to cause discomfort and ill health. Cure is provided by holy waters and benign spirits living in these very environments. At this level of thinking, human physical conditions are firmly tied to conditions on earth (mostly recognized by women) rather than to God's wrath and his heavenly space (mostly professed by the male savants of the church). Ecology is seen accordingly, and certain features such as single trees and forests have been preserved for the purpose.

God's land

This does not mean that God is not in control of the earth, heaven and hell and the inhabitants in these spaces. In a traditional narrative, Gennet, where Adam and Eve were created, had four rivers in it. One was the Ghion, the Geez name for the River Abay (Blue Nile), which flows out of Lake Tana in northwestern Ethiopia. This is identified with the River Ghion (Gen. 2:13), which "flows around the whole land of Cush" (Ethiopia). In spiritual songs and patriotic war cries, the River Ghion and highland Ethiopia are the primordial landscape, comparable only to the heavenly Jerusalem. The highlands in the region give the country a special place in the eyes of God: high land is what the meek of the earth will inherit.

Indeed, Ethiopia is God's chosen land, ruled and inhabited by the eldest descendants of God's favoured Israelites, the kings David and Solomon, through the Queen of Sheba, locally known as Makeda, who is said to have been born in what is now Eritrea. Makeda travelled to visit King Solomon and returned with a child from him. When her son, Menilek, grew up, she sent him back to Jerusalem to visit his father. When he returned, Solomon decided to send with him the first-born sons of Israel. Annoyed by this, the first-born sons stole the *tabota tsion*, "ark of the covenant", from the temple of Jerusalem and brought it with them. When the high priests discovered the theft, they gave chase, but a miraculous intervention by the archangel Michael enabled them to escape.[10] Menilek built a temple for the ark in his capital city Axum, where it still rests. His descendants ruled Ethiopia without interruption until the monarchy was overthrown in 1974.

On this account, then, not only does Ethiopia's old capital house the original ark which Moses had, but the country has been blessed by the presence of the first-born sons of Israel and their descendants, both as rulers and as ethnic groups. Despite evidence to the contrary,[11] one version of this narrative holds that the Falasha were descendants of those first-born sons of Israel who had not converted to Christianity. This led to a public uproar when the Falasha were spirited out of the country in the mid-1980s, for with their departure some people felt a vacuum in how they defined Ethiopia and its inhabitants.

Moreover, popular traditions also claim that the Holy Family visited Ethiopia during the flight to Egypt. The presence of both the Virgin Mary and the baby Jesus himself is thus seen as giving the country a special place in God's physical space. After being born of the Virgin Mary, dying and rising on the third day, Christ went to hell, saved all the souls consigned there in the "era of damnation", chained Satan, conquered death and saved humanity from our sins in the "era of mercy". The Virgin, who bore the Saviour, is thus seen as the second ark of the covenant; and by virtue of having visited Axum, both Christ and she have made a special association with the place where the first ark of the covenant has been resting.

As a result, the *tabot* at Axum is known as the Axum Maryam-Tsion Church. The Virgin, portrayed as the second carrier of God's covenant, is placed side by side with the Old Testament covenant of mercy. Until the

1840s, all the kings were crowned at this church, which remains an important and popular site of pilgrimage. It has a bath with holy water that has the power of giving fertility. Women are not allowed inside the church. Indeed, even priests are restricted to the outer circles of the concentric sections of the church. Only one holy priest, who lives out his life in this church, can approach the holy of holies: the *tabot* is said to emit a fiery heat that prevents others from getting near it. Once a year the *tabot* is brought out for public veneration. The designated priest carries it around.

All this imagery recalls God's presence in the burning bush that Moses saw. For Ethiopians, the church of Axum Maryam-Tsion represents the transition and link between Old and New Testaments and the physical presence in Ethiopia of important symbols literally associated with both the Old Testament and the New. Although other churches are not accorded the same status, respect and veneration are also expected to be accorded to them. For instance, all churches, being the places where the *tabots* are kept, are entered only with bare feet.

More to the point of ecological preservation, the grounds around churches are considered holy. Within a certain radius, depending on the size of the grounds, the wood and even the leaves are not to be cut and the land is not to be farmed or "bled". Monasteries have huge grounds which are kept holy; small churches often have only a small fenced-in compound immediately around them.

As a result, the surroundings of many churches are home to wild animals which have almost disappeared elsewhere. Around monasteries in the highlands one may see rare animals such as the colobus monkey, much hunted for its beautiful skin, baboons, leopards, huge snakes and birds of all sorts. The forests are still more or less intact. Many indigenous trees, which in some places have been destroyed completely over the last forty years, are still found standing on their own in the grounds of remote rural churches. Bees make honey inside the roofs of some churches without being disturbed, and doves and other birds make nests even on the ground.

Popular beliefs may attribute these natural consequences of the restrictions on using nature around churches to the inherent holiness of the grounds and its inhabitants. Monasteries are inhabited by monks, and when these holy men reach a high level of asceticism they are visible only to those who retreat for a number of days to pray and fast for the purpose of seeing them. They are popularly said to be holy if a swarm of bees rests on their shoulders. The colobus monkey is holy: it frequents churches. A big snake in a dream represents someone who is chosen by God. The leopard is not only found around churches but it is also so kind that if you lie still on your left side when you meet one and say that you have an eyesore, it will not attack you. Whenever a new church is made, the traditionally recommended trees for planting around it are two indigenous trees, the wild olive, *weira*, and the cedar tree, *ted*.

The spread of churches has thus imposed a symbolism similar to that of the Axum Maryam-Tsion on the whole country. Like the grounds of all churches, Ethiopia itself is literally considered holy by many people of the church and the environment is to be protected. Like the *adbar* trees, and at times almost competing with them in the people's attention, *tabots* (as churches are popularly referred to) spread around the country are important symbols of social life and activity as well as of spirituality.

Historical links are deliberately maintained between all the churches, for example by putting one old and one new *tabot* in a newly dedicated church. The old *tabot* is to be brought from as near as possible to one of the old churches near Axum. Such historical links maintain a chain of continuity through time and space. Also linking the various churches are hermits who continuously travel the length and breadth of the country, bringing ash from burnt incense (supposed to have special healing power) from Axum and other important churches and monasteries. In addition they carry all sorts of information from one part of the country to another.

This inter-relatedness between the physical environment and God's symbolic presence in it is also reflected in peoples' attitudes towards severe climatic and weather conditions. Over the past two decades the effects of the southward push of the Sahel have caused frequent drought and untimely and unpredictable rains. Coupled with that has been the spread of intensive farming, unwise government agricultural policy, and impoverishment of topsoil.

Many people in parts of central and northern Ethiopia strongly believe that these climatic and environmental difficulties are God's response to their relationship with him or neglect of it. [12] As a result, rural people engage in supplication for rain. The general Orthodox population conduct special prayers for mercy, *egziota*, often bringing out the *tabot* and other church paraphernalia. The *dabtara* also claim to know special prayers to conduct the clouds wherever they want them to be, while followers of polytheistic religions engage in more serious rituals of rain-making. It is part of the practical and day-to-day affirmation of physical inter-relatedness between people's spirituality, their environment and God.

This is accompanied by a continuing attempt to define the country in terms of Ethiopian Orthodox Christianity. Discovery in the 1890s of church sites in areas of the southern highlands where there was no semblance of the Christian religion or political and economic ties with the Christian north, were said to indicate thirteenth-century evangelization by a monk from the monastery of Debre Libanos. There have been similar finds in the 1980s and 1990s. Orthodox priests make the most of these discoveries to emphasize that the church had historically flourished in these southern regions of the country. The public is excited by more sites for pilgrimages, holy water and prayer. In the process, the idea of defining the highlands as the chosen land of God is being reaffirmed and the tradition of making churches and planting trees, thereby providing sanctuary for the rest of nature, is being maintained. People share the veneration of these sites. Muslims, who have a tradition of making pilgrimages to the graves of their own holy men, also travel to certain churches such as that of St Gabriel at Qulubi in Bale; similarly, Islamic holy sites in Harar and Bale are visited by Christians.

Followers of polytheistic religions participate in both and interact with Christians and Muslims. To a large degree, they have sustained and shared the tradition of using the ecology for venerating spirits. Although thousands of pilgrims to these sites contribute to the degradation of the immediate area once a year, the idea of enriching the place with trees has been ecologically positive, and the fact that it is part of a shared and commonly recognized practice gives it continuity.

Ecology and Orthodox Christianity

It is clear that Ethiopian Orthodox Christianity understands nature in a holistic manner. Nature includes human and invisible beings, trees, waters, forests and other land features, even air and invisible space and political structures such as a country. Perceptions about the causes of disease and misfortune which make certain features of the environment dangerous for human life are incorporated into the natural order. Dangers emanating from the inaccessible forests of the highlands, from the heat and fevers of the lowlands, from invisible sources in the rivers and other surface waters and unpredictable climatic and weather conditions are seen as instigated by natural spirits which need to be placated. What is more, all aspects of nature and human experience can be derived from Orthodox theology.

Partly as a result of the holistic way of perceiving nature, the religious practice of Orthodox Ethiopians is both inclusive and exclusive of other religious systems as well as humanity and ecology. Without relaxing the main tenets of Christian worship, therefore, Orthodox Christians also venerate nature. Holistic perception has encouraged them to mix Christian symbols with those of Old Testament Judaism and has allowed incorporation of the spirit cults. The presence of *tabots* to mark Christianity and the emphasis on the inheritance from the first-born sons of Israel are unmistakable adaptations of Judaism to Christianity, while attributing spirits to the encounter between God and Eve is an example of adapting Christianity to the basic African spirit cults. Overall, this holistic approach has favoured respect and veneration of nature, enriching and systematizing ecological preservation along with humanity and the rest of God's creation.

Because of the belief that human beings are the centre and height of God's creation, the definition, use and preservation of nature have been popularly intertwined with the maintenance of human welfare. This has pervaded the social and economic systems. Socially, it informed the pattern of human settlement on the environment. People built houses on raised grounds, and preferred to live on the highlands. However, they related to the rest of the environment and nature through the respect and veneration of trees, lakes or other features which they hold as symbolizing the unitary nature and continuity of human and other life.

The story of creation defines the relationships of Ethiopians with the world that they know in an inclusive manner, while the centrality of humanity to nature gives this definition an inward looking and exclusive, almost chauvinistic view (for instance, in terms of the *tabots* defining the "Christian lands" and descent from Israel defining the legitimacy and nature of the political system).

Politically, both the story of creation with human beings at the centre of it and the descent of Ethiopians from the chosen people of God define and give a sense of continuity and stability to the country and the old monarchy, but within the limited ambit of that part of Africa. It also gives a religious foundation to the way the country and its political system have been defined. Of course, this definition has also been influenced by the geopolitical position and history of the country.

Economically, the dualistic perception defines and limits the exploitation of the environment for the benefit of human beings. Ownership of and access to land and belonging in a community are essentially defined in terms of one's birthplace, but exploiting it excessively is regulated by restrictions about observing holy days, holy grounds and venerated sites.

The gender relations that cmcrgc from this system of perception have the most immediate day-to-day consequences. Women, who are responsible for the well-being of the family, resort to popular theology to use the landscape to the fullest possible extent. To be on the safe side, they try to placate God, human beings and invisible spirits by acknowledging the space provided for them and venerating them in different features of the environment. Their role as mothers links them to the surroundings in which they bring up their families. Theirs is the initiative in supplicating the *adbar* and the goddess Atete, thus sustaining the positive relationship that Ethiopians have with their environment. This contrasts sharply with the role that men played until the end of the nineteenth century in destroying wildlife from the lowlands and forests when they went hunting to prove their valour.

The inclusivist-exclusivist perception and mode of behaviour also comes through in the way popular Orthodox Christianity facilitates positive linkages with tradition, including those of the political system and other religions and between people in the geographical area of Ethiopia and generally in northeast Africa. Through accommodating the *adbar* and responding to the discoveries of the *tabots*, aspects of this dualism — historicity and symbolism — are still being encouraged with formal acknowledgment by the church. Indeed, the dualism and the process of adapting religion to human experience probably also explains the current emphasis on tree-planting by the Ethiopian Orthodox Church Development and Inter-Church Aid Department (EOC-DICAD), as well as by the laity at large.

NOTES

[1] I am greatly indebted to Dr Getatchew Haile, who read the draft of this article and drew my attention to further and important tenets and sources of the formal theology of the Ethiopian Orthodox Church. James E. Hug and Maria Riley kindly shared comparative material from other Christian churches, and Dr Hailu Fulass and Peter Esmonde offered useful comments and additional material on popular Ethiopian attitudes towards nature.

[2] This is discussed in detail below. Several scholars have taken this claim literally and tried to verify it; the latest is Graham Hancock, *The Sign and the Seal: A Quest for the Lost Ark of the Covenant*, London, 1992.

[3] Cf. D. Crummey, *Priests and Politicians: Protestant and Catholic Missionaries in Orthodox Ethiopia, 1830-1868*, Oxford, 1972; Tadesse Tamerat, *Church and State in Ethiopia, 1270-1527*, Oxford, 1972.

4 Indeed, formal scholarship even explains away God's creation of Eve from a rib bone of Adam's "right" side. In a commentary on creation as described in Genesis, an ancient Ethiopian scholar says that Eve's creation is analogous to our death as the blood and water which flowed out of the right side of Christ is to our resurrection. Cf. Getatchew Haile and Misrak Amare, trs, "Beauty of the Creation", *Journal of Semitic Studies*, Monograph 16, University of Manchester, 1991, pp.82-83.

5 On the commentaries, see Haile and Amare, *ibid.*, p.1.

6 I.M. Lewis, *Ecstatic Religion: An Anthropological Study of Spirit Possession and Shamanism*, Harmondsworth, UK, Penguin, 1971, pp.71-79; he refers to S. Messing, "Group Therapy and Social Status in the *zar* Cult of Ethiopia", *American Anthropologist*, LX, 1958, pp.1120-27.

7 Tsehai Berhane-Selassie, "Of Grass and Ritual: Reflections on the Lake Side Ceremony", *Sociology and Ethnology Bulletin*, Addis Ababa University, I, no. 1, March 1991, pp.13-15.

8 For reports of trip to the site cf. *ibid.*, Vol. II: Mirgissa Kaba, "Pilgrimage to Zeqwala Abbo", pp. 3-4; Alula Pankhurst, "Field Trip to Mount Zeqwala", pp.5-10; Getie Gelaye, "My Impressions of Dalaga: A Ceremony on Mount Zeqwala", pp. 11-12.

9 The conclusion to "Beauty of the Creation" (*loc. cit.*, pp.86-87) has a holistic formula for understanding creation, especially that concerning the classification of visible and invisible space: "It is said [that] the living place of the creations underneath the earth, underneath the abyss, is darkness. And above the darkness is wind. And that carries the fire. And the fire carries the water. And the water carries the earth. In this manner God harmonized the creations [which are] antagonistic to each other, in order that his deed... may be admired and his omnipotence known. Furthermore, the earth carries the horizon; and the horizon carries the firmament; and the firmament carries the water which is above it. From there upward exists the heaven of heavens. However, underneath all, above all and the carrier of all is God alone."

10 Cf. E.A. Wallis Budge, *The Queen of Sheba and Her Only Son Menyelek*, London, 1932, pp.77-78.

11 Cf. S. Kaplan, *The Beta Israel (Falasha) in Ethiopia: From Earliest Times to the Twentieth Century*, New York University Press, 1992.

12 Cf. Mesfin Wolde Mariam, *Suffering Under God's Environment: A Vertical Study of the Predicament of Peasants in North-Central Ethiopia*, Berne, 1991.

4.

Insights
from Eco-feminism

Ecology, Feminism and African and Asian Spirituality

Towards a Spirituality of Eco-Feminism

Chung Hyun Kyung

Silence,
my soul,
these trees are prayers.
Rabindranath Tagore

One of the most important items on the agenda for our time is how we can live with our mother earth in a way that promotes sustainability, diversity and balance. The earth is in danger. It is being destroyed with alarming speed. If this process is not stopped, the next generation of living beings will have no livable earth to inherit. People who want to protect the earth and to promote a sustainable life-style started the ecological movement, which challenges us to examine our way of thinking about nature, development and scientific progress. Ecologists enable us to see our anthropocentric sinfulness in relation to other living beings. They call us to a new pattern of relations with all beings in the cosmos based on mutuality, interdependence and life-giving values.

Feminist movements all over the world have also raised a radical cultural critique of our way of living. They have identified the cause of women's pain and struggle with the conceptual framework of patriarchy — a hierarchical system of domination in which men with power rule all other beings in the cosmos drawing on the ideological support of sexism, racism, classism, cultural imperialism and androcentrism. This system of

• This article was written as a summary of discussions on ecology at a consultation on African and Asian spirituality (cosmic and indigenous) in Colombo, Sri Lanka, in June 1992. After discussion with the participants, Chung Hyun Kyung wrote it with her own interpretation and language, and it was then reviewed and affirmed by all participants. It forms part of a longer consultation statement published by the Socio-Pastoral Institute, P.O. Box 439, 1099 Manila, Philippines.

"domination-submission" has promoted war, injustice and ecological disaster in world history.

When the ecological movement and the feminist movement joined together to work towards justice, peace and the integrity of creation, they discovered that they share many basic premises — such as their world-view, analysis, method, life-style and vision of the future. Both movements oppose "power-over" relationships which promote dualistic and hierarchical oppression among all beings. They envision liberated and liberating relationships which encourage "power from within" and "power with" other beings. They think the rape of women and the rape of the earth come from the same root: the violence of "power over" which is the main characteristic of the man in power: he destroys the right relationship among all beings.

People who share both feminist and ecological worldviews and participate in the movement for a feminist and ecological new world call themselves eco-feminists and their worldview eco-feminism. They draw their resources for struggle from more egalitarian, body-affirming, nature-respecting religions, cultures and ideologies. They are searching for a spirituality which promotes the immanence of God, the sacredness of this world and the wholeness of body, sensuality and sexuality. They want to rediscover the holiness of matter, which has been prominent in many tribal and indigenous religions of the world. In their yearning for holistic spirituality, eco-feminism and cosmic spirituality can empower each other.

Spirituality of primal religions

Many eco-feminists reject the spirituality of traditional Western Christianity, which is based on Greek and Hellenistic dualism, hierarchy of beings and an androcentric bias. Creation theology in this tradition put human beings, especially man, at the centre of the universe. Man has "dominion over" all other beings in the cosmos, and God has increasingly become the transcendental Other who has power over the whole universe. This God has been used by men colonizers as an ideological weapon for domination, exploitation and oppression. When God becomes a white, rich European man, white European man becomes a god for all other people and beings in the universe. Therefore, eco-feminists are looking for an alternative spirituality which is able to respond to their need for affirming the sacredness of the cosmos.

Where can we find the resources for this cosmic spirituality? Many agree that institutionalized, patriarchal, otherworldly religions cannot be the main source of holistic spirituality and have turned to the spirituality of indigenous people in Asia and Africa. This spirituality gives full value to creation as a dynamic and highly integrated Web of Life. It exudes life-giving values: sacredness of the land, reverence for all creatures, judicious use and conservation of the earth's resources, compassion for the weak, oppressed and marginalized. These cosmic values, rituals and practices are often considered "superstitious". But they capture a cosmic interwovenness that can become a healing and transforming experience for all of us.

A web of relationships

This cosmic interwovenness is a wholesome, harmonious and compassionate web of relationships: intra-personal and interpersonal, communal and societal, global and planetary. These relationships are based on justice: no exploitation, manipulation or oppression, but mutuality, deep respect and delicate balance. For example, when African and Asian people approach or pass rivers, trees, mountains, or when they plant, fish or harvest they often ask permission from the spirits of the land, the mountains, the plants and trees, the rivers and streams. They do not take from nature more than they need or without asking for what they need for life. They try to return to nature in some other way what they have taken, as if to repay this debt.

Therefore, when we incorporate African or Asian indigenous spirituality to eco-feminist spirituality, we begin to perceive the meaning of nature, God and humanity in a fresh new way. First of all, nature stops being a non-feeling, dead place. It becomes a God-infused and God-breathed place. We begin to feel deep respect, even a sense of awe before the life-giving, yet fragile interwovenness of the earth. The earth becomes sacred. The rhythmic ebb and flow of the rivers and seas becomes God's dance. The life-giving fecundity of the land with the water is the source of food coming from God's bosom. The wind and air become God's life-giving breath. Then we cannot destroy earth since God is there. God is the life-giving power. The cosmos is God's "womb". This intimate relationship between God and the cosmos is exploding with the seminal energy that generates and regenerates life. God energizes the cosmos, and the cosmos in return moves with the creator in a cosmic dance of exquisite balance and beauty. In this cosmic unfolding of ongoing creation, human beings become co-creators with God and nature.

This envisioning of right relationships among God, human beings and nature cannot just remain at the level of empowering image in a world of poverty. It should be incarnated in our people's struggle for survival and liberation, empowering their life and movement. The feminist movement has always emphasized that "the personal is political". When we ground our spirituality of eco-feminism in everyday personal and political life, orienting its energy to the liberation of the poor in the Third World, we will develop a concrete green life-style, politics and economics.

The cries of nature from mountains deforested, rivers poisoned and air polluted due to Western-style development, multinational corporations and capitalism break our heart. The cries of women and children who become victims of sexual violence, tourism and poverty make us weep. Reaffirming our commitment to the struggle of liberation of our people and nature, we would share the symbol of a tree as the most inspiring symbol for the spirituality of eco-feminism.

The tree captures the life-giving thrust and power of the eco-feminist movement. Its roots go deep into the soil of mother earth, strengthening it against erosion yet sucking its life-giving moisture. Its trunk thrusts upwards into the freedom of the sky with consummate uniqueness in its texture, shape and size, its leaves, roots and branches. The leaves transform death-dealing, poisonous carbon dioxide into life-giving oxygen. They provide shelter and shade for the life and growth of diverse insects, plants, birds, animals and humans. Its fruit gives food for the body and its flower gives food for the soul. Then, its leaves die and become compost to re-create the soil. This cyclic, rhythmic process of creating, nurturing, healing and re-creating life symbolizes the aspirations of the cosmic spirituality of eco-feminism.

> *I asked the tree,*
> *Speak to me about God,*
> *And it blossomed.*
> Rabindranath Tagore

Women, Economy and Ecology

Aruna Gnanadason

For too long, those of us involved in issues of justice have tended to treat concern for creation as secondary to what we presume to be priority issues. In India in the last few years, however, the environmental movement and the women's movement have revitalized this concern, which has engaged people throughout our history. The urgency with which we need to act cannot be overemphasized. Forests in India are disappearing (we lose 1.3 million hectares per year); soil conditions are deteriorating; water and wind produce erosion (56.6 percent of India's land has suffered); floods and drought cause serious damage every year; indiscriminate use of water resources is causing a fall in the level of ground water. Pollutants and chemical wastes as well as fertilizers and pesticides are eating into the core of our environment.

Bina Agarwal helpfully describes some of the key factors which have brought about this situation.[1]

• *"Scientific" forest-management.* Since colonial times, the state has taken over the forests and land curtailing the community's traditional customary rights. These forestry programmes, unfortunately, concentrate on growing commercially profitable species. There has been indiscriminate felling of trees for profit and for building a service infrastructure of trains, bridges and ships, benefiting a few. Women had in many communities been the protectors of forests as they had derived livelihood from them.

• *Privatization.* In earlier times, members of a community nurtured the piece of land to which they communally had a right. What the government termed "land for the landless" programmes have in fact encouraged exploitation by individuals, most of whom of course are men.

• *Erosion of community resource management.* Traditional institutional arrangements for resource use have been undermined. When the community worked the land, responsibility for resource management was linked to resource use, which was controlled by the community, and women had access to the resources.

• *Population growth*. While this is one cause, it is not the primary reason. Poverty associated with environmental degradation induces a range of fertility-increasing responses. The direct link between the low status accorded to women and increasing population and environmental degradation cannot be overlooked. But women would assert that an anthropocentric view of creation is what damages creation the most.

• *Agricultural technology and production systems*. The choice of these systems cannot be separated from the dominant "scientific agriculture", which is part of the development paradigm that has ignored the integrity of creation and is based on the abuse of the land. Over the years there has also been a systematic devaluation and marginalization of indigenous knowledge about species varieties, processes of nature and sustainable forms of interaction between people and nature. Women's knowledge and creativity have been completely ignored.

I have intentionally included the word "economy" in the title of this paper as a reminder that for women in India, as in most of the Third World, ecology and the protection of the environment and its resources are issues of livelihood and survival. The majority of women in India are poor. They are the backbone of the subsistence economy which sustains rural India. As feminist ecologist Vandana Shiva puts it, poor women in many parts of India are those who "work daily in the production of survival".[2] Although victims of the degeneration of the environment, they are also active in movements to protect it from the onslaughts imposed by "development" on the earth and its resources.

Women and girl children are most affected by environmental degradation because sex role divisions of labour ensure that women do the most strenuous kinds of work related to the resources of the earth: food-gathering, water-collecting and fetching of water from distant places. They are expected to care for the needs of their families, often single-handedly, in contexts where men live wasteful lives. When resources are depleted, women need to go even further in search of food, water and livelihood. Bina Agarwal also speaks of

systematic gender differences in the distribution of subsistence resources (including food and health care) within rural households, as revealed by a range of indicators: ... mortality rates, hospital admissions data and the sex ratio (which is 93 females per 100 males for all India).[3]

Added to this is the fact that women in India do not have access to resources, land or production technology. Women have been unable to compete in the labour market, being seen as a cheap reserve army of unorganized, unskilled labour. The development pattern adopted by India ensures that women are pushed to the periphery where they must engage in a daily struggle for survival.

This has engaged the women's movement in a critique of the entire "development" paradigm, from which neither women nor any of the other subjugated identities, Dalits or tribals, have benefited. A model that views "development" largely from the perspective of economic growth operates to the detriment of large sections of marginalized people, including women, and all of creation. Thus it is clear why women articulate their fears in this way. To quote Vandana Shiva again:

> We perceive development as a patriarchal project because it has emerged from centres of Western capitalist patriarchy and it reproduces those patriarchal structures within the family, in community and throughout the fabric of Third World societies. Patriarchal prejudice colours the structures of knowledge, as well as structures of production and work, that shape and are in turn shaped by "development" activity. Women's knowledge and work as integrally linked to nature is marginalized or displaced, and in its place are introduced patterns of thought and patterns of work that devalue the worth of women's knowledge and women's activities and fragment both nature and society.[4]

Yet we often hear governments and development agencies attempting to integrate women into this dominant development process, using phrases like the "women's component" or "women in development" — even though this dominant model does not in fact "develop" them in any way. Because of their frustration and disillusionment with these processes, many rural women in India have formed their own cooperatives, trusting in their organized power to opt out of mainline development processes and setting up their own small-scale informal structures to afford some small respite.

New economic policy: the environment and women

The discussion of the effects of the economy on both women and creation take on special significance in India in the context of recent economic policy shifts along the lines of recommendations from the World Bank and the International Monetary Fund. The resulting trend towards privatization and monetarization is posing a tremendous burden on the people and the resources of the earth. Gabriele Dietrich warns that:

Ecological concerns get usurped in the process and the regulations on intellectual property rights outlined by the General Agreement on Tariffs and Trades (GATT) violently curtail and appropriate people's alternative knowledge systems.[5]

A market-oriented, industrial economy requires increased energy production, which implies more dams and nuclear energy projects. Recent history has shown how these affect the environment and people's lives in deleterious ways. Women will no doubt be most affected, as they are the ones who must deal with the shortages of water and food that result. The Chipko movement, in the Utharkhand region of the Himalayas, is a largely tribal women-centred struggle, in which local people clung to trees in order to protect them from the saws of the contractor's men. They had also struggled against mining operations in the mountain region. This long struggle, which is a symbolic call to heed the knowledge of women, is beautifully described by Vandana Shiva:

> The Chipko movement started mobilizing for a ban on commercial exploitation throughout the hill districts of Uttar-Pradesh because the over-felling of trees was leading to mountain instability everywhere. In 1975, more than 300 villages in these districts faced the threat of landslides and severe erosion.
>
> The movement for a total ban was spurred by women like the 50-year-old Hima Devi, who had earlier mobilized public opinion against alcoholism, in 1965, and was now moving from village to village to spread the message to save the trees. She spoke for the women at demonstrations and protests against auctions throughout the hill districts: "My sisters are busy in harvesting the kharif crop. They are busy in winnowing. I have come to you with their message. Stop cutting trees. There are no trees even for birds to perch on. Birds flock to our crops and eat them. What will we eat? The firewood is disappearing: how will we cook?"
>
> Bachni Devi of Adwani led a resistance against her own husband who had obtained a local contract to fell the forest. The forest officials arrived to browbeat and intimidate the women and Chipko activists, but found the women holding up lighted lanterns in broad daylight. Puzzled, the forester asked them their intention. The women replied, "We have come to teach you forestry." He retorted, "You foolish women, how can you who prevent felling know the value of the forest? Do you know what forests bear? They produce profit and resin and timber." And the women immediately sang back in chorus:
>
> > What do the forests bear?
> > Soil, water and pure air
> > Soil, water and pure air
> > Sustain the earth and all she bears.

> The Adwani satyagraha created new directions for Chipko. The movement's philosophy and politics now evolved to reflect the needs and knowledge of the women. Peasant women came out openly, challenging the reductionist commercial forestry system on the one hand and the local men who had been colonized by that system, cognitively, economically and politically, on the other.[6]

I have quoted extensively here to illustrate how any act against creation breaks the spiritual bond between women and creation. In pre-Aryan thought in India, nature was symbolized as the embodiment of the feminine principle. The dynamic feminine principle *shakti* (energy, power) is the source and substance of everything. *Prakriti* (nature) manifests this primordial energy. Throughout the centuries women have drawn their *shakti* from *prakriti*. Common concepts such as *bhudevi* (goddess earth) and *bhumatha* (mother earth) emphasize this.

Itwari Devi, a woman leader in the struggle against mining operations, describes how women have drawn energy from nature to sustain their struggles:

> Our power is nature's power, our *shakti* comes from *prakriti*. Our power against the contractor comes from these inner sources, and is strengthened by his trying to oppress and bully us with his false power of money and muscle. We have offered ourselves, even at the cost of our lives, for a peaceful protest to close this mine, to challenge and oppose the power that the government represents. Each attempt to violate us had strengthened our integrity. They stoned our children and hit them with iron rods, but they could not destroy our *shakti*.[7]

The shattered bond

But this intrinsic bond has been broken and abused. Indian culture, which is in essence very patriarchal, has reduced women to subordinate roles through their traditional mothering and nurturing. This has contributed substantially to the abuse of both women and creation. It is assumed in the Indian patriarchal mindset that since women are able to give birth to and suckle new life, and since they have traditionally been the ones most affected by the depletion of natural resources, their responsibility is to care for children and to find the water and fuel the family needs. This has imposed restrictions on women, domesticating them and holding them in hostage to the precarious survival of their families. It has also been the basis for associating women and nature with the base, the inferior, the degraded — to be appropriated, used, abused and discarded. Indian religions have given quasi-divine legitimation to this abuse.

A holistic vision of interdependence

One important characteristic of the feminist paradigm is that although women are the special victims of environmental degradation, they do not speak merely as victims when they participate in environmental movements. They speak here of a whole new creative way of understanding life and doing theology and resolving the conflicts, schisms and dualisms that have been generated. The new insight provided by the participation of rural and tribal women in struggles to save the earth makes clear that women contribute not in passive resignation to the hard life they bear, but in creative actions for sustaining life.

The eco-feminist vision emphasizes the life that is in everything, the value of all God's bounty. It challenges limited views of development that measure the value of the gifts of creation only in terms of their use in the marketplace. Many of the environmental resources we should value (the clean air we breathe, the poetry of a tree or of a mountain) are excluded from economic measurement. Yet their exploitation (as in the tourist industry) or destruction and the costs of cleaning up after the destruction are labelled "growth" and "production".

An eco-feminist theological vision therefore affirms the sacredness of all God's gifts in creation — the animate and the inanimate. It rejects anthropocentric worldviews, which legitimate and even seek biblical sanction for the extraction of more and more from the life-giving mother earth.

In Jesus we see an affirmation of the "small things" of life. He drew inspiration from them in his teachings and his ministry — a lily in the field, a stone, a child, a mustard seed, grains of wheat, fish and loaves of bread, pigs, spit and mud, the birds in the air. Women in the dailiness of their lives have also been in close contact with life's little things, tending and caring for an environment which will enhance the growth and health of their families or communities.

An eco-feminist theological vision also emphasizes the connectedness between women and nature, as between humanity and nature. This poses radical challenges to the Aristotelian dualisms of mind-body, spirit-flesh, culture-nature, man-woman which have informed much of Western patriarchal theology and to the hierarchical theories of "chain of being" and "chain of command". Such a philosophy has legitimated the domination of humanity over the rest of nature and other forms of domination based on gender, race, class and caste. The colonial expansion, the white man's urge to "civilize" the world, the growth of market-based industrial development, the exploitation of the labour of the marginalized in our societies, the gross forms of violence and injustice against women — all these are consequences of this.

Five thousand years ago India was an agricultural country in which the bonds between humanity and the soil were nurtured and the earth therefore gave of her plenty. India continues to be an agricultural country. This must be protected from attempts to destroy the basis of life by senseless acts of aggression in the name of progress and development. The earth our mother cries out for protection. The church and all concerned people will have to heed the voice of women and the environmental movement before it is too late.

NOTES

[1] Bina Agarwal, *The Gender and Environment Debate: Lessons from India*, Vacha Study Circle Readings no. 16, SETV Centre for Social Knowledge and Action, 1992, pp.131-35.
[2] Vandana Shiva, *Staying Alive: Women, Ecology and Survival in India*, Delhi, Kali for Women, 1988, p.210.
[3] Agarwal, *op. cit.*, p.137.
[4] Shiva, *Let Us Survive: Women, Ecology and Development*, Sangarsh, 1986, p.5.
[5] Gabriele Dietrich, "Emerging Feminist and Ecological Concerns in Asia", *In God's Image*, XII, no.1, Spring 1993.
[6] Vandana Shiva, *op. cit.*, pp.74f., 27.
[7] Cited by Shiva, *ibid.*, pp.208f.

A Tide in the Affairs of Women?

Anne Primavesi

Recently a passage from Shakespeare's *Julius Caesar* surfaced in my mind again after many years:

> There is a tide in the affairs of men
> Which, taken at the flood, leads on to fortune;
> Omitted, all the voyage of their life
> Is bound in shallows and in miseries.
> On such a full sea are we now afloat;
> And we must take the current when it serves,
> Or lose our ventures (Act IV, scene iii).

These lines came to mind when reading documents from the United Nations Conference on Environment and Development (UNCED). I found there commitments to including women in environmental decision-making, planning, technical and scientific advisory services and management, promoting women's literacy, education, training, nutrition and health and disseminating gender-relevant knowledge to both women and men.

This "tide in the affairs of women", if "taken at the flood", will lead to their inclusion in the decision-making processes necessary to preserve the human habitat on this planet. If it is "omitted", it will not only be women's lives that will stay "bound in shallows and in miseries". Many see the absence of women from environmental planning as a justice issue. Worldwide, but especially in the South, women are in double jeopardy: they and their children are the most vulnerable physically to the effects of environmental degradation while they are the most powerless politically to do anything about them. Current political, social and economic structures deprive women of the power to implement the changes necessary for them to have a supportable life. The most obvious indication of this is the disparity between what governments spend on arms (killpower) and what they allocate to health, education and environmental research programmes (lifepower). [1]

The UNCED process was described by one participant at the preparatory World Women's Congress for a Healthy Planet as "seesawing constantly between small, homey examples of women's environmental activism and the awesomely daunting spectre of the global power wielded by men".[2] The women at the congress saw this tension between the personal and the political as a blueprint for incorporating the women's dimension into local, national and international decision-making from now on into the next century. What is this dimension and what difference do they intend it to make? In this article I will reflect on some developments in women's scientific, philosophical and theological education which may make a difference not only in local, national and international environmental decision-making, but also in academic and ecclesiastical institutions. The following developments in particular will be traced: the concepts of constructivism in science education and of contextualism in theology, together with ecological and feminist philosophies based on a relational, nonviolent worldview. Their interweaving as the article progresses will be a conscious attempt to "take the current when it serves".

A constructivist model

The constructivist model of science education rests on the premise that the ways in which we build up our knowledge of our experiential world can be explored, and that an awareness of these ways can help us to explore it differently and perhaps better.[3] Since opportunities for learning and discovery are culture-bound and time-specific, knowledge-building can then be seen as a fabric woven by choice out of necessity. The choice usually applies to the present and the future; necessity, interior as well as exterior, often derives from the past, whether it be our personal, social, political or religious inheritance.[4]

There is a sense, however, in which environmental decision-making today is driven by the need to arbitrate between the claims of present necessities and those derived from the future. The tension between the two claims is evident in the perceived need to use finite resources for development, especially in societies where the quality of life is so bad that people cannot reach their full potential, and the need to conserve those resources for a sustainable future. Whether the problems present themselves as demographic trends, illiteracy, bonded labour, militarism or climate change, we must now make decisions that will be determinative for life on the planet in coming generations. A constructivist approach helps us to be aware of the scope and limitations of our decisions: to distinguish between "information" and knowledge; to acknowledge the personal worldview or environment within which we use and interpret the facts and figures presented to us. By understanding how we shape the future we can take responsibility for doing so.

This differs from traditional approaches to knowledge-building, in which the activity of "knowing" centres on the knowing subject conceived of as a "pure" entity in the sense that it is essentially unimpeded by biological or environmental conditions, that is, by personal context. In company with feminist theory, constructivism deliberately breaks that conventional framework and, by taking biological and psychological factors into consideration, commits what professional philosophers and theologians more or less disparagingly dismiss as "psychologism". A further expansion of context is brought about through an ecological perspective, which takes environmental factors into consideration as well.

The traditional disregard of physiological and contextual factors in knowledge-building ignores the fact, central to a constructivist model, that significant learning is likely to occur only if the learner construes the "facts" to be learned as having personal relevance — if they are in some way bound to personal experience and evaluated against personal criteria. Personal knowledge is built up and expanded through transactions between a person and the environment.

A corollary to this, bearing directly on decision-making, is that any programme of knowledge-building neither can nor should be sealed off from everyday life, its institutional or environmental setting or its future effects. How a programme is conceived or carried on, for whom we do it, what we think about its possible effects and what we choose to see as important in it can never be insulated from the environment of that programme. The boundaries of that environment become even more fluid once the results of the programme are communicated. Whether through environmental laws, papal encyclicals, mathematical symbols, metaphors or clichés, they call forth other issues, make connections with and have impacts on other environments unknown to those who conceived the original programme.

Responsible programmes of knowledge-building thus include such questions as how far into the future the enquirer must consider consequences of decisions made on the basis of his or her conclusions. A current scientific example is the decision to develop atomic power, leaving us and future generations with the problem of disposing of nuclear waste in its many manifestations and the continuing production of weapons-grade plutonium. A religious example would be teachings about the human body which have reduced sexuality to its reproductive function. Through this write-off of sexuality our lives continue to be contaminated by negative sexual energy. What influence does this have on the kind of decisions being taken now about genetic engineering and reproductive technologies?

The empowering character of the constructivist model is that it forces us to see and to take responsibility for the power we have to make decisions whose effects we can neither compute nor control. It also presupposes that present social, religious and ideological constructs can be changed, therefore creating different kinds of communities, flawed though they may be; arriving at different perceptions of truth, incomplete though they may be.

A contextual model

The differences between constructivist and traditional approaches are exemplified in the tensions between contextual theologians in the South and ecclesiastical centres of power in the North. Until recently, theological programmes in the North have been conceived and carried through without acknowledgment either of the determining factor of their own context or of the differences between it and the context in which they are received. Within both contexts, a further exclusion — that of women — meant that theological programmes, methodologies and conclusions were dismissive of if not hostile to women's experience. The effects of this continue to be felt by women within the unjust, sexist infrastructures of the theological academy and of the churches, North and South.

In the North, these tensions appeared overtly in the rejection by some theologians of Professor Chung Hyun-Kyung's presentation at the World Council of Churches assembly in Canberra in 1991. They surface continually in debates about the ordination of women. From the Southern context, Leonardo Boff has likened the Vatican's new "universal catechism" to a Big Mac hamburger — the same the world over, with the same sins decried and the same virtues advocated at the North Pole, in the Amazon tropics, in Rome, in Bangkok and in Tahiti. Like many of the non-governmental organizations involved in the UNCED process, who link Northern economic hegemony, typified by McDonald's, with the destruction of indigenous cultures, Boff as a Southern theologian connects this hegemony with that of Northern ecclesiastical power systems.

The late Swedish theologian Per Frostin, after working in Africa, analyzed this tension between constructivist and traditional theological knowledge-building programmes, which is exemplified in Northern suspicion of contextual theologies and Southern reactions to Northern universalist claims, in terms of differences in methodology. Northern theologies deal with ideas: of God, of salvation, of sin. Contextual theologies deal with the social, economic and political impact of ideas on people, on their lives, on their bodies, on their possibilities for survival and growth, on their habitat.[5] This is another way of describing the tension between the "pure" knowledge of traditional philosophy and theology and what is dismissed as "psychologism".

A feminist model

Tensions also surface whenever women claim primacy for their experience. This latter claim resonates with the constructivist assumption that the knower, through inherent activity and organization, actively participates in the construction of known reality. The radical element in constructivism calls into question any cognitive theory which sees the relationship between knowledge and reality in terms of correspondence. Such correspondence is assumed in scientific, philosophical or theological discourse which uses terms such as "seen", "discovered", or "revealed" for the outcome of cognitive process. Knowledge then becomes a reflection or a picture of a world that is already there — that is, which exists before any consciousness sees it or experiences it in any other way than the one which has been presented by men as definitive.

Philosopher of science Helen Longino points out that the scientist's task in this tradition — from Plato's philosophers discovering the fixed relations among forms to Galileo's scientists discovering the laws of geometry written in the language of the grand book of nature — is the discovery of fixed relations.[6] Analogous to this, in my view, has been the assumption that the task of Christian theologians is to discover the fixed relations between the world, humankind and God written in the languages and canonical texts of the Bible.

This assumption ignores other ways in which those relations have been conceived in the rest of the world, especially in the South, for example in mythic narratives or ritual. This dismissal of indigenous religious perspectives needs to be taken seriously as an eco-theological issue, for the wisdom of native peoples, bound inextricably to their religious traditions, has much to teach us about the un-wisdom of our own devaluing and destruction of natural resources. Acknowledgment of our limited perspective is a necessary act of ecological humility. It is also vital to the kind of global decision-making called for by the UNCED documents. How, for instance, are the relations between God and world conceived in the other cultures in the Asia-Pacific region where Christians make up only 3 percent of the population, and specifically in the world's fastest growing economy, China?

The Chinese context

This last question points to a further example of Northern theological hegemony, discussed by Chinese theologian Kwok Pui-Lan in her book *Chinese Women and Christianity: 1860-1927*. She recalls the unsettling debate about "the term question" — how to render the word "God" into the Chinese language. William Milne, an early Protestant missionary, noted that "the Chinese language possesses no single appellation expressive of the ideas which Christians connect with the words elohim, God, deity, etc.". (Milne did not mention that the word "elohim" would express a very different "idea" for the Jews who coined it.) In the seventeenth century the Jesuit missionaries proposed to use *tian* (heaven) or *shangdi* (supreme ruler), but the Dominicans and Franciscans insisted on using *tianzhu* (master of heaven). When the Protestant missionaries arrived in the early nineteenth century, they sought another term for God that would distinguish their religion from Roman Catholicism. They used *shen* and *shangdi*, with the British favouring *shangdi* and the Americans preferring *shen* translated sometimes as God, sometimes as Spirit. Even today, Chinese Roman Catholics use *tianzhu*, mainline Protestants use *shangdi* and Evangelical Christians prefer the term *shen*. Kwok comments:

> But the difference in language only reflects the deeper divergence in mental categories and thought processes. The missionaries believed there is a supreme being, who creates and rules the universe, and God is the name for this "self-existent, eternal, almighty Being, the Creator of heaven and earth". In contrast, the Chinese conceive of cosmogony as a dynamic, continuous and organismic process in which there is no creator who stands outside the universe. "The analogy behind their thinking is not a man making a pot," as A. C. Graham vividly describes it, "but rather a tree growing from its hidden root and branching out".[7]

This reminds us in the North how much our speech betrays us. The content of our word "God", understood from another context, describes a being who rules and masters the universe and is defined by and on behalf of sectarianism, nationalism and sexism. Feminist theology, also done within the context of exclusion from Northern ecclesiastical power, experiences the force of that understanding and struggles to replace it with nonviolent, inclusive content. Seen from within Europe by our Jewish brothers and sisters, our God rules through the terror of the pogrom and the horror of Auschwitz. From the Chinese perspective, he is a God who creates while standing outside the universe, that is, objectively, and as such is, in Kwok's words, "totally unintelligible".

The model of objectivity

This dominating, "objective" God is a hallmark of Western Christian models of divine relationship with the world. It is also, as criticisms from many quarters have forced Christians to acknowledge, a hallmark of European colonizing relationships with the rest of the world. It has been characteristic, too, of "ideal" relationships between citizen and government, husband and wife, scientist and whatever is being researched. The conceptual and practical content of such claims to dominating objectivity, whether attributed to our relations with each other or with God, to knowledge and its communication or to anything else, need to be rigorously examined. Helena Kennedy describes the "ideal of objectivity" within the legal system as a masculine value which has come to be taken as a universal one. Often when the law fails people, she says, it is because "judicial objectivity" has meant a denial of the female or black or working class experience.[8] Evelyn Fox-Keller, writing on subject-object relations as a component of scientific objectivity, argues that not only in the denial of interaction between subject and other but also in the access of domination to the goals of scientific knowledge, one finds the intrusion of a self we begin to recognize as partaking in the cultural construct of masculinity.[9]

The conjunction between the impulse towards domination and effective domination both of the female and of nature as female is well documented.[10] The emphasis here is on the concept of objectivity in our relations with each other and in conceiving God's relationship with the world, and on how this functions as a controlling factor in making decisions. Mary Midgley describes claims by scientists to have no "emotional attachment", bias or wish-fulfilment in their work as a triumph of hope over experience, since it is a claim that the subject-matter of the physical sciences is remote from human concerns (and, by extension, divine concerns) and can be handled with impartiality.[11]

There is however a need for an objectivity that allows the object of our attention to be what it is, to retain its identity in our regard. How do we achieve such an "inclusive" objectivity in our knowledge-building? For we cannot develop fully on the basis of subjective experience alone but need and must create "objective" concepts to filter, shape and share experience with others.

Empowering models

Nelle Morton empowered women in such an enterprise, describing it as the dynamic between the personal and the political.

> We know solidarity with other women and all women simultaneously as most exquisitely personal and powerfully political. Often our first utterance was a cry or agonizing gesture, but in that movement we knew that we had been heard and understood even before the cry was uttered. Our tongues were loosened and we experienced ourselves speaking a new speech — boldly, perhaps, or haltingly, but authentically for the first time in our lives. We experienced a speech that follows hearing, as opposed to the going logic that demands precise speech for more accurate hearing to take place. Hearing, for us, became a personally transitive verb that evoked speech. [12]

This passage presents "hearing into speech" as a hearing engaged in by the whole body, a process that, Morton says, resists analysis and explanation. [13] It is the process experienced and recorded by the women who took part in the Women's Congress at Miami. Over four days fifteen hundred women "heard into speech" dramatic testimonies, which were presented on the fifth day to UNCED secretary general Maurice Strong as a women's political environmental agenda.

Philosopher of language Gemma Fiumara advocates similar attempts to retrieve the functions of listening. These may, she says, allow for truer forms of dialogue than the dialectical dismantlings which tend to re-propose what has been demolished. [14] Through emphasis on hearing/listening, respect for individual difference, for context, is safeguarded. Evelyn Fox-Keller, discussing the interaction between emotional and cognitive experience, defines dynamic objectivity as a form of knowledge that grants the world around us its independent integrity but in a way that remains cognizant of, indeed relies on, our connectivity with that world. She quotes Piaget in support of a pursuit of knowledge that makes use of subjective experience in the interests of a more effective objectivity. [15]

This form of knowledge-building enables us to weave rafts by choice out of necessity whose structural integrity is strong enough to take us out from the shallows and to set us afloat on the full sea. Traditionally the emphasis in theories of knowledge has been on the who and the what, the subject and object of knowledge. Environmental theory extends our horizon to encompass the nature of the knower (who), the process of knowing (how), the context within which the process takes place (where and with whom), as well as the thing known (what). In this communal environment, effective objectivity can be reconceived as a function of the communal structure of knowledge-building rather than as an individual property.[16]

This resonates with Nelle Morton's description of what she called Piaget's "organic approach, refusing to separate the mind from the body and the individual from the world [environment]".[17] Otherwise, she says, the intellect is without roots and nourishment, tantamount to the body being cut off from the spirit and the mind. Morton tackles some of the false theological problems which come from setting boundaries between emotion and thinking. Responding to an essay by a prominent male professor of theology, who declared that women cannot have it both ways, "organic and transcendent", she points out that for women, organic does not mean "staying with the gut, nor is it limited to the senses as nouns". *Transcendent*, evoking static immobility, she replaces with *transcending*, which arises out of the organic in process of reshaping self and society. In a statement that sums up much of a woman's environmental theological agenda, she says:

> Thus spiritual is experienced profoundly as sisterhood in its loftiest and most universal sense and, we may add redundantly, political action of the most radical sort on behalf of and ultimately including all humanity — women, children and men.[18]

I would add: and all living beings.

It is possible now to see how a constructivist-environmental approach to knowledge-building, with its emphasis on personal experience and its refusal to separate that experience from construction of the world, shares a common agenda with the kind of knowledge-building women can and must bring to decision-making processes. The call for the inclusion of women in those processes by various groups responsible for pre- and post-Rio documents appears not only as an act of justice but as positively significant. In the context of an ecological philosophy which holds that the human person is compounded of interactions between elements of which we partake, it is a call to conscious awareness of those interactions and the necessity for sustaining them in a non-violent way. By crossing the boundaries between emotion and what is conventionally classed as thinking, the cognitive act becomes a non-violent act of understanding love between us, between us and all living being, between us and God.[19]

Empowering theology

In the theological context, it is possible now to see how "the term question" forces us to ask not only about our use of the word "God" but also about its content, the doctrines it depends on and supports. In particular we need to question its assumptions about the nature of the relationship between God and world. Ecological philosopher Arne Naess defines an environmental relationship as an intrinsic relation between two things A and B such that the relation belongs to the basic definitions of A and B. Without the relation, A and B are no longer the same things. [20] If the relation between us and the environment is such that we cannot define ourselves or the environment without it, is the same true for the relation between it and God, between God and ourselves, as the Chinese think? If so, then the "where" and "with whom" we know God has to be considered.

The cognitive jolt which comes from doing so — and thus realizing the limitations of one's theological presuppositions — is well illustrated by Diana Eck's experiences in India. Growing up in the United States, she shared a common Christian perception of mountains — Sinai, Tabor, Zion — as "where" God "spoke". She was astonished to find that in India the mythic cosmic mountain, said to anchor the universe at its very centre, has a greater circumference at the top than at the bottom. Who had ever imagined such a mountain? Inverting our usual image of a mountain peak, it spread out at the top, making room for the cities of a whole host of gods.

For Diana Eck, schooled in the religious imagination of the West, the archetypal mountain peak of Sinai had room only for one God. This conforms with our notion that anything truly important should be unique, singular, not part of a set of seven or twelve. Musing on this, she discovered and confronted her own distinctively Western habit of thought, grounded in the Western monotheistic tradition: the expectation and valuing of singularity and uniqueness. The singular is accepted as the proper number for Truth, for God, for Son of God, for church. This is a myth, Eck says, in the sense that it is a powerful story we tell about reality, so powerful that we do not recognize it as our story. The question of how many gods is not really a question of numbers, but of viewpoint. The singular is not the world-shaping myth of religious people alone, but is a particular way of seeing and evaluating in the West that has shaped the worldviews of Marxists, scientists, humanists and atheists. It affects our way of thinking about authority and about truth questions. [21]

It also affects our thinking about ourselves, about our behaviour as the norm, or as a departure from it. Anne Hunt-Overzee expresses this succinctly when she says that it has been through her experience of a non-Christian spiritual tradition that she has come to understand her own spiritual growth and wholeness — indeed, "salvation" in terms of embodiment. [22] We tend to think of our self as singular, not as intrinsically relational. We tend then to make decisions on the basis of our singular perspective rather than allowing for a diversity of perspectives.

A conscious attempt to counteract this tendency is beginning to be accepted as fundamental to a global religious ethic. In particular, it seems to me, it calls for Christian theologians to extend their horizons beyond interchurch dialogue to interfaith pilgrimage. Lois Wilson made such an appeal at the November 1993 Re-Imagining Conference in Minneapolis (USA). Attendance at the Parliament of the World's Religions in Chicago in August 1993 convinced her that all faiths are in pilgrimage and this must be acknowledged. The churches' failure to do so signals a lack of respect for diversity and the loss of their prophetic voice. They must address the question posed to religious leaders at the Parliament:

> What are the traditional teachings within your faith tradition concerning a proper relationship with those who differ in race or gender (conditions one cannot change), or culture, politics, or faith? [23]

The power of difference

If we try to have a proper relationship with those who differ from us in these ways, we find that respect for and encounter with contexts different from our own serve as both a clue to new modes of connectedness between us and an invitation to engagement with others. We also deepen our awareness of the suffering of the other. Our pain has different forms, but there is a very real need for Christians especially to perceive the injustice experienced by their Muslim, Jewish or Hindu neighbours. [24] This mode of knowledge-building constitutes a principle for ordering the world radically, theologically, in an all-encompassing compassion and respect, content with multiplicity. [25]

This kind of knowledge invigorates and bears us on to new ventures, to a fusion of horizons in which, recognizing diverse contexts and respecting differences, we are invited to a form of engagement with the future, with the yet-to-be-experienced. Difference empowers, offering potential for innovation, for new structures, concepts and combinations. [26] Something which does not fit or appear to fit with our own experience challenges us, not only to create a larger multi-dimensional pattern into which it might fit but also to see possibilities not available to us within our own context. Differences then offer understanding of ourselves and of others while allowing for the preservation of the individual. Transcending them, in Nelle Morton's sense of organic process which reshapes self and society, we find that richness and diversity of life forms are indispensable to the flourishing of human and non-human life on earth. Life itself, as a process over evolutionary time, implies the potential for increase of diversity and richness.[27] This is ground for hope, a theological virtue which responds to the needs of an environmentally depleted world.

Evelyn Fox-Keller remarks that in the relationship which scientist Barbara McClintock describes with plants, as in human relations, respect for difference constitutes a claim not only on our interest but on our capacity for empathy — in short, on the highest form of love: love that allows for intimacy without the annihilation of difference. The crucial point was that she could risk the suspension of boundaries between subject and object through this kind of love, precisely because scientific knowledge for her was not premised on that division:

> Self and other, mind and nature survive not in mutual alienation or in symbiotic fusion but in structural integrity. This is a mode of access, honoured by time and human experience, to reliable knowledge.[28]

For me, this structural integrity in knowledge-building enables us to venture our rafts onto the flood tide in affairs, and, we hope, to take them on to fortune.

NOTES

[1] Cf. Ruth Sivard, ed., *World Military and Social Expenditures, 1991*, Washington DC, World Priorities, 1991, which has a special section on the environment.

[2] See Official Report of World Women's Congress for a Healthy Planet, New York, WEDO, 1991.

[3] I rely here on many insights gained from fruitful discussions with Carol Boulter, a friend who lectures in science education at Reading University. Cf. M. Pope and J. Gilbert, "Personal Experience and the Construction of Knowledge in Science", *Science Education*, LXII, no. 2, 1983, pp.193-203; A. Jon Magoon, "Constructivist Approaches in Educational Research", *Review of Educational Research*, XLVII, no. 4, Fall 1977, pp.651-93; M. Pope, "Constructivist Goggles: Implications for Process in Teaching and Learning", paper presented at Bera conference, Sheffield, Aug. 1985; P. Watzlawick, ed., *The Invented Reality*, New York, Norton, 1984.

[4] See W. Ong, ed., *Knowledge and the Future of Man*, New York, Holt, Rinehart & Winston, 1968, pp.22f.

[5] Cf. Per Frostin, *Liberation Theology in Tanzania and South Africa*, Lund, Lund University Press, 1988, pp.6-26.

[6] Helen Longino, "Can There be a Feminist Science?", in *Women, Knowledge and Reality*, eds A. Garry and M. Pearsall, Winchester, MA, Unwin, 1989, pp.203-216.

[7] Kwok Pui-Lan, *Chinese Women and Christianity: 1860-1927*, Atlanta, Scholars Press, 1992, pp.31f.

[8] Helena Kennedy, *Eve was Framed: Women and British Justice*, London, Chatto and Windus, 1992, p.266.

198   ECOTHEOLOGY: VOICES FROM SOUTH AND NORTH

[9] Evelyn Fox-Keller, "Feminism and Science", in Garry and Pearsall, *op. cit.*, pp.175-86.

[10] Cf. Rosemary Ruether, *Gaia and God*, San Francisco, Harper & Row, 1992, ch. 7; and ch. 2 and 3 and the sources quoted in my book, *From Apocalypse to Genesis: Ecology, Feminism & Christianity*, Tunbridge Wells, Burns & Oates, 1991.

[11] Mary Midgley, *Science as Salvation*, London, Routledge, 1992, p.23.

[12] Nelle Morton, *The Journey is Home*, Boston, Beacon Press, 1985, p.99.

[13] *Ibid.*, p.128.

[14] Gemma Fiumara, *The Other Side of Language: A Philosophy of Listening*, London, Routledge, 1990, p.13.

[15] Evelyn Fox-Keller, *Reflections on Gender and Science*, New Haven, Yale University Press, 1985, p.115.

[16] Cf. Longino *op. cit.*, p.208.

[17] *Op. cit.*, p.24.

[18] *Ibid.*, p.98.

[19] Arne Naess, *Ecology, Community and Lifestyle*, Cambridge University Press, 1989, p.63.

[20] *Ibid.*, p.36.

[21] Diana Eck, *Encountering God*, Boston, Beacon Press, 1993, pp.59f.

[22] Anne Hunt-Overzee, "I Am My Relationships: a Personal Reflection on Creating Theology in a Multi-Faith Context in Feminist Theology in a European Context", *Yearbook of the European Society of Women in Theological Research*, eds Annette Esser and Luise Schottroff, Mainz, Grünewald and Kampen, Kok Pharos, 1993, pp.129-37.

[23] Cf. the report on the parliament in *Earthkeeping News: Newsletter of the North American Conference on Christianity and Ecology*, III, no. 2.

[24] Hunt-Overzee, *loc. cit.*, p.133.

[25] Fox-Keller, *Reflections on Gender and Science*, p.163.

[26] Michael Polanyi, *Personal Knowledge*, London, Routledge and Kegan Paul, 1958, p.259.

[27] See James Lovelock, "A Numerical Model for Biodiversity" *Phil. Trans. R. Soc.*, B, 1992, 338, pp.383-91. "What seems important for sustenance is not so much biodiversity as such, but potential biodiversity, the capacity of a healthy system to respond through diversification when the need arises" (p.390).

[28] Evelyn Fox-Keller, *Reflections on Gender and Science*, p.165f.

Eco-feminism and Theology

Rosemary Radford Ruether

What is eco-feminism? What is the relationship between eco-feminism and theology? I would begin to answer these questions by discussing three topics: the ecological crisis, feminism and theology.

The *ecological crisis* refers to a number of interconnected crises: air, water and earth pollution, the exhausting of nature's basic resources, overpopulation, or, in other words, hunger and increasing poverty of half the world's population, especially in the so-called Third World. These phenomena can be understood as components of the crisis in the modern development model, a model that exploits nature but is uninterested in restoring its resources or in promoting justice among human beings.

Feminism is the critique of the cultural and socio-economic system that defines women as an inferior group to be marginalized from public life. Feminist theology reveals how traditional theology underlines these patriarchal patterns within society and the church and its teachings; for example, the idea that woman was created in second place and that she committed the original sin, resulting in expulsion from paradise. Women, therefore, must be subject to men both because of their nature and as punishment for Eve's sin.

The *theology* of eco-feminism brings feminist theology into dialogue with a culturally based critique of the ecological crisis. Patriarchal ideology perceives the earth or nature as a female or as a feminine reality. As such, nature is considered to be inferior to men. As a material being having no spirit, no life in and of itself, nature is only a tool to be exploited by men. The cultural roots of the ecological crisis can be found in this common perception of both women and nature as realities without spirit and tools to be exploited by the dominant males.

The worldviews of both the Greeks and the Hebrews reflect this perspective on women and nature. According to the story of the creation of the cosmos found in Plato's *Timaeus*, there were in the beginning two realities, the reality of ideas or the intellectual world and the reality of matter. The creator moulded the matter according to the patterns of the ideas. First of all, the creator established the cosmos as a round and hierarchical being composed of descending levels. On the highest level, outside the cosmos, was the intellectual world of ideas. The region of the fixed stars was established as the highest level within the cosmos. Under the stars were the seven planets, the last of which was the moon. Under the moon was the air and finally, on the lowest level, the earth. The regions above the moon were said to be immortal, but the life forms below it were mortal.

The creator then created the soul of the world and breathed it into the cosmos so that it began to rotate. Then the creator took what was left of the soul of the world and cut it into pieces; he put these pieces in the stars so that the soul could learn the truth about ideas. The creator ordered the gods of the planets to create the bodies of men. The souls were incarnated in these bodies and were put on the earth. Each soul was given the task of controlling the passions of the body. If the soul was successful in this task, it would return to its star and there enjoy a blessed life. But if the soul was unable to fulfill its task, it would be incarnated after death in the form of a woman or an animal. This teaching clearly demonstrates the relationship in Plato's worldview between cosmic hierarchy and gender hierarchy. There is a parallel between the hierarchy of spirit-matter and soul-body and the hierarchy of male-female and human-animal. For Plato and the other Greek philosophers, woman is akin to matter and its irrational passions, while man is akin to reason and the spirit. Reason must dominate the body just as man must dominate woman.

The Hebrew worldview is somewhat different, but reveals a relationship between God and human beings that is representative of the relationship between man and woman and between human beings and nature. According to the Genesis creation narrative, God created the cosmos, the heavens and the earth from an initial state of chaos. Several words can be used to express this chaos: "emptiness", "darkness", "the abyss", "the waters". God exists outside the chaos, shaping it. God is the active principle; chaos is the receptacle of the creative power of God. The Spirit of God moved over the face of the waters.

God creates by means of his word of command. God said, "Let there be light", and there was light. Chaos does not resist God's commands, but is totally at the disposal of God's command. God created the world in six days and rested on the seventh; thus establishing as a standard for the human race and for all of creation that we must work six days and no more and rest on the sabbath.

God gave human beings, male and female created on the sixth day, sovereignty over the earth, over the fish of the sea, the birds of the sky, the beasts of the land, the plants and trees. God said to them, "subdue the earth and reign over the animals of the sea, the air and the earth". This emphasis is now called "anthropocentrism", due to its perception of the human being as lord over creation and the culmination of God's creative work.

Today we know that human beings have inhabited the earth only recently. The earth has existed for five billion years, whereas *homo sapiens* has been here for only one hundred thousand years. Only in the last ten thousand years have we domesticated plants and animals, thereby becoming the dominant species on the earth.

The Genesis creation narrative took shape during a primitive phase within the process of the domestication of plants and animals. The text expresses confidence in the rights of human beings over other beings and all living things on the earth. In the light of the present ecological crisis, we may ask ourselves if this attitude of human dominance over the earth, the plants and the animals may not have contributed to the exploitation and destruction of nature that we see today.

The Genesis narrative assigns human beings the role of governors over nature, God's representatives on earth. The image of God in the human race is understood in relation to this role: human beings as God's representatives on earth and his governors over nature. But apparently the first chapter of Genesis does not give man this same type of sovereignty over woman. On the contrary, male and female were created at the same time and together partake in the image of God. It is therefore logical to assume that they must share equally in the task of representing God in the governing of nature.

The first chapter of Genesis seems to indicate that in the original creation there were no dominant-subordinate relationships between men and women or between groups of human beings, such as classes or races. This concept of humanity as the collective image of God, a shared image without distinction between individuals, has been a key concept for modern equality movements, those in favour of human and civil rights for oppressed races, the abolition of slavery and the emancipation of women.

But this interpretation of Genesis 1:27 is a product of recent thought. Hebrew culture did not understand the text in this way; it assumed that the task of representing God in the administration of the earth should be carried out by male heads-of-households. The story of the creation of Eve in Genesis 2 and the laws of Israel found in Leviticus and Deuteronomy make it clear that the subjugation of women, as well as slaves, was a constant in Israel. As in other patriarchal societies of that time, Israelite men considered women, slaves, animals and land as private property to be governed by male heads-of-households.

Is the Bible, therefore, responsible for the ecological crisis? Must we find in the teachings of the Bible the source of the mandate that promotes the domination of women and nature? Will it be necessary to reject the religion of the Bible in favour of a spirituality of mutuality between men and women and between human beings and nature? This tendency to blame the religion of the Bible for these evils is often found in eco-feminist writings.

In my opinion, this accusation against the Bible is much too simplistic. These attitudes of domination over women and nature existed in all the other patriarchal societies of that time. In no way were they specific to Israel. In addition, these classical cultures, including the Hebrew culture, also established regulations for the care and maintenance of the earth as a way of limiting its exploitation. Let us not forget that ancient technology did not allow the extreme abuse of the earth that we see today.

Only in modern times, with the simultaneous appearance of industrialism and colonialism, have we seen the development of a worldwide capacity for exploiting the earth and other people groups that is capable of leading to a survival crisis for the human race on this planet. At the same time, scientific ideology has eliminated the ancient restrictions against the exploitation of the earth that were a part of the classical cultures. It is therefore possible today to conceive of unlimited exploitation of the earth's resources.

We might say that the classical patriarchal cultures have provided certain roots for the development of today's crisis, but it was sparked and fed by modern industrialization and colonialism. We must therefore urgently seek to rebuild our development model, which is based on industrialization, as well as the roots that maintain it, roots that include the classical patriarchal culture of the Hebrews and the Greeks.

But at the same time we recognize positive elements in the culture of the Bible that can be rescued in the creation of a new eco-feminist culture. What are these positive elements? In my opinion there are various aspects of biblical tradition and classical Christianity that can provide ecological values for correcting the exploitation of women and the earth. I want to mention two specifically: the concept of a covenant between God, humanity and nature, and the concept of the cosmos as the body of Christ.

In the Bible we find that the covenant between Israel and God includes all members of the family, including women and servants. It also includes nature, animals, plants and the earth. Male property-owners are restricted in their use of these people or beings. In addition, every sabbath all people, servants, male and female, the animals and the earth must rest in order to be restored.

The laws of the Bible also recognize that unjust relationships develop in history. God requires, therefore, that these unjust relationships be dismantled regularly and that just relationships between human beings, animals and the earth be restored. The biblical ideal is that the earth's resources be shared equally among human beings. Biblical teaching provides for a continuous process of periodic rest and restoration of the earth.

This process of righting relationships climaxes with the year of jubilee. Every fifty years all slaves must be set free, expropriated land must be returned to those who have fallen into slavery and the animals and land must be given over to rest. All relationships between human beings and with nature must return to a just equilibrium.

The concept of the year of jubilee is reflected as well in the teachings of Jesus at the synagogue in Nazareth. Jesus referred back to the concept of the year of jubilee as found in Isaiah in his announcement of the present day of salvation: "The Spirit of the Lord is upon me... to bring good news to the poor. He has sent me to proclaim release to the captives and recovery of sight to the blind, to let the oppressed go free, to proclaim the year of the Lord's favour" (Luke 4:18-19).

The New Testament theme of the cosmos as the body of Christ can be found in several of Paul's epistles as well as the gospel of John. In the first chapter of the gospel of John, the Word of God is revealed as the true beginning of the world. The world does not know him, but the Word comes to the world to restore it and to return human beings to their true identity as God's creatures, sustained by his Word, the beginning of life.

In the epistle to the Colossians, we find a vision of the fullness of salvation in which the cosmos is restored as the body of Christ: "He is the image of the invisible God, the firstborn of all creation; for in him all things in heaven and on earth were created — all things have been created through him and for him... For in him all the fullness of God was pleased to dwell, and through him God was pleased to reconcile to himself all things, whether on earth or in heaven, by making peace through the blood of his cross" (1:15-20).

Such visions of restored justice and a sanctified cosmos through Christ suggest several elements for a new spirituality of love and the protection of all creation. But this new spirituality makes clear the need to develop an eco-feminist culture within the context of today's ecological crisis. For this eco-feminist culture we would need to design and create new relationships between women and men, new relationships between social classes, new relationships between countries on the international scene and new relationships between human beings and nature — relationships of mutual support, of life and not violence or exploitation.

In the gospel perspective, all these transformations are part of the call to salvation which Christ makes to us, a salvation that culminates with the coming of the kingdom of God to earth. But today, perhaps, these symbols from the Bible are not enough. It is also necessary to respect and learn from other cultures, especially the ancient cultures of the indigenous peoples, which often preserve elements of a vision of community among humans, plants, animals and spirits, a vision of a cosmic community that has been lost by modern culture.

In order to create an ecological culture and society, we must transform relationships of domination and exploitation into relationships of mutual support. This transformation will not occur without a parallel change in our image of God, our image of the relationship between God and creation in all its dimensions. We must reformulate our concept of God, no longer to be seen as an imposing power that commands relationships of domination, but as a power of mutual support, the source of a true life of mutuality. This God must be a creator who structures mutually supportive relationships between human beings as well as between people groups in global society and between humans and nature. Only when we have come to understand that God is the source and the foundation calling us to live in relationships of mutual support can we effectively rebuild our vision of the world.

5.

Insights
from Indigenous Peoples

Through the Soles of My Feet
A Personal View of Creation

Rob Cooper

Throughout the world, indigenous people are desperately searching within traditional wisdom for the means to survive. Inevitably, ancient beliefs reassert themselves, teaching once again that truth, when centred on God, creates its own eternal durability. And yet, the truth of creation cannot be confined to one tradition or culture, for despite the human genius of cultural and theological interpretation, the beauty, mystery and grand diversity of the Spirit of God ultimately defy definition.

Precisely because the pulse of life has its origin in God, however, we are driven by an innate need to honour and praise the creator. God is true spirit and therefore cannot be completely defined in human terms. We inevitably find ourselves praising and honouring God in ways we can understand. Those ways arise from within us and reflect our cultural nature and comprehension of life. The following reflection is an expression of the understandings of one Maori, born and bred within God's plan for the world, as lived out in the islands of Aotearoa-New Zealand.

Once, at a bi-cultural dialogue on spirituality, a *Pakeha* (white New Zealander) asked me where I got my spirituality from. Without hesitation I replied, "Through the soles of my feet". It was a spontaneous reaction that had not arisen from any deep reflection. Yet such an insight has its origins in experience, growth and learning about oneself in relation to the world. For me, that growth and understanding was a long time coming. Along with four brothers, I had grown up in Auckland, the nation's economic capital. Our mother was of Irish descent; our father was a Maori from the Northern Ngapuhi tribe. It is through him that we claim our Maori ancestry; and it is through Maori tradition and wisdom that I learned to know, understand and love God.

The Maori creation narrative is both robust and poetically intriguing. In describing *Ranginui* as the sky father and *Papa tu a nuku* as the earth mother, it links Maori cultural understandings with similar indigenous cultures throughout the world. Sadly, we also share with them the experience of displacement from a position as rulers of our destiny to the status of a politically powerless coloured minority within our own country.

This is the bitter fruit of colonization. Yet the crucible of history has helped to refine, purify and invigorate our values and the concept of being Maori in today's world. *Te reo Maori*, our native tongue, is regaining importance as our most distinguishing cultural characteristic. *Marae*, our natural meeting places, are being rebuilt or refurbished. Most importantly, they are being reclaimed by our young. Here the essential essence of being Maori is inculcated and learned, and those lessons are inextricably joined with *Papa tu a nuku*, the earth mother.

Like all the world's cultures, we do not live in isolation. Our nearest "foreign" neighbours dwell within our own shores, having wrested political power from us through the simple process of outnumbering us. In earlier times we fought and, more often than not, defeated them in battle. Although we were never conquered by force of arms, our defeat through the weight of numbers was no less real. So crushing was this cultural invasion that literally thousands of Maori "turned their faces to the wall" during the late 1800s and quietly died. The scourge of disease took its deadly toll, prompting writers of the times to refer to us as a dying race.

Yet we survived. Intermarriage eventually occurred. Ultimately an uneasy social relationship was established, though the powerful underlying currents of racial prejudice are reflected in the white mono-culturally driven institutions of politics, commerce, religion and government. Of equal difficulty, however, are the deeply different sets of values that distinguish Maori and *Pakeha*. These differences are rooted in theological as well as sociological understandings.

Specifically, the individual ideas of salvation and the primacy of the individual reflected in British-based law are concepts of "people" that are foreign to Maori. Being Maori ties the individual to lines of genealogy that serve as the means for building *whanaungatanga* (relationships). These *whanaungatanga* enable us to make friends of strangers, to search within ourselves for the ways and means to belong, to rebuild our roots. We do not consider individualism to be important; indeed, an individualized Maori is considered to be at great social risk. Thus it is not difficult to comprehend the universal truth of the sisterhood and brotherhood of humanity. A Maori proverb asks: "*He aha to mea nui o te ao? Maaku e ki atu — He tangata; He tangata; He tangata!*" ("What is the greatest thing on earth? I reply, it is people, people, people!") People and their hopes, needs and dreams must always have priority above all else.

For Maori, Aotearoa-New Zealand is merely a microcosm of the world. From here we are called to live out those God-given values and that sense of unity with creation that should characterize our *whanaungatanga* with God. All the world is God's. And within our tiny part of it, surrounded by the seas that abundantly reflect the world's inheritance of love, we Maori have been blessed with some cultural insights into the beauty, truth and purpose of creation.

Our history convinces us that we are vital participants in God's plan. Even if our understanding of the complete picture is limited, we believe implicitly in our part within it. Therefore, it is utterly unthinkable that we do not govern ourselves, for our ways are not the ways of the *Pakeha*. Nor are they the ways of exploiting, desecrating and despoiling our environment.

How lunatic it is that humankind, seemingly in search of the tranquillity and peace of nature, invades the atmosphere with noisy helicopters that buzz like angry hornets and wasps above the sacred heads of our snow-capped mountains! How perversely high-rise buildings reach into the sky, casting deep shadows on the bosom of *Papa tu a nuku*, making her surface inhospitable. No wonder that so many of the world's cities become no-go areas after dark, for is not the night merely a more complete sunless inner city day? And *Tangaroa*, the name we give to God's guardian of the seas, must look with bewilderment upon the scale of greed and selfishness that characterizes the plunder and pollution of the oceans. What madness is it that drives people excessively to eat, drink, inhale, inject and consume the gifts of God in a seemingly endless orgy of self-destruction? Why does technology so readily become the servant of the beast?

The answers to these questions and the solutions to these problems have all been given long ago. What is lacking is the will to act. Within our midst are people who could be the catalysts for change. Anthropologists call them "indigenous"; and they are the keepers and guardians of a simple, obvious and critically important truth: the world is not merely some gigantic quarry to be worked at the whim of those who would translate its resources into power and wealth. *The world is the only home of humanity*.

This simple truth comes home to me every time I walk barefoot upon the earth (a safe and enjoyable pastime, given the geographical location, climatic conditions and absence of dangerous reptiles, insects or animals underfoot in Aotearoa). Walking or standing barefoot upon the earth provides the conduit for my spiritual enrichment. To stand on the hills of my ancestors still fills my heart as it did when I was a child. There is something about it that inspires reverence. Gripping the earth, grass or field flowers with one's toes is extremely reinvigorating for the soul.

To know this feeling of life is to understand more significantly the meaning of death. Despite the violent deaths of many of my forebears, some of whom perished in defence of our right to be what God created — that is Maori — their *wairua*, or spirit force, still lives in Aotearoa. We understand the spirits of our dead, gentled by the reunification of their bodies with their earth mother, *Papa tu a nuku*, still to belong within God's plan.

That plan of God proceeds. Despite the reckless selfishness of the First World and its would-be followers, there is growing evidence of greater international appreciation for mother earth. Those who say they do not believe in God are nevertheless perplexed by what is happening to planet earth. Those who do believe feel dreadfully apprehensive over the consequences of our lack of responsibility and stewardship for creation.

We are the creatures of a love-filled, generous and forgiving creator. But we are called to be responsible, above all by creation, because it is central to God's purpose and our being. In Maori belief, the earth is not to be conquered as if it were an enemy, but to be loved and co-operated with as if it were our mother. Of course, there will be conflicts of interest, but ultimately the earth will have its way, as it must. For above all else, it is the means of life for all. Therefore, no selfish individual, race, nation or class of people can command the earth, its seas or skies. At best we can co-operate, and when at our best we do so, we are enthralled with the results.

The beautiful simplicity of this truth was brought home to me once while observing some road construction (an admittedly unlikely place to witness co-operation with nature). Two men, one of them a Maori, were operating bulldozers independently of each other, yet working towards the same goal, which was cutting a road into the hillside. The Maori operator seemed to be "nosing" his machine around on the hillside, as if sniffing out the most suitable place to cut. The other operator was shifting large volumes of soil through the simple device of frontal attack.

A casual observer would reasonably have concluded that the Maori was not making the best use of his machine. While the other operator had enlarged a substantial platform on the hillside, from which he was literally attacking the mass of earth, the Maori continued to poke and prod. Here and there he made some exploratory cuts, wielding the blade of his machine in almost surgical fashion. Suddenly, the roar of the machine changed to a lower pitch. The cuts, still precise, sliced into the hillside. Layer upon layer of earth peeled from the flank of the hill, tumbling like wool from the belly of a prostrate sheep. Now the Maori operator demonstrated his skill, his patient search for a seam paying off in the ease with which the earth tumbled down the hillside. Soon he had surpassed the volumes shifted by his partner. Clearly his preliminary preparations and understanding of strata had enabled him to bring man, machine and the living earth into co-operation in the task. Despite sitting on a bloodless giant machine, he could still employ the intuition of ages and coax from his earth mother a form and shape of greater service to her offspring.

Technology is not the measure of human development. That is always evidenced rather by the ways we love and treat the young, the regard and reverence we have for the old and, most specifically, the status, love and respect we accord to women. Yet none of these human values can be compartmentalized, any more than we can differentiate our lives from the world we live in. To attempt to do so is to dishonour our creator and to cease to live in harmony with creation.

But creation is not static nor imposed upon us. We are part and parcel of its dynamics, naming, describing and reshaping it in glorious attempts to make sense of it. Too often however, our human cultures, no matter how refined, limit our horizons. Somehow we cannot conceive of a world beyond the village, a world to which we all belong. Yet the limits of our cultural nature are the framework from within which we understand the world. Therefore we are called to excel at that which we understand, namely our own culture. Somehow or other we indigenous minorities must make sense of our circumstances. Meaning must be given to our experiences, which often seem so overwhelmingly depressing. The humour and ironies of our age offer insights into the future, for as the old adage has it, "many a true word is spoken in jest".

What then are we to make of our introduction into the Western way of life? Why have we been introduced so relatively late into that world? What is it within God's grand plan that brings us to these times?

Our hope is that in coming so late into a world mad with materialism, our identification of ourselves as literally "people of the land" and our harmony with our environment will reflect the way the world could be. There remains within Maori culture, in the way we live, that sense of unity in creation. Identifying every hill, mountain, valley, stream, lake and river by name is not merely an act of power. It is, more importantly, the placing of such natural features within the hearts and lives of our very existence. Naming and knowing our world distinguishes us from the brutes. It also joins us together in responsibility for it — and them. Every part of the world matters, and everyone of us is called simultaneously to be its keeper and child. The pulse of the world is real. It lives with and for us, yet we are not merely parasites upon it, despite the evidence of human actions.

Indigenous people are still largely in touch with these realities. Every tribe throughout the world can identify and describe its tribal territory. All know, or are re-discovering, their tribal resources and their profound connections to the very earth upon which they dwell. Huge expanses of sea, ice and supposedly barren wastelands are home to people whose links with the creator and creation cannot be fully grasped beyond an exclusive membership of indigenous people. Ultimately, however, every single one of us must come to understand our commonality in God. Our very survival as a species is in our hands.

The coupling of technological, scientific and indigenous experiences and skills is not merely desirable but essential. To achieve this will not be easy, but we must try. The whole world is the Lord's, and we are called to be co-operators with this wonder in creation and re-creation.

An Aboriginal Perspective on the Integrity of Creation

Stan McKay

Aboriginal culture is passed from one generation to the next by story telling. The philosophy of life is passed on to the young mainly by their observation of the elders. Many of the most profound teachings are passed on without words.

Our elders say that when our thoughts and dreams are put into written form they lose life. We are people of the oral tradition and it is a struggle to put our teachings into written form. Thus there is a sense of compromise in writing an article which seeks to reflect our spiritual insights on paper. But the turmoil of these days has brought us to the point that our elders advise us to share the insights and even to risk writing them. It is urgent for all people to come together for a healing vision for the earth, our mother.

Art Solomon, an Annishinabe (Ontario, Canada) spiritual elder, wrote the following prayer for a 1983 World Council of Churches meeting in Mauritius which brought together people representing various faith communities to prepare for the WCC's sixth assembly in Vancouver:

Grandfather, look at our brokenness.
Now we must put the sanctity of life as the most sacred principle of power, and renounce the awesome might of materialism.
We know that in all creation, only the family of man has strayed from the sacred way.

We know that we are the ones who are divided, and we are the ones who must come back, together to worship and walk in a sacred way, that by our affirmation we may heal the earth and heal each other.

Now we must affirm life for all that is living or face death in a final desecration with no reprieve.

We hear the screams of those who die for want of food, and whose humanity is aborted and prevented.

Grandfather, the sacred one,
> we know that unless we love and have compassion the healing cannot come.

Grandfather, teach us how to heal our brokenness.

What Art Solomon has shared in this prayer allows the reader to ponder how simple our spiritual world view is — and how profound. The purpose of this paper is to develop some themes that support the renewed ecumenical emphasis on the creation, particularly in the World Council of Churches. Much of this does affirm a Native North American view of creation, but there are also some areas which have not been developed that I could add to the scope of the discussion. Moreover, there are subtle differences in terminology and emphasis which can be confusing and at times contradictory.

"All my relations" (or ants and uncles)

For those who come from a Judaeo-Christian background it might be helpful to view Aboriginal peoples as an "Old Testament people". Like them, we come out of an oral tradition rooted in the creator and the creation. We, like Moses, know about the sacredness of the earth and the promise of land. Our creation stories also emphasize the power of the creator and the goodness of creation. We can relate to the vision of Abraham and the laughter of Sarah. We have dreams like Ezekiel and have known people like the Pharaoh. We call ourselves "the people" to reflect our sense of being chosen.

Indigenous spirituality around the world is centred on the notion of relationship to the whole creation. We call the earth our mother and the animals are our brothers and sisters. Those parts of creation which biologists describe as inanimate we call our relatives. This naming of creation into our family is an imagery of substance, but it is more than that, because it describes a relationship of love and faithfulness between human persons and the creation. This unity as creatures in the creation cannot be expressed exclusively, since it is related to the interdependence and connectedness of all life.

The next logical reflection is that because of our understanding of the gift of creation we are called to share in the fullness of life. It is difficult to express individual ownership within the Native spiritual understanding. If the creatures and the creation are interdependent, it follows that it is not faithful to speak of ownership. Life is understood as a gift, and it makes no sense to claim ownership of any part of the creation. Our leaders have often described how nonsensical it is to lay claim to the air, the water or the land; because these are related to all life. Chief Dan George expresses it this way in *My Heart Soars*: "Of all the teachings we receive, this one is the most important: Nothing belongs to you of what there is; what you take, you must share."

Reference to the earth in our culture is not individualistic so as to indicate ownership. Our words indicate sharing and belonging to the earth. The coming of Europeans to the land which we used in North America meant a conflict of understanding which centres on the ownership of land. The initial misunderstanding is not surprising, since the first immigrants thought of themselves as coming to take "possession" of a "vacant, pagan land". The incredible fact is that this perception continues after five centuries. Equally surprising has been the historical role of the Christian church in this process of colonization, which basically was a dividing up of the earth so it could be a possession.

The developments of our own generation may alter the pattern of non-communication with indigenous peoples about the earth and life. It may be that we have entered into a time of survival which will not allow people to pursue ownership of the earth without perceiving that this path leads to destruction of life, including their own. The most obvious example has been the nuclear threat, but more important for Native people are the depletion of resources and pollution of the environment. We understand this activity to be insane, since we live in an environment which gives life but is sensitive to abuse.

Our elders have told stories about the destruction of mother earth. In their dreams and visions they have known from time immemorial about a deep caring and reverence for life. Living in very natural environments they taught that we are to care for all life or we may die. The elders say: "If you see that the top of the tree is sick you will know that it is dying. If the trees die, we too will die." The earth is our life. It is to be shared, and we know the creator intends it for generations yet unborn.

The process in political circles and in government that has come to be known as "land claims" is devastating to our cultural values. In order for us to participate in the process, our statements become sterile and technical. Our documents must be in language suggested by lawyers and understood by judges. This legal jargon contains concepts of ownership which do not carry our spiritual sense of life. As marginalized peoples, forced to live on tiny plots of land, we encounter the worldview of the wealthy and powerful and are forced to compromise or to die.

Yet we maintain the earth is to be shared, and we continue to challenge faceless corporations to be faithful to their humanity. Even as we are being pushed into the "land claims" process, we maintain our heritage and are motivated by a love of the earth and a concern for the survival of the creation. Our earth mother is in a time of pain and she sustains many thoughtless children.

The circle of life

My remarks thus far may not make sufficiently clear what the spiritual relationships to earth are for us. It is necessary to say that we feel a sense of "Amen" to the psalmist's words, "The earth is the Lord's and all that is in it" (Ps. 24:1). The value that informs the spirituality of my people is one of wholeness. It is related to a view of life which does not separate or compartmentalize. The relationship of health with ourselves, our community and with all creation is a spiritual relationship. The need of the universe is the individual need to be in harmony with the creator. This harmony is expressed by living in the circle of life.

There is an awareness that the Spirit moves through all of life. The Great Spirit is in fact the "cosmic order". Aboriginal North American spirituality draws this cosmic order together with human life in a very experiential way. Our view of the creation and the creator is thus an attempt to unify the worldview of human beings who are interdependent. We are a part of all life. Dogmatic statements are not relevant, since the spiritual pilgrimage is one of unity in which there are many truths from a variety of experiences.

I find the image of living on the earth in harmony with the creation and therefore the creator a helpful one. It means that "faithful" living on the earth will be moving in the rhythm of the creation. It means vibrating to the pulse of life in a natural way without having to "own" the source of the music. It is our experience that the creator reveals truth to the creation and all may share in it. We have ceremonies and symbols of what may be true for us. We have developed myths and rituals which remind us of the centrality of the earth in our experience of the truth about the creator. We seek to integrate life so that there will not be boundaries between the secular and religious. For us, the Great Spirit is in the daily earthly concerns about faithful living in a relationship with the created order.

Each day we are given is for thanksgiving for the earth. We are to enjoy it and share it in service of others. This is the way to grow in unity and harmony. Central to the movement into harmony with other communities is the idea of respect. Respect allows for diversity within the unity of the creator. Dialogue can then take place in a global community which does not develop defensive arguments to protect some truth. The situation will be one of sharing stories instead of dogmatic statements and involves listening as well as talking.

Mending the hoop

Many teachings of the aboriginal North American nations use the symbol of the circle. It is the symbol of the inclusive caring community, in which individuals are respected and interdependence is recognized.

The Christian church has been unclear in its relationship to the creation. The church's earliest understanding of the second coming of Christ was that it was imminent, so that we should disconnect ourselves from the things of creation. Apocalyptic thought becomes part of a philosophy of "hatred of the world", which holds up spiritual salvation as the goal. The result has been a Christology from Europe which interprets biblical references to God's love for the world as being *only* about human salvation. The North American refinement of this incomplete Christology has been to explain that this is a teaching about *individual* human salvation. This entire message of hope is detached from the creation which in the beginning was "good" and which is a part of the world that God "so loved".

The Industrial Revolution and recent technological development have brought us into a mindset which fits our theology. Economic gain is more important than caring for the creation. The pursuit of short-term gain renders the created order disposable. Materialism and militarism are served by science and technology. There is a critical imbalance in the circle of life when our life-style does not reflect a holistic and inclusive vision of the creation.

Aboriginal teachers speak of our individual wholeness which is discovered in a balance of body, mind and spirit. The discovery of the self leads to an understanding of our interdependence with the whole creation. The integrity of creation is a faith statement about our intention to live in balance and harmony with creation. The elders say "you do what you believe". Anthropocentric philosophies and theologies cannot accommodate a holistic balanced approach. They describe the natural order as enemy and seek to destroy the mystery of hope itself.

The Full Circle of Liberation

An American Indian Theology of Place

George Tinker

This is a challenge to hear the voices of indigenous peoples. We make up a Fourth World, if you will, oppressed by both the powerful nations and the so-called developing nations. We share with our Third World relatives the hunger, poverty and repression that have been the continuing common experience of those overpowered by the expansionism of European adventurers and their missionaries five hundred years ago. What distinguishes us from them are deeper, more hidden, but no less deadly effects of colonialism, which impact our distinct cultures in dramatically different ways. These effects are especially felt in the indigenous spiritual experience, and our struggle for liberation is within the context of this distinctive spirituality.

Our liberation struggle has been overlooked until recently in Third World liberation theology models of social change, which often remained inappropriate and ineffective in the struggle of indigenous people for self-determination. In fact, most themes in liberation theologies have been derived from the modes of discourse of the Western academy itself, against which indigenous peoples have struggled for centuries. These modes — whether theological, legal, political, economic or even from the so-called social sciences — have shaped colonial, neo-colonial and Marxist regimes which, in the name of development, modernization or even solidarity, have inflicted spiritual genocide on Fourth World peoples.

Gustavo Gutiérrez, perhaps the foremost liberation theologian, argues that liberation theology (a) should focus on the "non-person" rather than on the non-believer; (b) is a historical project that sees God as revealed in history; (c) makes a revolutionary socialist choice on behalf of the poor; and (d) emerges out of the praxis of the people. The emphasis on praxis is perhaps the most enduring and pervasive gift of liberation theology.

A Native American theology finds the emphasis on the historical unsuitable and begins with a much different understanding of Gutiérrez' category of the non-person. Moreover, Native American culture and spirituality imply political solutions that differ from those currently imposed by any socialist paradigm. In the context of these differences, my hope is for constructive dialogue leading to mutual understanding and solidarity between Third and Fourth World peoples and an advance of genuine and holistic liberation.

Resistance to class categories

In an early essay Gutiérrez argued that much of contemporary theology seeks to respond to the challenge of the non-believer, the one who "questions our religious world and faces it with a demand for profound purification and renewal". By contrast, the challenge to theology in Latin America comes primarily from the person who is not even recognized as a person by the existing social order: the poor, the exploited. This challenge is aimed first of all at our economic, social, political and cultural world; "therefore it is an appeal for the revolutionary transformation of the very bases of a dehumanizing society."

But this powerful naming of the alienation of marginalized poor and oppressed peoples as the impetus for a liberation theology falls short of doing justice to the particularities of indigenous people's suffering of non-personhood. The very affirmation of Third World "non-persons" tends to continue what has been, in praxis, a disaffirmation of indigenous people for now five hundred years in the Americas.

While avoiding the language of explicit political programmes, Gutiérrez like other Latin American theologians identifies the preferential option for the poor with socialist and even implied Marxist solutions that analyze the poor in terms of social class structure. This overlooks the crucial point that indigenous peoples experience their very personhood in terms of their relationship to the land. The liberation theologians' analyses are powerful and effective to a point, but by reducing the non-person to a class of people that share certain universal attributes, they disregard some more telling attributes.

Native American peoples resist categorization in terms of class structure. Instead, we insist on being recognized as "peoples", even nations, with a claim to national sovereignty based on ancient title to our land. Classification, whether as "working class" or "the poor", continues the erosion of our cultural integrity and national agenda. Just as capitalist economic structures — including the church (missionaries) and the academy (anthropologists) — have reduced Native American peoples to non-personhood, so, too, the Marxist agenda fails finally to recognize our distinct personhood.

Reducing our nation-ness to class-ness imposes upon us a particular culture of poverty and especially a culture of labour. It begs the question of whether indigenous peoples desire production in the modern economic sense in the first place. To put the means of production into the hands of the poor eventually makes the poor exploiters of indigenous peoples and their natural resources. Finally, it seriously risks violating the very spiritual values that hold an indigenous cultural group together as a people. I am not suggesting that we simply discard Marxist or other tools of analysis. Rather, this is a constructive critique of these tools and the implicit hegemony they exercise in much of the Third World.

Failure to recognize the distinct personhood of Native American peoples has a history as long as the history of European colonialism and missionary outreach in the Americas. In particular, the church's failure to recognize the personhood of Native Americans was the most devastating. Less directly than the military (yet always accompanied by it), missionaries consistently confused the gospel of Jesus Christ with the gospel of European cultural values and social structures. They saw our cultures and our social structures as inadequate and needing to be replaced with what they called "Christian civilization".

Many liberation theology and socialist movements promise indigenous peoples nothing better than continued cultural genocide. From an American Indian perspective, the problem with modern liberation theology, as with Marxist political movements, is that class analysis gets in the way of recognizing cultural discreteness and even personhood. Small but culturally unique communities stand to be swallowed up by the vision of a classless society, an international workers' movement or a burgeoning majority of Third World urban poor. This, too, is cultural genocide and signifies that indigenous peoples are yet non-persons, even in the light of the gospel of liberation.

God in place and time

Gutiérrez argues that God reveals God's self in history. I would assert that this is not only *not* a self-evident truth, but that Native American theology that is true to our culture must begin with a confession that is both dramatically different from and exclusive of Gutiérrez' starting point. Essentially, a Native American theology must argue out of spiritual experience and praxis that God reveals God's self in creation, in space or place, and not in time.

The Western sense of history as a linear temporal process means that those who heard the gospel first have and always maintain a critical advantage over those of us who hear it later and have to rely on those who heard it first to give us a full interpretation. This has been our consistent experience with the gospel as it has been preached to us by the missionaries of all denominations — just as it has been our experience with the political visions proclaimed to us by revolutionaries. The problem is the assumption of a hegemonic trajectory through history that fails to recognize cultural distinctions. With the best of intentions, solutions to oppressed peoples' suffering are proposed as exclusive programmes that do not allow for diverse possibilities.

Whatever the conqueror's commitment — to evangelization and conversion or to military subjugation and destruction — it was necessary to make the conquest decisive, at military, political, economic, social, legal and religious levels. And just as the conquest had to be decisive, so too must modern revolutions be decisive. They allow no room for peoples who consider themselves distinct — economically, politically, socially and culturally — to find their own revolution or liberation.

A prime example was the situation of the Miskito Indians during the Sandinista revolution in Nicaragua. Summarily relocated from their coastal territories, where they had self-sustaining local economies, to high-altitude communal coffee plantations, Miskito peoples were forced to labour as culturally amorphous workers without regard to the abject cultural dislocation they had suffered. The Miskito Indians had been a *people*; removal from their land reduced them to a *class* whose cultural identity could not be a factor.

Whether in capitalist or socialist guise, then, history and temporality reign supreme in the West. On the other hand, Native American spirituality and values, social and political structures, and even ethics are rooted not in some temporal notion of history but in spatiality. This is perhaps the most dramatic (and largely unnoticed) cultural difference between Native American thought and the Western intellectual tradition.

The issue is not whether time or space is missing in one culture or the other, but which is dominant. Of course Native Americans have a temporal awareness, but it is subordinate to our sense of place. Likewise, the Western tradition has a spatial awareness, but it lacks the priority of the temporal. Hence, progress, history, development, evolution and process become key notions that invade all academic discourse in the

West, from science and economics to philosophy and theology. History becomes the quintessential Western intellectual device.

If Marxist thinking and the notion of a historical dialectic were finally proved correct, then American Indian people and all indigenous peoples would be doomed. Our cultures and value systems, our spirituality, even our social structures would give way to an emergent socialist structure that would impose a notion of the good on all people regardless of ethnicity or culture.

Drawn together in creation

One could argue that we Native American peoples must learn to compromise with the "real world", that to pursue our own cultural affectations is to swim against the current of the modern socio-economic world system. When rightists or capitalists of any shade assert this, they are arguing the self-interest or prerogatives of those who own the system. When Third or Fourth World peoples make the argument, I am curious how readily some of us concede to Western categories of discourse. How easily we internalize the assumption that Western, Euro-American philosophical, theological, economic, social, spiritual and political systems are necessarily definitive of any and all conceivable "real" worlds.

Native Americans think that our perception of the world is just as adequate, perhaps more satisfying and certainly more egalitarian than the West's. In order to sense the power of our culturally integrated structures of cognition, a beginning understanding of Native American spirituality is necessary, for all of existence is spiritual for us. That is our universal starting point, even though we represent a multitude of related cultures, with a great variety of tribal ceremonial structures expressing that spirituality.

That the primary metaphor of existence for Native Americans is spatial does much to explain the fact that American Indian spirituality and American Indian existence itself are deeply rooted in the land, and why our conquest and removal from our lands was so culturally and genocidally destructive to our tribes. There is, however, a more subtle level to this sense of spatiality and land-rootedness. It shows up in nearly all aspects of our existence, in our ceremonial structures, our symbols, our architecture and in the symbolic parameters of a tribe's universe.

The fundamental symbol of the Plains Indians' existence is the circle, a symbol signifying the family, the clan, the tribe and eventually all of creation. Because it has no beginning and no end, all in the circle are of equal value. In its form as a medicine wheel, with two lines forming a cross inscribed vertically and horizontally across its whole, the circle can symbolize the four directions of the Earth, and more important, the four manifestations of *Wakonta* (the sacred mystery, creator, God) that come to us from these directions. Native American egalitarian tendencies are worked out in this spatial symbol in ways that go far beyond the classless egalitarianism of socialism.

In one layer of meaning, these four directions hold together in the same equal balance the four nations of two-leggeds, four-leggeds, wingeds and living-moving things — encompassing all that is created, the trees and rocks, mountains and rivers, as well as animals. Human beings lose their status of primacy and "dominion". In other words, American Indians are driven implicitly and explicitly by their culture and spirituality to recognize the personhood of all "things" in creation. When the Lakota peoples of North America pray *Mitakuye ouyasin*, "for all my relatives", they understand relatives to include not just tribal members, but all of creation.

This matrix of cultural response to the world, which we might call spirituality, continues to have life today in North America among our various Indian tribes, even for those who remain in the church and continue to call themselves Christian. More and more frequently today, Indian Christians are holding on to the old traditions as their way of life and claiming the freedom of the gospel to honour and practice them as integral to their inculturated expression of Christianity.

Today there can be no genuine American Indian theology that does not take our indigenous traditions seriously. This means, of course, that our reading of the gospel and our understanding of faithfulness will represent a radical disjuncture from the theologies and histories of the Western churches of Europe and America — as we pay attention to our stories and memories instead of to theirs.

This inculturation of an indigenous theology is symbolic of American Indian resistance and struggle today. More than symbolic, it gives life to the people. However, we also see the possibility that our interpretations can prove renewing, redeeming and salvific for Western theology and ecclesiology.

An American Indian theology coupled with an American Indian reading of the gospel might provide the theological imagination to generate a more immediate and attainable vision of a just and peaceful world. Respect for creation must necessarily result in justice, just as genuine justice necessarily is the achievement of peace.

We understand repentance as a call to be liberated from our perceived need to be God and instead to assume our rightful place in the world as humble human beings in the circle of creation with all the other created. While Euro-cultural scholars have offered consistently temporal interpretations of the gospel concept *basileia* ("kingdom") of God, an American Indian interpretation builds on a spatial understanding rooted in creation. If *basileia* has to do with God's hegemony, where else is God actually to reign if not in the entirety of the place that God has created?

While God revealing God's self in history holds out some promise for achieving justice and peace at some future moment, the historical-temporal impetus must necessarily delay any full realization of the *basileia* of God. Instead, American Indian spirituality calls us to image ourselves here and now as mere participants in the whole of creation, with respect for and reciprocity with all of creation, and not somehow apart from it and free to use it up at will. The latter is a mistake that was and is epidemic in both the First and Second Worlds and has been recklessly imposed on the rest of us in the name of development.

This understanding of *basileia* and repentance mandates new social and political structures, genuinely different from those created by either of the dominant Euro-cultural structures of capitalism or socialism. The competition generated by Western individualism, temporality and paradigms of history, progress and development must give way to the communal notion of inter-relatedness and reciprocity.

I am not espousing a value-neutral creation theology in the style of Matthew Fox or a New Age spirituality of feel-good individualism. Rather, this is ultimately an expression of a "theology of community" that must generate a consistent interest in justice and peace.

If I image myself as a vital part of a community, indeed as a part of many communities, it becomes more difficult for me to act in ways that are destructive of these communities. The desire or perceived necessity to exert social, political, economic or spiritual control over each other gives way to mutual respect, not just for individuals, but for our culturally distinct communities.

If we believe we are all relatives in this world, then we must live together differently from the way we have. Justice and peace, in this context, emerge almost naturally out of a self-imaging as part of the whole, as part of an ever-expanding community that begins with family and tribe, but is finally inclusive of all human beings and all of creation. Such is the spirit of hope that marks the American Indian struggle of resistance in the midst of a world of pain.

6.

Ethical Implications

Letting People Decide
Towards an Ethic of Ecological Survival in Africa

Edward P. Antonio

> Insofar as there are any significant connections between poverty and environmental degradation, it is poverty as development, not poverty as underdevelopment, that is the problem.
>
> *The Ecologist*

A fairly common theme in discussions of those political theories which concern themselves with the nature of democracy is "participatory democracy". In what follows I shall use the principle of "participatory democracy" to develop a brief general critique of how many popular environmental theories and practices have paid little more than lip-service to the idea of involving indigenous peoples in the design and execution of environmental projects, and to derive from that critique an ethic of survival informed by a Christian and African "humanistic" vision of what it means to "get people involved". What I offer is a series of reflections about several related themes within the context of my concern with the question of popular participation, in the hope that they may provide some basis for conversation and dialogue between Northern and Southern theologians. The paper is divided into two main sections: the first deals with popular participation, sustainable development and the co-optation of environmental concerns by the World Bank and the corporate sector; the second reflects on the tensions between the demands of modern institutions and what, following the Ecologist, I shall call the moral economies of popular participation.

Why "participatory democracy", one might ask. Robin Sharp has noted a number of reasons which necessitate discussion of this issue; I would like to begin with his observation that "people's rights and responsibilities form the crux of any discussion of sustainability".[1] Sharp argues that this is a function of the nature of sustainable development itself, which requires the participation of people in matters that concern their livelihoods. Although I make extensive use of Sharp's article in developing my own reflections and agree quite substantially with his argument, I question the suggestion that it is sustainable development itself which provides the rationale for the attempt to encourage popular participation. For this is to make popular participation a consequence of a recent mode of thought. The concept of "sustainable development" has come to us fairly recently and belongs to a set of discursive practices whose provenance is basically Western. This also applies to other reasons Sharp offers for broaching the question of participatory democracy: reasons such as the fact that both the Arusha Declaration on Popular Participation in Development (1990) and the Manila Declaration on People's Participation and Sustainable Development (1989) affirm the need for getting people involved in making decisions about matters which directly affect their livelihoods. Both these declarations and the wave of demands for democracy which have swept through sub-Saharan Africa since 1989 are embedded in the discourse and institutions of modern economies and political structures.

Popular participation, sustainable development and the co-optation of environmental concern

But while Sharp's reasons for concerning himself with participatory democracy are valid, it is a mistake to give them the status of a starting point. Popular participation is not new to many rural communities in Africa. It is in fact the means by which communities have always sustained themselves and their relationships to nature over long periods of time. Their social objectives were not "development" but simply living, getting on with the business of being around — or, to use the jargon, subsistence. The idea of sustainable development is of course a useful conceptual tool in dealing with the reality of impending ecological disaster, but to make it the starting point for a search for political models that will allow for popular participation is to take away from rural and indigenous communities a practice already very familiar to them. We risk ending up with a definition of popular participation in terms of the needs of sustainable development models and not necessarily in terms of the needs of peoples and communities. We might thus either ignore the reality of existing practices of popular participation or silently co-opt them, redefining them by investing them with a foreign moral content and then imposing them on people.

One of the most powerful and worrying features of capitalism in its "post-modern" phases has been its capacity to co-opt and reproduce the critical discourse of opposition and marginal groups. The languages of both environmental concern and "participatory democracy" have been so co-opted. Both the World Bank and the International Monetary Fund have in recent times spoken in terms of the ecological crisis.[2] Big business and multinational corporations have also jumped onto the bandwagon.[3] The idea of "free market environmentalism" is no longer the pariah it once was.

The assumption behind this sudden discovery is a false kind of democratic utopianism which says that the challenge to survival posed by the environmental crisis is so colossal that we cannot afford to let social and economic differences stand in the way. Whether you are an (allegedly) irrelevant and outmoded church or an illiterate, poverty-stricken villager in some remote part of the world or the IMF itself, the environmental crisis equalizes all. Before it, all must acknowledge the frightful possibility of a common catastrophe or the late recovery of some opportunities for a common future.[4]

On this scenario, survival requires a "by any means necessary" ethic. If the survival of the rich and powerful is to be assured, it does not really matter what means are used. These can range from dumping toxic wastes in Zambia to pretending that Northern governments and economic institutions are genuinely concerned about the plight of the poor and the destabilization of fragile environments in the South. In some parts of the Third World this "by any means necessary" ethic has meant imposing on people — often in the name of the people — certain environmental programmes. The debate on the commons and the issue of enclosures has been a response to this phenomenon. The logic here hardly differs from that used in earlier times to impose "development" on village-dwellers.

Is it really survival or the environmental crisis which is the concern of multinationals, aid agencies and Northern and Southern governments? Here of course we must guard against cynicism. We must be humble enough to acknowledge that we as the people of God do not have a monopoly on genuine concern over the fate of our small planet and our place within it. But it is not cynicism to recognize that the institutions which have now co-opted prophecies of common doom and proclaim a new ecologically sound future for all are the very same institutions which have been responsible for the reproduction of inequalities in the world.

Modern institutions and the
moral economies of popular participation

My point here is not, of course, to deny the universality of the problem. I do not deny that the inhabitants of planet earth are living beyond their limits or gainsay the real achievements of ecological movements and groups in both the North and the South. Indeed, there is a fundamental sense in which it is the successes of these movements and groups which have forced capitalism and those who support it to co-opt the language of environmental survival. Nevertheless, the universalistic language of ecological concern ("the environmental crisis", "our common fate", "our common future"), which has a strong theological appeal for Christians because of the universalism of their own faith, obscures a number of important factors.

The first, which pertains to my concern for popular participation, is that the universalism implied in these phrases does not allow for recognition that "the environmental crisis" is experienced differently by different people, depending on their cultural and economic contexts.[5] And to overlook this is to fail to recognize that the solutions we envisage will also vary according to culture. To accept this is to agree that what the World Bank or a given non-governmental organization regards as the answer to a particular problem in a particular area will not necessarily be so regarded by the inhabitants of that region.

The second point often obscured by universalizing ecological solutions is that ecologies are invariably tied up with people's livelihoods, which are themselves always understood and maintained in terms of rules, regulations, structures and institutions hedged on the one hand by strategies and techniques of problem-solving and on the other by a framework of ethical and moral knowledge about the requirement for sustainable relationships with nature. In rural communities people quite literally live off nature, and they do so in a more immediate and direct sense than their counterparts in urban settings. Their knowledge of the world and their sense of reality are shaped by how they interact with the natural environment. They are moulded by what the Ecologist has so appropriately described as the "moral economies" of local peoples.[6]

"Participation" here is not a programmatic process for facilitating the adoption of modern institutional frameworks to improve the lot of the wretched. Rather it is a natural process, a way of being in the world. Participation is not just concerned with making the right kinds of decision about who should participate, when and under what conditions or about how much power they should be given (although that is obviously an important part of it).[7] It is primarily about relationships between peoples and their natural environments. To speak of traditional, communal styles of participation as ways of being in the world or as culturally sanctioned ways of being in conversation with nature will not make sense unless we see these forms of participation in the context of the connection between ecologies and people's livelihoods, that is, unless we understand them in terms of their "survival value".

Survival is more than physical subsistence. It encompasses the world of the ancestors and their relationships to nature, relationships which themselves provide the moral framework in terms of which members of the present generation define their own ways of dealing with each other and with nature. Here, a good harvest is not simply a matter of hard work or good fortune, just as the rains on which a good harvest depends are not spiritually or morally neutral; for they point beyond themselves to the fact that both the social and natural orders are still morally integrated. At this level, the stability of the society is a function of obedience to the requirements of the sacred order written into natural processes. These processes offer themselves as a kind of ethical or juridical text containing rules and regulations for behaviour. Certain rivers, mountains, trees or animals are sacred; the names of clans and the identities of families and individuals are inscribed into the natural processes so that the self-knowledge people have is inseparable from nature. The system of totems which Durkheim discusses in *The Elementary Forms of the Religious Life*, and which is also widespread in Africa, illustrates the point well.

What is being suggested is not that we should believe in ancestors or adopt a totemic system in order to obtain ecological salvation, but rather that if we universalize environmental problems we will succeed only to the extent that we destroy other people's cultures and identities. To put it another way: to ignore the extent to which ecologies are for traditional communities a matter of livelihood is to precipitate the environmental crisis and not to alleviate it. For the environment is much more than just nature or the "objective world". It includes our attitudes towards each other and towards nature.

If we are going to help others to cope with the enviromental crisis, which has come about largely as a result of the impact of Westernization, we need to take their local cultures and moral systems seriously: first to try to contain some of the disruptive consequences of Westernization and second to see if we ourselves cannot learn from these cultures' ways of saving our planet.

This is exactly what modern political institutions have *not* done in dealing with ecological and development problems at both national and international levels. They have often ignored local cultures on the basis that these are an obstacle to development.[8] They have pretended in the name of development and modernization that "the ecological problem" can be resolved simply by imposing solutions minted elsewhere. The trouble is that the economic practices and political structures associated with modernization and development have descended from a system of profit-derivation that has called into question our humanity, our capacity to care for one another and for creation. These practices and structures have brought us up against not only our finiteness and the finiteness of creation, but also against our own sinfulness, our will to power. This will to power, whose manifestations are the domination of nature and of other peoples, has created a severe tension between "political involvement" and "popular participation", between "macro-economic" structures and "community structures".[9]

This tension is not a tension simply between the (supposedly) objective, technical and democratic institutions of modernity and the value- and ritual-driven structures of (supposedly) "backward" rural communities. It is rather a tension between value systems that understand and value nature differently. Adjectives like "democratic", "objective" and the like hide cultural beliefs and values mortgaged to a moral discourse which underpins a powerful globalizing technologism — itself the best ideology of development and modernization. For these latter terms bespeak something "better", "progressive" and "liberating"; they offer us a moral vision of a materially better world. On the other hand, in the traditional cultures of southern Africa nature is not a limitless resource to be conquered and manipulated for the sake of science and progress. Nature is a friend, a mother who gives and sustains life.

I do not wish to romanticize traditional communities or to pretend that they have unencumbered access to a pristine reservoir of ecological values which existed before the advent of Europeans and which might somehow pull us back from the precipice of ecological disaster. But I do believe that at the heart of these communities still lies a moral awareness, existentially, though not necessarily epistemologically, sensitive to the dynamism of the first and second laws of thermodynamics.[10] And this, if taken seriously, offers us the possibility of finding a path into a sustainable future. This contains a nature-based ethic alert to the rhythms of death and life or decay and renewal. It is an ethic that requires life-styles that are attuned to those rhythms. Nature is a tutor who offers us hints about how best to forge such life-styles. Being attentive to her tutoring by being attuned to the rhythms of natural processes will, I believe, enable the survival of the earth and of ourselves.

It is important to grasp how nature can be understood as a tutor. I suggested ealier that for traditional communities nature is a sort of ethical-juridical "text". What I meant is that the way people interact with each other is predicated on the larger context of the elaboration of their self-knowledge and social identities as legitimated by a complex network of religio-totemic configurations which specify which animals are to be preserved for which clan and which parts of the natural world are to be kept inviolable or protected because of their sacral significance. One implication of this is that behaviour and even life-styles are tacitly read off these religio-totemic patterns. To understand one's social identity properly is a matter of maintaining an ethically and indeed a spiritually correct disposition towards one's ancestors and their totemic line; it is to have a place in nature which one acknowledges and respects as a necessary part of one's physical as well as spiritual existence.

Perhaps the underlying assumption of this way of thinking is the recognition that we cannot push nature too far without bringing terrible consequences upon ourselves. In other words, nature is a tutor because in the dialectical relationship between nature and culture we are made aware of the limitations imposed on what we can or cannot do in our relationship with nature.

I am not arguing here that we should not get involved with indigenous communities because to do so is to interfere with their cultures and livelihoods. I recognize that culture is not something frozen in time — just as I recognize that many (though by no means all) development and environmental projects do interfere, often in destructive ways, with local modes of ethical cognition and traditional systems of economic production. My point is that if we allow this destruction to go on, even in the name of sustainability, we are in fact contributing to the destruction of a large and significant part of the environment. For the environment is not just nature; it is also people, their livelihoods and ways of going on in the world. In other words, the environment is the specific conjuncture of relationships between people, their local knowledge, the social structures in which these subsist and the outside world of rivers and trees, soil and land, space and time. In this regard Falloux and Talbot are quite right to remind us in their analysis of the national environmental action plans of various African countries that "knowledge of societies is an essential starting point". They express a hope for a cultural revolution in modern institutions if a participatory approach is to be found.[11]

But such hope is vain if the "knowledge of society" envisaged is simply "anthropological" or "sociological" knowledge and is not formed as a result of conversation with the endogenous structures of traditional communities and the moral economies which have carried them through the generations. The trouble with merely sociological or anthropological methods of comprehending these communities is that they usually carry and convey the powerful assimilative possibilities of modernity, so that the superiority of modern institutions is frequently implied. Thus environmental and development projects define goals for popular participation which require the integration of indigenous peoples into the global political and economic systems. It is these models which are used in describing and justifying those systems. The peoples' own self-understanding is then made ancillary to the objectives of environmental development. In this way it becomes unnecessary and impossible for development agencies to learn from the moral economies of indigenous systems of knowledge and practices.

NOTES

[1] R. Sharp, "Organizing for Change: People's Power and the Role of Institutions", in Johan Holmberg, ed., *Policies for a Small Planet*, London, Earthscan Publications, 1992, p.40.

[2] Cf. The Ecologist, *Whose Common Future? Reclaiming the Commons*, London, Earthscan Publications, 1993, p.111.

[3] *Ibid.*, ch. 5; all the essays in this volume show clearly how even at the UNCED meeting in Rio the corporate sector had a special relationship with the secretariat.

[4] For a critique of this way of thinking, see *ibid.*, p.2.

[5] See for example M. Jacobs, *The Green Economy: Environment, Sustainable Development and the Politics of the Future*, London, Pluto Press, 1991, pp.17-19.

[6] *Op. cit.*, p.2.

[7] See for example François Falloux and Lee M. Talbot, *Crisis and Opportunity: Environment and Development in Africa*, London, Earthscan Publications, 1993, p.109.

[8] Cf. Samir Amin, *Mal-Development: Anatomy of a Global Failure*, London, Zed Books, 1990, p.96.

[9] Sharp, *op. cit.*, pp.42,52.

[10] Cf. Jacobs' lucid account of the laws of thermodynamics and their implications for environmental economics, *op. cit.*, pp.11f.

[11] Falloux and Talbot, *op. cit.*, pp.109,115.

Social Ecology: Poverty and Misery

Leonardo Boff

We hear much today of the many crises we face: the economic crisis, the energy crisis, the social crisis, the educational crisis, the moral crisis, the ecological crisis, the spiritual crisis. In reality all these individual crises are part of a larger crisis of the society we have created over the past four hundred years. This is a global crisis in that this model of society has been transmitted to or imposed on practically the entire globe.

The first visible characteristic of this type of society is that it produces poverty and misery on the one hand and riches and the accumulation of wealth on the other. This phenomenon can be observed globally as well as within each individual country. There are a few rich countries and many poor countries. It is especially obvious within individual countries that a minority benefits from a great abundance of goods (food, health care, education, housing) while the majority lack the elements essential for life and dignity. Even in the Northern industrialized nations we find areas of poverty, just as there are wealthy sectors in the Third World. Why are things this way? The following critical responses will give us the answer.

Three critical responses to today's society

There are three main lines of thought which criticize the prevalent social model:

1. The *liberation movements* of the oppressed say that this society is not built on life, the common good, participation or solidarity among human beings, but on economy, the powers and instruments that create wealth through the ravaging of nature and the exploitation of human beings. This economy seeks unlimited growth in the shortest possible time with a minimum investment and maximum profit. Those who are able to survive within this dynamic and follow this logic will accumulate capital and become wealthy, but as a result of a permanent process of exploitation.

The economy is directed by an ideal of development that is encompassed by two infinite quantities: the supply of natural resources and a wide open future of unlimited possibilities. Within this type of growth economy, nature is simply a supply of natural resources, raw material for the satisfaction of human desires. Workers are the human resources necessary to attain a production goal. As described, this vision is instrumentalist and mechanical: people, animals, plants, minerals, in short, all living beings lose their autonomy and intrinsic value. They are reduced to a means by which to meet an end that has been subjectively established by those human beings who consider themselves to be the centre of the universe and who seek riches and the accumulation of wealth.

The primary critique posed by liberation thought is that this model is not capable of creating wealth without at the same time generating poverty. It cannot stimulate economic development without at the same time producing social exploitation, internally and globally. Nor is it democratic, because it establishes a political system designed for control and dominance — by the elite in liberal, representative democracies or under military tutelage. It is not a democracy in the sense of a social organization based on the interests of the majority, geared towards the well-being of the many through a participation that creates increasing equality and solidarity.

Out of this critique were born the liberation movements of the oppressed, including the struggle of the landless and the homeless as well as well-organized and combative unions. From this critique is born a culture of citizenship, democracy, participation, solidarity and liberation. It proposes a development that responds to the demands of all, and not only of the strong.

2. *Pacifist* and *active non-violence* groups note that a society of unequal development generates violence within societies and nations and internationally. This violence is a direct consequence of the domination of those countries with technological and scientific power over those which are further behind. This generalized conflict has thousands of faces. The best known are class, ethnic, gender and religious conflict.

This model of society promotes not solidarity but competition, the struggle of all against all. Human potential for sensitivity towards others, tenderness towards life and wholehearted co-operation are set aside to make way for the baser sentiments of exclusion and class or personal advantage. To maintain a minimum of cohesion within a society that is internally unstable, military bodies must be established to control and repress. Globally, the different blocs of nations create a military-industrial complex, fostering an arms race and the militarization of all existence. Even after the end of the cold war, one to three million million dollars are invested each year in the industry of death; and only 130 thousand million dollars for the preservation of the planet. This has led to the development of peace and active nonviolence movements who propose models of society that seek justice through social democracy.

3. *Ecological* movements maintain that current society and the prevailing type of development cannot produce wealth without at the same time ravaging the environment. The most abundant by-products of the industrial system are garbage, toxic and radioactive wastes, atmospheric contamination, acid rain, deterioration of the ozone layer, poisoning of the land, water and air — all adding up to a deterioration of the quality of life. Hunger, disease, lack of housing and education, and family and social crises are ecological aggressions against the most complex being of creation, the human being. This is true especially of the weak, the poor and the marginalized.

These preoccupations are giving birth to an ecological culture, a collective awareness of the responsibilities we have as human beings for the survival of the planet and of animal and plant life. It emphasizes our responsibility for the misery and poverty in the world and for promoting relationships that allow life and well-being for all human beings and all of nature.[1]

It is important today to articulate these different critiques of the dominant system. We must urgently seek to develop a new paradigm for society which does not repeat the mistakes of the old but integrates all human beings in a more humane way and establishes more benevolent relationships with the environment.

An immense equilibrium: social ecology

Our topic is ecology, poverty and misery. Poverty and misery are social issues, not natural or predestined phenomena. They are produced by the way in which society is organized. Today we are aware that social issues have to do with ecology in a very broad and real way. Ecology has to do with the relationships between all things in every dimension. Everything is interconnected. There are no closed compartments of environment on one side and social issues on the other. Social ecology seeks to study the relationships that a society establishes between its members and its institutions and between these and nature.

First of all some cautions are necessary:

• Ecology is far more than conservationism. It is not enough to conserve a species threatened by extinction, as if ecology were concerned only with "endangered species". Today the entire planet must be conserved, because all of it is in danger of extinction.

• It is not enough to preserve, through reserves or natural parks, regions where nature's equilibrium is maintained. This leads merely to ecological tourism and results in very limited behaviour changes: we behave with respect and veneration towards nature only in certain places and not in others.

• Environmentalism is not enough, as if ecology involved only the natural environment, plant life, water and air. Such a perspective can become anti-humanistic, favouring nature without the presence of human beings who are considered to be the "Satans" of the earth. This vision is common in the North, where, after dominating the world politically and economically, a need is felt to purify it. The truth is that human beings are part of the environment. They are part of nature and have the capacity for changing nature and themselves and in this way creating culture.

• We must beware of a political environmentalism which seeks harmony between society and the environment only in the interest of developing techniques for plundering the environment while affecting the human habitat as little as possible. This vision upholds the idea of plundering the earth; that human beings must dominate nature. More than permanent harmony, therefore, it seeks a truce in which nature can heal its wounds so that we can then resume plundering it. What is important today is to overcome the devastating and de-energizing paradigm of modern society and develop a new alliance between human beings and nature in which we become allies in an effort for conservation and assurance of a common destiny.

• It is not enough to speak of a human ecology that is preoccupied with human actions and reactions on a universal level only. It is important to consider the mental categories that determine our level of benevolence and/or aggression, but human beings do not live in generalities but in the midst of deteriorating social relationships. Their very mental and psychic predispositions have an eminently social nature. For this reason we must seek a social ecology that is capable of articulating social justice. It is within the framework of social ecology that issues of poverty and misery must be discussed. Poverty and misery are social issues that must be resolved socially.

1. *What is social ecology?* There has been much written on the subject of social ecology. We have the contributions of Charboneau Rhodes's French encyclopedia of ecology and the works of social anthropologist Edgar Morin. The contributions of M. Bookchin from North America and A. Naess from Norway are also important. In Latin America, reflection on social ecology developed particularly after the UN's first international conference on the environment in Stockholm in 1972. At this conference two basic perspectives were considered, that of the North which tended towards environmentalism, and that of the South, emphasizing the social and political aspects. A strong current of Latin American social ecology developed in Peru with Carlos Herz and Eduardo Contreras and in Uruguay with the work of Eduardo Gudynas.

Gudynas defines social ecology as "the study of human systems in interaction with environmental systems".[2] Human systems include individuals, societies and societal systems. Environmental systems include natural elements (jungles, deserts, plains), civilizations (cities, factories) and human beings (men, women, children, ethnic groups, social classes).

2. *The basic issues of social ecology.* Gudynas proposes the following basic hypotheses:

• Human beings, individually and socially, interact intensely with the environment. One cannot be studied apart from the other. There are aspects that can be understood only from the perspective of this mutual interaction: the secondary forests, the variety of grains (wheat, corn, rice, etc.) and fruit that are the result of thousands of years of genetic development.

• This interaction is dynamic and takes place within time. The history of human beings is inseparable from the history of their environment and the interaction between them.

• Each human system creates its suitable environment. Each is different and has its own representations.

• Social ecology is interested in issues such as the instruments with which human beings act upon nature. Is it with intensive technology such as agrotoxins or with organic fertilizers? How do human beings appropriate natural resources for themselves: in solidarity, participatively, or in an elitist fashion with exclusive technologies? How are these resources distributed: proportionally in accordance with the work of each person, equally in response to the basic needs of all, or in an elitist and exclusive way? How does unequal distribution affect human groups? What kind of language do those in power use to justify the unequal relationships that owners of capital in seeking better work conditions in urban and rural areas?

The discussion of social ecology encompasses the misery and poverty of marginalized populations, the concentration of land in rural and urban areas, agricultural and farming techniques, population growth and the process of urban sprawl, the disintegration of the ozone layer, the enhanced greenhouse effect, the diminishing of tropical forests and the threat to the Northern forests, the poisoning of the water, the soil and the atmosphere.

3. *A holistic ecology.* From a holistic viewpoint, society and culture also belong to the ecological complex. Ecology is the relationship between all living and non-living things, natural and cultural, and between them and their environment. Within this perspective economic, political, social, educational, urban and agricultural issues come under consideration as a part of social ecology. The basic ecological issue is always present: to what extent does this or that science, social activity, institutional or personal practice help maintain or destroy the equilibrium of all things? We, along with everything we are by nature and everything we have created through culture, are part of an immense equilibrium, the ecosystem.

Ingemar Hedström, a Swedish social ecologist who has lived many years in Costa Rica, has written:

> Ecology became a criticism and even a denouncing of the functioning of modern societies. Among the things that have been denounced is the over exploitation of the southern hemisphere... by the comparatively rich countries of the North. In this sense, to create awareness concerning the global ecological problem must mean to create awareness of the socio-economic, political and cultural situation of our societies, which means to recognize the exploitation of the southern countries by the industrialized nations of the North. [3]

Today's social system is anti-ecological and produces misery

Within the parameters of social ecology we must denounce the deeply anti-ecological character of the social system we live in — the worldwide capitalistic order. Every phase of this system has been and is based on the exploitation of human beings and nature. The avid search for unlimited material development has led to inequality between capital and work, creating exploitation of workers and the accompanying deterioration in the quality of life.

This violence was planted in Latin America with the sixteenth-century standard of labour and a relationship with nature that implied ecocide, the devastation of our ecosystems. We were incorporated into a larger reality, that of the capitalist economy. Our capitalist system is an economy of dependent exportation.

Private ownership of the sources of wealth — the land and its riches and its water — was introduced. This appropriation took place in a profoundly unequal and irrational way. A minority owned the best lands; the poorest land was left for the majority who, in order to survive, had to exploit and exhaust the soil, thereby causing deforestation and disrupting the natural equilibrium. Black slaves, freed by judicial decree, were not compensated in any way but were thrown directly from the big house to the shanty towns. They were forced to occupy the hills, clear them of timber, dig open sewerage trenches and live under the threat of sickness and disease. All these manifestations are forms of social aggression against the environment.

Today the conquest continues, especially in the form of the foreign debt, which is in essence aggression against social relationships, social devastation of the poor and the contamination of the biosphere. It is ever clearer that the foreign debt has a fundamentally political meaning. The banks are protected against the non-payment of this debt. But it is maintained because of its political importance as a means of control, assuring increasing dependence on the nations of the North. The interest on the debt causes the system to perpetuate itself. It requires a kind of development that privileges mega-projects and mono-cultures (soya in Brazil, cattle in Central America, fruit in Chile) by offering credits and financing for such projects from the World Bank and the International Monetary Fund.

The payment of the debt and the interest on it is financed through exports, but the income received from the products exported depends on the global market and therefore the debt is not honoured. As a result, state investment in social areas is reduced in order to pay off the debt. This strategy produces social tragedy as it affects public policy concerning food, health, employment and urban organization.

Along with this social perversity we find an environmental deficit. The poor occupy the most dangerous areas of the city and the agricultural frontiers, where they destroy the forests in an effort to survive and pollute the rivers seeking gold. The inability of the debtor nations to pay forces them to take out new loans at higher interest rates to pay interest on the old. The cycle of dependence, neo-colonialism and domination begins again.

Cancelling the debt will not solve the problem as long as the dominant developmental model remains, ravaging human beings and nature, looking outward, producing what the rich want us to produce for them to consume and not responding to the internal market. The vicious circle continues with the same perverse consequences.

US economist Kenneth E. Boulding calls the capitalist economy the "cowboy economy" in that it is based on the assumption of unlimited resources and empty spaces to invade and settle down in. It is unrestrained anthropocentrism. He argues that we must move instead towards what he calls the "spaceship earth economy". On this spaceship, as on any airplane, the survival of the passengers depends on the balance between the carrying capacity of the vehicle and the needs of the passengers. This means that human beings must become accustomed to solidarity as a fundamental virtue and find their place in the ecological equilibrium, in the sense of being able to produce and reproduce their life and the life of all other living beings and to help preserve the natural balance. The earth is a closed, balanced system, not an open one allowing any type of anti-ecological adventure.

Chico Mendes proposes a developmental model that combines social and environmental elements. He understands that jungle peoples (social issue) need the jungle in order to survive (environmental issue). He also identifies two types of violence: ecological violence against the environment and social violence against the indigenous peoples and rubber-gatherers. Both respond to the same logic, the logic of accumulation through the domination of people and things. How then must development take place? How can a society of jungle peoples be established that breaks with this logic? In the first place it must respect, support and reinforce the knowledge of the jungle that these societies (indigenous peoples and rubber-gatherers) have developed during their many centuries of history — their knowledge of nature, of the trees, of the herbs, of the soil, of the wind, of the noise of the jungle. At the same time it must incorporate new technologies that provide social benefits while maintaining environmental and social equilibrium.

A social-environmental ethic

From this context it is apparent that there is an urgent need for an ethic that restricts not only the behaviour of human beings among themselves, but also their relationship with the environment (air, land, water, animals, plants.)[4] Going beyond the North's current understanding of environmental ethics, we must overcome our anthropocentrism, limit the violence against nature present in our paradigm of unlimited development, accept the otherness of all created beings and develop reverence for all nature. From this ethic can emerge a new benevolence and even restoration of the enchantment lost to technology and secularization.

Valuable as such an environmental ethic is, it omits a fundamental element: the social context, with its contradictions. The environment does not exist alone. Within it are human beings, socialized in unequal and unjust ways of living, working, distributing goods, acting and reacting to it. In this social context there is violence and there are those who are condemned to a deplorable quality of life, breathing polluted air, drinking infested water, living on poisoned soil. This is a new type of aggression.

Our ethic must therefore be social and environmental, since our environment is affected by social elements and society by the environment. We discern two types of injustice: social-economic-political injustice, the consequence of violence against workers, against citizens, against the lower classes; and environmental injustice, violence against the air, the ozone layer, the water. Social injustice affects people directly; environmental injustice indirectly and perversely attacks human life, producing disease, malnutrition and death not only for the biosphere, but also for the entire planet.

This new social-environmental ethic must avoid the two extremes that disrupt the ecological equilibrium: naturalism and anthropocentrism. Naturalism understands nature as a hypostatic subject, with sacred and unchangeable laws to which human beings must submit. Anthropocentrism, by contrast, treats human beings as the sovereigns of creation. They may interfere as they wish without feeling tied to or limited by nature. Both of these perspectives separate what must go together. Nature and human beings are always interdependent. One is within the other; together they are part of a greater whole.

Human beings, as a fundamental part of the environment, have a singular characteristic. They are the complex species of living beings that are moral subjects; in other words they are capable of acting freely, of making judgments, of taking stands as a result of specific interests but also because of solidarity, compassion and love. The human species may think and act in the interests of others. It may sacrifice personal gain in the interest of solidarity and friendship. It may interfere with the rhythm of nature. All this makes the human being a responsible being, and responsibility is what makes humans ethical beings. They may be guardians of nature, heirs responsible for the inheritance received from the creator, or the Satans of the earth, destroying, disrupting equilibrium and devastating the living species of the planet and even their own kind.

Throughout the historical-cultural process, human beings have interfered with the environment. Violence has been applied, as well as ingenuity in seeking to improve certain species for their own benefit. Little concern has been evident for the impact on nature, except perhaps when nature has been devastated to the point of the self-destruction of culture itself. But with industrialization during the past four centuries the aggression has been increasingly stronger and more systematic, transforming everything into a tool for accumulation, mostly for the benefit of those who are owners of the means of production and only secondarily, if at all, for the rest. The result has been devastating. Human beings have developed an unjust and humiliating relationship with nature. The earth can no longer resist the machinery of death.

Ecological justice acknowledges that human beings have a duty of justice towards the earth. The earth has dignity and otherness; it has *rights*. Having existed for millions of years before human beings appeared, the earth has the right to continue to exist in well-being and equilibrium. Ecological justice proposes a new attitude towards the earth, an attitude of benevolence and mutual belonging, while at the same time seeking to repair the injustices committed by the technical-scientific project.

Ecological injustice is transformed into social injustice by producing social oppression, exhaustion of resources, contamination of the atmosphere and the deteriorating quality of life that touches all human beings and all of society.

A new socio-environmental ethic can be implemented only if we develop a new planetary conscience, an awareness of common responsibility for the common destiny of all human beings. From this awareness grows slowly a new ecological culture, a new paradigm that is more reverent and holistic in its approach to the environment. Philosopher Hans Jonas has formulated this with a paraphrase of Kant's famous "categorical imperative": "Behave in such a way that the effects of your actions are always compatible with the permanence of nature and of human life on the earth."[5]

Theologically, we may speak of ecological sin. Attitudes that compromise the ecological equilibrium and provoke perverse consequences for living creatures and human beings are not restricted to the present but reach into the distant future, touching those who have not yet been born. The biblical precept "You shall not kill" (Ex. 20:13) may also refer to biocide and ecocide of the future. We are not permitted to create environmental and social conditions that produce disease and death for future living creatures, human and non-human. From this perspective we may understand generational solidarity — actions and attitudes that will allow those who do not yet inhabit this planet the right to live without disease and to enjoy a preserved and holistic environment.

One proposal reflecting this new ethical awareness calls for the "reconversion" of foreign debt in the form of policies to protect the natural and social environment of debtor nations. The suggestion is that part of the foreign debt would be cancelled as governments and businesses make an effort to protect the environment and maintain more equal and just social relationships. But the reconversion of the foreign debt for governments and large business is not enough. To be socially just it must also involve social movements and their representatives. They should be the subjects of an economic, political and social transformation that would respond to their historic demands and permanently articulate social and ecological justice.

It is pharisaical and unjust, however, for the rich nations of the North to demand that the South focus on the environment without providing technical means to facilitate ecological preservation. What is required is the transfer of technology to poorer nations so they can produce for internal and international markets but with considerably less ecological damage.

Just as conventional ecology developed unrelated to its social context, current theologies, including liberation theology, have developed without reference to the environmental context. It is important now to complement these perspectives with a coherent and holistic vision. The logic that leads the dominant classes to oppress peoples and discriminate against persons is the same as that which leads to the exploitation of nature. It is the logic that seeks uninterrupted and accelerated progress and development as the means to create the conditions necessary for human happiness. But this way of seeking happiness consumes the very foundations that sustain happiness, nature and human beings.

To reach the root of the evils that confront us as well as to find a solution for them, we need a new theological worldview that sees this planet as a great sacrament of God, the temple of the Spirit, the place of creative responsibility for human beings, a dwelling place for all beings created in love. Etymologically, ecology has to do with dwelling place. Taking care of it, repairing it and adapting it to new threats, broadening it to allow new cultural and natural being — this is the task of ecology and its mission.

Addendum: three examples of mutually negative relations between social and environmental elements in Latin America

1. *The death of birds in Brazil.* In 1985 a phenomenal dying off of almost 50,000 pigeons and hawks was documented in Minas Gerais, in the central region of Brazil. It was determined that these birds had visited a rice plantation recently sprayed with Furdan, an insecticide produced by the Guaicuhy Agricultural Company. A similar event occurred in Mexico city, in 1986, when millions of pigeons and migratory birds suddenly died. Specialists stated that they died as a result of a thermal inversion which did not allow the cadmium and lead by-products of a petroleum refinery in the northeastern part of the city to dissipate in the air. Millions of children were also contaminated and many died.

2. *Thermal inversion.* In Sao Paulo and especially in Mexico City we find examples of thermal inversion. Mexico City is located at an altitude of 2500 metres on a huge plateau surrounded by cliffs. Thermal inversion occurs because the layers of dense contaminated air cannot rise into the stratosphere and remain close to the surface of the city, forming a dense fog or smog. This inhibits the circulation of air, asphyxiating the people. Walking the streets of Mexico City is said to be equivalent to smoking forty cigarettes. It is known that 4000 people died during the great thermal inversion in London in 1952. Approximately thirty thousand children and 100,000 adults die yearly in Mexico City as a result of thermal inversion.

Along with the thermal inversion come the acid rains of summer. The air, contaminated with acids, sulfur, nitrogen and carbon dioxide contaminates the cloud water, and when it rains this water in turn poisons streams, lakes, plantations and animals.

Acid rain may also be caused by chemical reactions in the atmosphere which is loaded with industrial acids. These chemicals then contaminate the earth with zinc, lead, mercury and aluminum, metals which are highly toxic to human life. They are absorbed by the water, by vegetation and plant life, by the air. Not only is human life affected, but also plant life, lakes, water animals, plantations and cities. The food chain of the lakes may be interrupted. Water plants which absorb the toxins are then eaten by small fish, which are in turn food for large fish, which are caught and eaten by human beings.

3. *The "hamburgerizaton" of the forests.* The creation of the McDonalds chain of fast food restaurants in 1955 began an enormous ecological problem for all of Central America. In order to make the hamburgers cheaper for North Americans, McDonalds began importing

cheap meat from Central America. The meat exporters cut down trees for grazing land in order to raise more beef cattle. Between 1960 and 1980 the exportation of beef grew 160 percent and the green belt of Central America decreased from 400,000 square kilometers to 200,000. Ingemar Hedström calls this the "hamburgerization" of Central America.[6]

In much the same way, the Amazon was affected by the famous Daniel Ludwig and Volkswagen projects. In Jari de Ludwig two million acres of forest were cut down. Volkswagen chopped down 144,000 acres to place 46,000 heads of cattle. Each head of cattle had 30,000 square meters of land. The projects failed. No one benefited, and the forests were lost to all.

NOTES

[1] Cf. J.R. Regidor, "Giustizia sociale e giusticia ecologica nei rapporti Nord-Sud", *Emergenze*, IV, 1988, pp.22-26.
[2] Eduardo Gudynas, *Social Ecology: The Latin American Route*, Montevideo, CIPFE, 1990.
[3] Ingemar Hedström, *We Are Part of a Great Equilibrium*, San José, DEI, 1985, p.12.
[4] Cf. J.R. Regidor, "Etica ecologica", in *Nuevi paradigmi*, I, 1991, pp.61-73.
[5] Hans Jonas, *Das Prinzip Verantwortung*, Frankfurt, Insel Verlag, 1984, p.36.
[6] Ingemar Hedström, *op. cit.*, pp.46-47.

African Independent Churches Face the Challenge of Environmental Ethics

M.L. Daneel

The significant role of African Independent Churches (AICs) in terms of Africanized mission methods, growth rates and development of a contextualized theology, in which the interaction between the gospel witness and African religion and worldviews is paramount, is increasingly recognized. This article will focus on the contribution AICs in Zimbabwe are making in the field of applied environmental ethics.

While the Justice, Peace and Integrity of Creation emphasis of the World Council of Churches is stimulating theological reflection and thought-provoking study on the role of Christ's church in relation to environmental issues, the AICs are making a complementary contribution by tackling environmental problems in the field. They are not in the first place producing environmental literature, but they are proclaiming a widening message of salvation which encompasses all of creation, and in their services of worship they are dancing out a new rhythm which, in its footwork, spells hope for the ravaged earth. They have not worked out a new ethic on paper, but they are "clothing the earth" (*kufukidza nyika*) with new trees to cover its human-induced nakedness. In so doing they have introduced a new ministry of compassion; they live an earthkeeper's ethic.

The "war of the trees" offers an ecumenical platform to unite the churches in a "green army" and to launch environmental reform in terms of the liberation of creation. The "lost lands" which have been politically liberated now need to be recaptured ecologically. In the new struggle ecclesiastical structures are changing, new perceptions of ecological responsibility are emerging and innovative liturgical procedures are being introduced to integrate environmental ethics and church praxis.[1]

An environmental offensive from an ecumenical platform

Since the formation in 1988 of ZIRRCON (Zimbabwean Institute of Religious Research and Ecological Conservation), AICs in the country have been challenged on the basis of their Christian faith to engage in tree-planting activities. But the roots of Zimbabwe's ecumenical earth-keepers movement are in the country's liberation struggle and in Fambid-zano, the ecumenical movement of Shona Independent Churches, founded in 1972.[2]

The AICs in fact have a rich tradition of enacted liberation theologies.[3] For many years their leaders resisted oppressive rule. Their prophets participated in *chimurenga* (the war of liberation), helped the guerrilla fighters to purge village communities of so-called wizards (counter-revolutionaries), fed and treated wounded fighters and helped to devise — in the name of the Holy Spirit — feasible guerrilla tactics on the war front.

With this background of transcending ecclesial barriers for the sake of a common cause, the climate was conducive for ecumenical ecological mobilization. Some *chimurenga* "war prophets" came to the fore here, including Bishop-prophet Musariri Dhliwayo, whose church headquarters during the war was an operational centre for guerrilla fighters in the Gutu district, who was elected patron of the Christian army of earthkeepers.

For many years churches affiliated to Fambidzano have engaged in united action under the leitmotif of John 17:21,23, which combines Christian unity and witness.[4] Many agreed that the devastation of the environment constituted sufficient grounds for the formation of a new movement. Early in 1991 the Association of African Earthkeeping Churches (AAEC) was established. It is affiliated to ZIRRCON as its think-tank and fund-raiser, and within a year more than a hundred AICs, representing a formidable ecological work force of some 2 million members, had joined the movement.

A new environmental ethic was not formulated in detailed theological statements, but it surfaced in the practical objectives of the AAEC constitution:

• *afforestation* — the production of fuel-wood, the growing of fruit trees for personal and commercial use, exotic trees like blue gums for building operations, indigenous trees to clothe and protect the earth and the slow growing kiaat (*mukurumbira*) and red mahogany (*mukumba*) as a long-term investment for the coming generations;

• *wildlife conservation*, including the establishment of game sanc-tuaries in the communal lands where hardly any game is left;

• *protection of water resources* through the reclamation of catchment areas to prevent river and dam siltation, the prevention of river-bank cultivation, gully-formation, etc.[5]

AAEC's environmental objectives are seen as being undergirded by a divine mandate. During the founding ceremony I emphasized divine initiative with reference to one of our key texts, Isaiah 43:18-21 — "do not remember the former things... I am about to do a new thing":

> This association we are creating today is a new thing God is doing in our midst... It does not belong to us but to God. Therefore, if we are courageous and persevere, this new movement will perform great deeds.

A brief exposition of the Christological basis for our struggle characterized a focus which would later emerge in a tree-planting eucharist:

> Our mandate derives from our faith that we belong to the body of Christ. As members of that body we are not only commanded to build unity amongst ourselves as Christian churches, but to build new relationships with the entire creation in an attempt to avoid destruction and preserve life for all creatures. I say this because the body of Christ is more than the church... In him all things hold together, in him all things are created. That makes him the true guardian of the land (*muridzi venyika*), the great guardian of all creation. Read together with Matthew 28:18, where Jesus claims all authority in heaven and on earth, we take this twofold interpretation of Christ's body to mean that his presence and power pervade all creation... The implication is that when we as Christians partake of holy communion we express our unity in the body of Christ, that is the church. At the same time we reaffirm our responsibility for the body of Christ, in the sense of its presence in all creation. The sacrament therefore makes us earthkeepers, stewards of creation...

The association's first president, Zionist Bishop Machokoto, emphasized the ecumenical foundation of the envisaged environmental programmes:

> What I ask of God is a true sense of unity amongst us. We have to work together and avoid all forms of confusing conflict. Our unity must rest on convincing works. It is no use coming here to enjoy our tea and meals without engaging in development projects which show convincing progress. The basis of our work, according to God's word, is love, a love which reveals itself in works... Let us show our willingness and ability to work. Therefore, each of you, as you leave here, go and prepare yourselves for tree-planting... We the churches [of the AAEC] will have to make sacrifices for the causes to which we have pledged ourselves. Therein lies our unity...

This call for united action is the key to the kind of ecumenism developed by the AAEC. In a predominantly peasant society with a deforested, overgrazed and over-populated environment, AIC bishops and their churches have not joined forces to realize some abstract ecumenical ideal of church unity as an end in itself. Rather, ecumenicity has taken shape as churches share concretely a newly identified common commitment to healing the earth. In the "battles of the trees", developing nurseries with thousands of seedlings and planting and watering trees in the hot sun, lay the liberation from interchurch conflicts. Not that all the differences and conflicts of the past were suddenly resolved. But they paled into insignificance as the green revolution unfolded during annual conferences and meetings and in the joint labour and celebration of tree-planting ceremonies. A new brotherhood and sisterhood beyond the traditional ecclesial constraints had started to evolve — that between the creator God, earthkeeping humanity and the trees, plants and wildlife. A new myth, arising from the common, holistic subconscious of Africa and blended with Christian perceptions of a realized, observable salvation for all creation in the here and now, had started to emerge.

Changing perceptions of the church as healing institution

The prophetic AICs have always been popularly conceived of as healing and liberating institutions in Zimbabwe, as elsewhere in southern Africa, but there have been historical mutations in this concept as it relates to political and national developments. In the 1930s the Zionists and Apostles emerged as "hospitals", insofar as prophetic healers focused largely on contextualized faith-healing ministries which offered therapeutic solutions to a comprehensive range of human afflictions experienced in terms of African belief systems and worldviews.

Between 1965 and 1980 the AICs, increasingly drawn into *chimurenga*, evolved as socio-political healing and liberation institutions. The AIC headquarters still had their faith-healing "hospitals" or healing colonies, but the diagnostic and therapeutic thrust of many prophets had a direct impact on the guerrillas' militant field strategies, as the Holy Spirit was felt to guide positively on behalf of the cause of the oppressed.[6] God's presence translated into the provision of food, supportive prayers, care for wounded and mentally disturbed fighters, blessing of weapons with holy water and numerous related activities enabling harassed bush-fighters and suspect members of society to survive and retain some meaning in life in the midst of suffering and deprivation.

As the AICs became increasingly involved in development projects following independence,[7] the image of the church as deliverer from poverty and agent of socio-economic progress began to predominate. Newly built community halls became centres of vocational training and small-scale industries, such as clothing manufacture, sewing and carpentry, augmented in some cases by agricultural projects. Rather than causing fragmentation or secularization, such extension of the church's task in this world implied an expansion and reinterpretation of its healing ministry. The gospel good news, it appears, includes socio-economic healing — healing from poverty, agricultural stagnation and lack of opportunity.

The inception of the AAEC has shifted the focus to the church's healing of a suffering creation. A new perception of the divine-human encounter, emphasizing Christian stewardship in nature, has begun to emerge.

It should be noted that these historically conditioned mutations in the church's ministry have not involved radical ecclesiastical reforms or changes. Rather, the new insights and action programmes have served as modifying extensions and innovative elaborations of existing AIC ecclesiologies.

Tree-planting sermons illuminate how the earth-healing ministry of the AAEC churches is interpreted. These are considered to be environmental "teaching sessions". Consider, for example, the exposition during a tree-planting ceremony by Bishop Kindiam Wapendama, leader of the Sign of the Apostles Church, executive member of the AAEC and ardent advocate of the green revolution:

> Deliverance, Mwari says, lies in the trees. But in the first place the people have to obey. Mwari therefore sends his deliverers to continue here on earth with his own work; that is, all the work Jesus had started here. It is a divine mission. Jesus said: "I leave you, my followers, to complete my work. And that task is the one of healing!"
>
> We are the followers of Jesus and have to continue with his healing ministry. You are the believers who will see his miracles in this afflicted world. So, let us all fight, clothing the earth with trees! Let us follow the example of the deliverers sent by Mwari... It is our task to strengthen this mission with our numbers of people. You know how numerous we are. At times we count 10,000 people at our church gatherings. If all of us work with enthusiasm we shall clothe the entire land and drive off affliction... Just look at the dried out and lifeless land around you. I believe that we can change it!

These views are representative. God takes the initiative to restore the ravaged earth, but his divine commission to deliver the earth from its malady lies with the body of Christian believers, the church. The deliverance finds expression in *kufukidza nyika*, that is, "to clothe the land" with trees. This mission is clearly seen as an extension of Christ's healing ministry, which his disciples must fulfil. That this is a communal obligation is highlighted by the bishop's reference to the large church meetings as a potential green labour force. Wapendama's confidence that a mobilization of the AAEC's massive earthkeeping army can overcome the evil of earth-destruction is a significant move away from the fatalism found in peasant society, where little hope is left that environmental restoration is still possible.

True to prophetic perceptions of salvation as human well-being in all sectors of life, achieved through healing in this existence, the earth is to be salvifically restored under the directives of Mwari. But the new order is not one-sidedly ushered in by God; it is also dependent on being "worked out" by human endeavour. The church's mission is thus expanded. The good news extends well beyond soul-salvation and a futuristic eternal life for individual human beings. And the testing ground for the quality of individual conversion and spirituality lies in the ministry of earthkeeping.

Confession of ecological sins:
a sign of commitment to environmental reform

Confession of sins has always been prominent in the healing and sacramental ceremonies of the prophetic AICs. During faith-healing ceremonies the healer-prophet urges patients to confess their sins. Not only is this a way of placing the afflicted under the care of the Holy Spirit, but the revelation of the dark side in the patient's existence also enlightens the healer-prophet about the cause of affliction and the area in the patient's life which requires therapeutic treatment.[8] The confession of converts prior to baptism symbolically illustrates the neophyte's acceptance of the authority of the church, represented during the ceremony by the prophet's listening to the confessions, as well as the final mystical authority of the Holy Spirit which induces such confessions. Public confession prior to participation in the sacrament of holy communion is in a sense a mass demonstration of right-mindedness and obedience in relation to God.

Some AAEC-related prophets are already applying their newly gained insights about ecological stewardship to their guardianship over the morals of their churches. In the baptismal context they increasingly reveal that the Holy Spirit expects novices to confess not only their moral sins in a society of disturbed human relations but also their ecological sins: tree-felling without replanting, overgrazing, riverbank cultivation and the neglect of contour ridges, thereby causing soil erosion — in other words taking the good earth for granted, exploiting it without nurturing it or showing it reverence.

At "Jordan" it makes sense to the newly converted to confess ecological guilt, where the barren, denuded planes, the erosion gullies, the unprotected river banks and the clouds of wind-eroded dust are clearly in evidence. Crossing the River Jordan in baptism, after such confession, means more than individual incorporation into the body of Christ and the prospect of personal salvation in heaven. It also requires the new convert's commitment to help restore creation as part of God's plan, as a sign of genuine conversion and repentance in recognition of the gift of God's grace.

To many Independents, baptism is also a healing ceremony in which the life-giving water of Jordan, filled by the Holy Spirit, is drunk by baptizands for individual cleansing and curative purposes. Thus the baptismal ceremony offers a unique opportunity for interpreting the Spirit as healer both of the people and of the land. Baptism therefore becomes another feature of an extended ministry of healing — a changing ecclesiology. The drinking of "Jordan"-water symbolizes the shift from personal, individual benefit of the baptizand by the Holy Spirit's healing and saving powers to a ritual statement of solidarity with all creation, an affirmation of a new commitment, through individual conversion, to earth-healing.

Also significant is the combat of AAEC prophets against ecological sins in the context of tree-planting eucharistic ceremonies. During public confessions preceding the bread and wine, "green prophets" from a wide range of Zionist and Apostolic churches are increasingly branding offences that cause firewood shortage, soil erosion, poor crops and the absence of wildlife as a form of wizardry (*uroyi*) — the gravest of all sins, threatening not only human survival but all other forms of life. As the resolve of the earthkeeping churches and the conviction of the prophets that the Holy Spirit rather than human beings motivates and guides the green struggle grow, unrepentant ecological sinners (*varoyi*) in the AICs will increasingly find themselves barred from participation in the eucharist.

Discussions with these prophets, who are becoming Christian "guardians of the land", indicate that they generally have a clear idea of who the earth-destroying wizards in their society are: people in resettlement schemes who endanger the common good by indiscriminately felling as many trees as they can for a quick profit from selling firewood; those who refuse to accept the principle that firewood can be used only by those who plant the trees that supply it; those who resist government conservationist measures and tribal elders' prohibition of tree-felling in the traditional holy groves (*marambatemwa*) of the ancestors; and the destroyers of river banks.

The identification of ecological sin with wizardry and the insistence on public confession enable the church in its green struggle to identify the enemy outside and within its own ranks. Identification of wrongdoers enhances and concretizes the church's ethical code and control system. This is reminiscent of the *chimurenga* struggle, during which counter-revolutionaries and collaborators were branded as wizards. Alongside the traditionalist spirit mediums, AIC war prophets elicited confessions from suspects as part of the process of identifying wizard-traitors and singling them out for punitive measures. Unifying the ranks and cleansing the guerrilla cadres from internal subversion in terms of the idiom of wizardry indicated a relentless will to succeed and survive. For *uroyi* is an evil which brooks no compromise.

In the earthkeeping churches the response to wizardry is more nuanced than it was during the war period, when traitors were executed or tortured. Wanton tree-fellers or poachers of wildlife will, upon prophetic detection, either be temporarily barred from the eucharist, or, in the event of repeated transgression of the earthkeepers' code, be excommunicated. The AAEC is only too aware of the common guilt which in a sense makes all of us *varoyi* — earth-destroyers. Still there is a vast difference between admitting earlier guilt and continued deliberate deforestation or related destructive action in the face of a protective environmental code. This selfish environmental exploitation regardless of the will of the community and the destruction caused to nature is branded by the prophets as the evil of *uroyi*, to be stamped out at all costs.

Discussions about ecological *uroyi* and how to combat it stimulate emotive expression of views about the nature of an earthkeeping church. The characteristic attitudes and convictions may be summarized as follows:

• The earthkeeping function of the church is beyond doubt. As Bishop Darikai Nhongo of the AAEC-affiliated Zion Christian Church says: "The church is the keeper of creation."

• Part of the church's mission is to develop and apply strict rules against the destruction of the earth.

• The application of strict environmental laws implies authorization and empowerment of the prophets to expose the ecological wizards during public confessionals.

• Prophetic exposure is only the first step towards a process of church cleansing, so as to mobilize effectively a Christian "green army", eliminate subversion and realize environmental goals. Paramount is an element of judgment and punishment so that, as in *chimurenga*, the enemy outside and within can be clearly discerned. The church cannot usurp the divine function of final judgment, yet Peter's function as "holder of the keys" justifies expulsion of unrepentant tree-felling *varoyi* to give momentum to the earthkeeping cause.

Some AAEC leaders have proposed working with secular chiefs to act comprehensively against the wizards, not only excommunicating them from church but also having them expelled from their residences — one of the severest penalties imaginable. Not all would favour such radical punitive measures. Some would plead for a ministry of reconciliation, offering exposed ecological *varoyi* the opportunity to mend their ways without undue stigmatization. But it is clear that there is a growing commitment to what is considered a real liberation struggle, for which the church is seen as one of the most important mobilizing vehicles.

Eco-liturgical innovation

The best example of liturgical innovation in the AAEC churches in connection with the emergent environmental ethic is the tree-planting eucharist. This ceremony, which supplements rather than supersedes well-established liturgical procedures for holy communion, is of interest for several reasons. First, the participation of numerous churches in each ceremony and the sharing of ritual officiant roles on an interchurch basis strengthen environmentally focused ecumenism. Second, the integration of eucharist and tree-planting binds environmental stewardship, often treated as peripheral in Christian tradition, into the heart of church life and biblical spirituality. Third, this ceremony highlights characteristic trends of an emergent AIC theology of the environment. And, fourth, the new liturgies are imaginatively contextualized in relation to African religious holism and worldviews. Thus an earthkeeping model is developed which could well challenge AICs elsewhere in Africa to assimilate environmental stewardship through similar liturgical innovation.

In a tree-planting liturgy drafted by AAEC general secretary and Zionist Bishop Rueben Marinda, preparation for the eucharist begins with the digging of holes for tree-planting in the vicinity of an AIC headquarters or local congregation. The lot, sometimes fenced in, is referred to as "the Lord's Acre".

While the communion table, with neatly pressed tablecloth, bread, wine and several seedlings on it, is being prepared, groups of dancers dance around the bulk of the seedlings to be planted, which are stacked nearby. Dance and song bring praise to Mwari the great earthkeeper, encourage the green fighters to be vigilant in the struggle and even implore the young trees to grow well. The service includes several earthkeeping sermons by AAEC bishops and ZIRRCON staff members, as well as speeches by visiting government officials.

The sacrament itself is introduced by the public confession of ecological sins. Participants, including church leaders, line up behind a band of prophesying prophets to confess their guilt and listen to prophetic admonitions. After they file slowly past the prophets, they pick up a seedling and move to the communion table to partake in the sacrament.

The following excerpt is part of the liturgy read out to the congregation in Shona:

> Look at the stagnant water
>   where all the trees were felled.
> Without trees the water-holes mourn,
>   without trees the gullies form.
> For the tree-roots to hold the soil...
>   are gone!
>
> These friends of ours
>   give us shade.
> They draw the rain clouds,
>   breathe the moisture of rain.
>
> I, the tree... I am your friend.
> I know you want wood
>   for fire:
>   to cook your food,
>   to warm yourself against cold.
> Use my branches...
> What I do not need
>   you can have.
>
> I, the human being,
>   your closest friend,
>   have committed a serious offence
>   as a *ngozi*, the vengeful spirit.
> I destroyed you, our friends.
> So, the seedlings brought here today
>   are the *mitumbu* [bodies] of restoration,
>   a sacrifice to appease
>   the vengeful spirit.
> We plant these seedlings today
>   as an admission of guilt,
>   laying the *ngozi* to rest,

strengthening our bonds with you,
  our tree friends of the heart.

Indeed, there were forests,
  abundance of rain.
But in our ignorance and greed
  we left the land naked.
Like a person in shame,
  our country is shy
  in its nakedness.

Our planting of trees today
  is a sign of harmony
  between us and creation.

We are reconciled with creation
  through the body and blood of Jesus which brings peace,
he who came to save
  all creation.

At this point the sacramental bread and wine are served. Each participant, holding a seedling in his or her hand while receiving the sacrament, then proceeds to the holes in the new woodlot. Prior to the actual planting the bishop walks through the woodlot, sprinkling holy water on the ground, saying:

This is the water of purification and fertility.
We sprinkle it on this new acre of trees.
It is a prayer to God, a symbol of rain,
so that the trees will grow,
  so that the land will heal
  as the *ngozi* we have caused withdraws.

"Holy soil" which has been prayed over is then scattered in the woodlot with the words:

You, soil...,
I bless you in the name of Christ
  for you to make the trees grow
  and to protect them.
Provide the trees with sufficient food
  for proper growth.
Love the trees and keep their roots,
  for they are our friends.

The bishop then leads the green army into the Lord's acre to do battle against the earth's nakedness. The seedlings are addressed one after the other as they are placed in the soil:

You, tree, my brother, my sister,
   today I plant you in this soil.
I shall give water for your growth.
Have good roots
   to keep the soil from eroding.
Have many leaves and branches
   so that we can
   breathe fresh air,
   sit in your shade
   and find firewood.

To the Western mind this simple liturgy may seem of only relative significance considering the enormous, nearly impossible task of halting deforestation, desertification and soil degradation. As a spontaneous ecological ritual activity in the African cultural and linguistic context, however, it is a powerful statement of Christian commitment to the healing of all creation.

The close identification with water, soil and trees — elevating them ritually to the status of communication with human beings — reflects African religious holism. The holistic intuition of the past is taken to a level at which mutual interdependence is eloquently and meaningfully verbalized. In this overtly declared friendship, following admissions of human guilt for the mindless destruction of nature, mutual responsibility is reaffirmed: the new trees to provide shade and unpolluted air to sustain healthy human life, and the earthkeepers to water and protect their budding friends in the Lord's acre. The liturgy assumes responsible after-care by the community of believers commissioned to do so, in itself a strong incentive to the woodlot-keepers not to let the green army and its monitoring agents down. This imaginative stimulation of effective after-care, normally the Achilles' heel of grassroots African tree-planting endeavours, is already proving to provoke sustained, if sometimes mono-tonous, responsibility in the wake of the more exciting ritual experience of tree-planting.

Impersonating the vengeful *ngozi* spirit in terms of earth-destruction is as potent a way of accepting full responsibility for deforestation as is the confession of ecological wizardry. The *ngozi* is an aggrieved spirit of a murdered person or someone against whom a grave injustice has been perpetrated prior to death.[9] In customary law and traditional religion the *ngozi*, which creates havoc in the offender's family through illness and death, has a legitimate claim to full compensation in the form of up to ten sacrificial beasts, called *mutumbu*, literally "corpse" or "body", as they pay for the corpse of the deceased. In some cases the relatives of the offender also provide the *ngozi* with a young wife, who must sweep and tend to the small hut specifically erected for her disgruntled "spirit-husband". Presenting the trees to be planted as *mutumbu*-compensation for the *ngozi*-spirit provoked by wanton tree-felling is a thoroughly contextualized illustration of appeasement between humans and environment. The ritual, moreover, expresses compassion for the badly abused friends: trees, soil, water and, by implication, all of life in nature.

The *ngozi*-concept has several subtle connotations in the liturgy. It reflects the reckless and distorted spirit of the human "stewards" of the earth who attack nature with a single-minded "vengeance", like that of the *ngozi*, as if they are entitled to cause such havoc. There is also the suggestion that the "murdered" trees themselves exact retribution, like the *ngozi*, and that the seedlings are therefore the legitimate sacrificial replacement of the stricken tree-trunk corpses. Then follows the implicit suggestion in the sprinkling of water over God's acre that it is God who turns *ngozi* to the ecological offenders by retaliation through severe drought. Such an interpretation corresponds with the persistent traditional belief that the creator withholds rain in order to punish transgressions against nature and the guardian ancestors of the land, who are responsible for ecological equilibrium. In the admission of guilt, the ritual plea for the removal of divine discipline and the renewal of human resolve to heed the environment as ordained by God and ancestors, absolution is found. God responds by sending life-giving rain. Transformed as they are in the Christian liturgy, some of these traditional notions are still in evidence. Sprinkling holy water and soil over the barren earth earmarked for repair is a symbolic act of earth-healing. It accords entirely with prophetic faith-healing practice referred to above, thus demonstrating the ecclesiological shift which extends beyond human healing into the realm of healing or liberating all creation.

In the liturgy Christ is presented as the one whose blood works reconciliation between humanity and the rest of nature, the one who brings salvation to all creation. The reference is to Colossians 1:18-20. Although the liturgy here is not explicit on the twofold interpretation of the body of Christ as church and as creation, the central concept behind this Christological feature is that "in Christ all things hold together". The sacramental activity which unfolds around this concept suggests that at the point where believers give expression to their unity in the body of Christ as church through the use of bread and wine, they accept responsibility for the repair of the cosmic body of Christ to which they also belong and which they too have abused. Consequently, they proceed in unity as church to heal the stricken body through tree-planting in partnership with Christ, who as head of the believers is the real *muridzi venyika* (guardian of the land) — in contrast to or fulfilment of the traditional concept of ancestral guardianship.

In the tree-planting eucharist this close identification of Christ's body with the abused and barren soil makes sense. Traditionally, the ancestral guardians of the land belong to the soil. They *are* the soil. Their ecological directives issue from the soil, as expressed in the literal saying *Ivhu yataura* "the soil has spoken". In a sense Christ in this context is both guardian and the soil itself. New perspectives of Christ's lordship and his salvation of all creation can be developed from this essentially African expression of his pervading presence in the cosmos. In African peasant society, at any rate, Christ's reign as *muridzi* (guardian) of the land is an essential part of the gospel, for he is the one who is believed consciously to strike a balance between exploitative agricultural progress and altruistic, sacramental restoration of the land.

Here the AICs give ecological expression to what Moltmann calls the messianic calling of human beings:

> In the messianic light of the gospel, the appointment [of humans] to rule over animals and the earth also appears as the "ruling with Christ" of believers. For it is to Christ, the true and visible image of the invisible God on earth, that "all authority is given in heaven and on earth" (Matt. 28:18). His liberating and healing rule also embraces the fulfilment of the *dominium terrae* — the promise given to human beings at creation... It is to "the Lamb" that rule over the world belongs. It would be wrong to seek the *dominium terrae*, not in the lordship of Christ but in other principalities and powers — in the power of the state or the power of science and technology. [10]

The AICs would agree that their tree-planting eucharist expresses their "ruling with Christ" in his liberating and healing rule as fulfilment of the *dominium terrae*. Inherent in this view is an acute awareness of the incarnate Christ who, despite his lordship, shares the suffering of an endangered creation. The assertion that Christ's body is creation and that he is the fulfilment of all creation underlines the predominant interpretation of the cosmological inference of Colossians 1:15-20: "in Christ all things hold together." Whereas this logos doctrine remained unrelated to Western science and was neglected as a theological basis for referencing nature, according to Carmody,[11] the AAEC depends on it — in its own innovative and rudimentary way — as the cornerstone of its tree-planting eucharist.

In doing so there is no pretence that we, the earthkeepers, are the saviours of creation, for that we can never be. But as believers and disciples of the one who holds all things together, we are erecting not only symbolic but concrete signposts of life-giving hope in a creation suffering while it awaits redemption. For, as Duchrow and Liedke state:

> Spirit-endowed beings do not save creation, but creation looks to us. The way that we cope with its suffering shows how much hope there is for creation. When we increase the suffering of creation its hope sinks. When we sharpen the conflict between human beings and nature, and also the conflict between humans, then creation lapses into resignation. When, instead, in solidarity with nature and our fellow human beings, we reduce suffering, then the hope of creation awakes into new life.[12]

This is precisely what the AAEC hopes to achieve. Through the movement of the earthkeeping Spirit new patterns of solidarity between formerly opposing churches and between a pluriformity of religions in society is being established, thereby giving rise to an ecumenism of hope. This hope takes concrete shape in the form of a healing ministry that attempts to cover and nurture the afflicted land. Serious attempts to expose and discipline those who continue with the rape of the earth embolden the green combatants to intensify the struggle. Replacing the trees in sacramental recognition of the lordship of Christ — the ultimate guardian, who reigns over yet suffers within the stricken earth — brings life and celebration to creation.

NOTES

[1] Cf. M.L. Daneel, "The Liberation of Creation: African Traditional Religious and Independent Church Perspectives", *Missionalia*, Pretoria, Unisa, 2d ed., 1991; "Healing the Earth: Traditional and Christian Initiatives in Southern Africa", in R. Koegelenberg, ed., *Church and Development: An Interdisciplinary Approach*, EFSA, 1992; "African Independent Church Pneumatology and the Salvation of All Creation", *International Review of Mission*, LXXXII, no. 326, April 1993, pp.143-66; "Towards a Sacramental Theology of the Environment", *Zeitschrift für Missionswissenschaft und Religionswissenschaft*, LXXV, no. 1, Jan. 1991, pp.37ff.; "African Christian Theology and the Challenge of Earthkeeping", *Neue Zeitschrift für Missionswissenschaft*, XLVII, nos 2-3, Apr.-Jul. 1991, pp.129-42; 225ff.

[2] For the history of this movement see M.L. Daneel, *Fambidzano: Ecumenical Movement of Zimbabwean Independent Churches*, Gweru, Mambo Press, 1989.

[3] Cf. M.L. Daneel, *Christian Theology of Africa: Study Guide in Missiology*, Pretoria, Unisa, 1989, ch. 3.

[4] Daneel, *Fambidzano*, pp.30f.

[5] Cf. Muchakata Daneel, *ZIRRCON: Earthkeeping at the Grassroots in Zimbabwe*, Pretoria, Sigma Press, 1990.

[6] Daneel, *Christian Theology of Africa*, pp.66-72.

[7] Daneel, *Fambidzano*, ch. 8.

[8] Cf. M.L. Daneel, *Old and New in Southern Shona Independent Churches*, Vol. 2, The Hague, Mouton, 1974, pp.214f., 292f.

[9] *Ibid.*, Vol. 1, 1971, pp.133-40; M. Gelfand, *Shona Ritual*, Cape Town, Juta, 1959, p.153.

[10] J. Moltmann, *God in Creation*, London, SCM Press, 1985, pp.227f.

[11] J. Carmody, *Ecology and Religion: Toward a New Christian Theology of Nature.* Ramsey, Paulist Press, 1983, p.91.

[12] U. Duchrow and G. Liedke, *Shalom: Biblical Perspectives on Creation, Justice and Peace*, Geneva, WCC, 1989, p.61.

Ethics and Sustainable Development

David G. Hallman

The UN Conference on Environment and Development (UNCED) and its follow-up have engaged the global community in discussions about "sustainable development". Many of the issues that have arisen in this debate have profound ethical dimensions. How these problems are identified and addressed will have to reflect ethical understandings of full participation. Solutions will be effective only if based on ethical principles that respect the integrity of creation and give priority to the needs of the marginalized.

The church cannot claim a monopoly on ethics; indeed when it comes to applying ethics to environment and development, we find that some of our secular colleagues have done more serious thinking than have we. Nevertheless, there is still an important role for the church in raising ethical questions and proposing ethical directions or principles in discussions, planning and implementation of sustainable development approaches.

This role and responsibility derive from some of the basic facts of our faith. First, we believe that the word became incarnate and lived and lives among us. This world is important in God's sight. Some theologians understand this world as God's body. Second, the theological concepts we use to articulate our faith provide a basis for exploring the sufferings and liberation of God's creation and God's children. Our theology propels us into ethics. Third, ours is not only a rational faith but a spiritual one as well. Western Christians are beginning to appreciate how much we can learn about the spirituality of creation from aboriginal peoples. Living in a spiritual relation with creation requires a different life-style; and ethical discernment is a significant part of that process of learning to live differently.

Anna Marie Aagaard has described three stages in the process of applying ethics: "guiding principles" lead to "practical norms" (what is desirable, possible and appropriate in a given context) and then to "decisions about action".[1] This paper will look at two recent statements of guiding principles regarding environment and development, one from a Christian, the other from a secular source, then discuss two cases in which the churches have tried to move from guiding principles to practical norms and decisions about action: climate change and the role of transnational corporations in sustainable development.

Two ethical perspectives: "The Rio Declaration" and "One Earth Community"

One of the UNCED-related attempts to articulate ethical or guiding principles concerning environment and development emerged from the official UNCED negotiations themselves. Early on the organizers had the idea of preparing an "Earth Charter" for the government leaders to sign in Rio, a set of principles concerning the relationship of human societies to the earth that would be a counterpart to the Universal Declaration of Human Rights.

When it came to the actual negotiations, however, it proved impossible to reach agreement among the governments, in part because of the widely divergent views of what an Earth Charter should be. Northern governments wanted a poetic document to inspire the peoples of the world; the South was more interested in a practical, semi-legal text that could bind Northern governments to accept their responsibility for most of the ecological damage and address the economic disparity in the world. One delegate from the South commented, "You from the North want something that you can frame and your children can hang on their bedroom wall, while many of our children don't even have bedrooms." The compromise document that was agreed upon was the Rio Declaration, some of whose 27 principles were priorities for the North and some for the South.

During the same period, the World Council of Churches hosted an interfaith consultation to draft principles to be recommended for inclusion in the proposed UNCED Earth Charter. Later, the United Church of Canada reworked those principles after testing them with partner groups in Canada and in the South. The intention was to produce a statement of ethical principles on environment and development independent of the failed Earth Charter, which could be used as a guide for church programmes and for advocacy with government and industry. The document *One Earth Community* was the result.[2] We shall look briefly at a few of the principles of both documents, highlighting some of the commonalities and contrasts (the Rio Declaration is printed in full at the end of this article, as are substantial excerpts from *One Earth Community*).

The Rio Declaration	One Earth Community
Principle 1: Human beings are at the centre of concerns for sustainable development. They are entitled to a healthy and productive life in harmony with nature.	*Principle 1*: Human societies must bear a responsibility towards the Earth in its wholeness.
Principle 2: States have, in accordance with the charter of the United Nations and the principles of international law, the sovereign right to exploit their own resources pursuant to their own environmental and developmental policies, and the responsibility to ensure that activities within their jurisdiction or control do not cause damage to the environment of other states or of areas beyond the limits of national jurisdiction.	*Principle 2*: To be both people-oriented and ecologically sound, all development strategies must be founded on a just international economic order, with priority for the world's poor.
Principle 5: All states and all people shall co-operate in the essential task of eradicating poverty as an indispensable requirement for sustainable development, in order to decrease the disparities in standards of living and better meet the needs of the majority of the people of the world.	*Principle 3*: Life-styles of high material consumption must yield to the provision of greater sufficiency for all.

The first principle of the Rio Declaration represents a Southern victory in the negotiations. Many governments and non-governmental organizations (NGOs) from developing countries were concerned throughout the UNCED process that Northern interest in the environment reflected a selfish intention to protect affluent life-styles in the North from the consequences of ecological destruction while disregarding the poverty that riddles Southern societies. Principle 1 in the Rio Declaration places the well-being of human beings at the focal point of sustainable development. The phrase "in harmony with nature" expands this somewhat, but the principle still continues the anthropocentric tradition of focusing only on human need and viewing the rest of creation as having only utilitarian value. Such dominance of humans over nature is even more starkly apparent in Principle 2 of the Rio Declaration, which incorporates the Southern demand for affirmation of national sovereignty over natural resources. That may help reduce Northern infringement on Southern interests but at the risk of limiting global co-operation on global problems. The second half of the principle does recognize the responsibility of nations for the impact of their activities beyond their borders.

One Earth Community begins with responsibilities rather than rights. Understanding human societies (including their economic systems) as a subset of the broader ecosystem or creation, Principle 1 affirms the inherent value of all creation in its wholeness and mandates humanity to respect and care for it. It is followed immediately by one which proclaims the indivisibility of ecological sustainability and economic justice. Meeting the needs of the world's poor, as opposed to profit or increased affluence for overdeveloped societies, is to be the priority for development.

Principle 2 of *One Earth Community* is an appeal not for charity but for a systemic approach, "a just international economic order". The Rio Declaration also speaks of the need to eradicate poverty (Principle 5) but does not refer to the systemic nature of economic injustice which perpetuates poverty. Principle 12 refers to economic systems but only to promote the current approach. Indeed, a major frustration for many involved in the UNCED process was the unwillingness of industrialized nations seriously to discuss the negative impact on environment and development of currently dominant economic structures and processes such as the International Monetary Fund, the World Bank, trade agreements and transnational corporations.

A central issue in the ethics of sustainable development is raised by Principle 3 in *One Earth Community*. The primary source of environmental destruction in industrialized countries and the major threat to the global commons are the high levels of material and energy consumption by industry, the military and individuals in those countries. Further, as Indian economist Vandana Shiva has noted, development in the North has not come exclusively from its own resources but also from five hundred years of colonizing and exploiting much of the South. *One Earth Community* maintains that those levels must be reduced so that all may live with sufficiency. The Rio Declaration acknowledges only obliquely the greater stress placed on the environment by industrialized societies. President George Bush declared at UNCED that US life-styles were not open for negotiation.

While these comparisons (and others that could be made) suggest that *One Earth Community* is a more ethically advanced statement than the Rio Declaration, I do not wish to underestimate the value of the latter. In the erratic and arduous history of international negotiations on environment and development issues, the Rio Declaration is a significant step forward. Some of its principles could have far-reaching consequences — for example, the precautionary principle (no. 15) and the "polluter pays" principle (no. 16). The document as a whole can serve as an effective instrument for groups and individuals to use in demanding that their governments apply at home the principles they agreed to in Rio.

Global ethics and climate change

The issue of climate change is a classic example of nearly everything that has gone wrong in the human relationship with creation, illustrating simultaneously the ecological impact of an industrial life-style of over-consumption and the injustice inherent in the current structuring of the global economic system.

Climate change is being precipitated by the over-accumulation in the atmosphere of "greenhouse gases" emitted by a variety of human activities. There is a natural greenhouse effect provided by the atmosphere, which makes life possible by keeping some of the sun's warmth near the earth. But human activity over the past one hundred and fifty to two hundred years of industrialization has added more greenhouse gases to that natural blanket of gases, thus trapping more of the sun's heat.

The major greenhouse gas is carbon dioxide, and most of its anthropogenic sources are from the burning of fossil fuels (coal, oil and gas) in transportation, electricity-generation and industry. Chlorofluorocarbons (CFCs) — artificial chemicals produced for industrial and consumer purposes over the past fifty years — are not only responsible for the destruction of the ozone layer but also constitute one of the most potent of greenhouse gases. The other main greenhouse gases are nitrous oxide and methane from various agricultural and industrial practices.

The likely consequences of this process are being debated scientifically. But the largest-ever international co-operative scientific effort — the Inter-Governmental Panel on Climate Change — has been organized to try to answer some of the questions. More than a thousand scientists in one hundred countries have been collating research on causes and consequences. They have concluded that a process of climate change has begun as a result of human industrial activity and will lead, if unchecked, to a gradual rise in the earth's temperature. This gradual warming could precipitate major droughts in areas of large land mass such as sub-Saharan Africa, the US midwest and the Canadian prairies. Rising sea levels from melting polar ice caps could inundate vast coastal regions of many countries, affecting as many as 8 million people in Bangladesh and 10 million in the Nile delta in Egypt, and submerge entire island states such as the Maldives. The third major impact expected is an increase in the frequency and intensity of tropical storms. Over the past ten years, there has in fact been a higher number of serious storms throughout the world than would have been statistically probable.

The frightful injustice of climate change is that, while the problem is caused primarily by the high level of greenhouse gas emissions in the North, the consequences of global warming will affect the whole planet with the South suffering disproportionately. Droughts, rising sea levels and storms will affect Southern countries more not only because of their geography but also because they have fewer resources with which to adapt to the situation than the richer Northern countries.

A range of ethical issues are raised by the threat of climate change. To start with, climate change is one of the more blatant examples of how we have violated the first of the *One Earth Community* principles — the responsibility of human societies towards the earth in its wholeness. Until recently, development patterns pursued by industrialized societies in particular have given virtually no consideration to the consequences for the planet as a whole. Decisions about development patterns and specific projects have used narrowly defined anthropocentric criteria based on maximizing profit and local or national interests. Negotiation of international agreements such as the Montreal Protocol on ozone depletion and the Climate Change Convention represents a step in the move from guiding principles to a practical norm. Nations are being pushed to incorporate a wider vision of their responsibilities as a result of the mounting scientific evidence on global warming and pressure from their people. But progress to date, as represented by the climate convention, has been very inadequate; as a practical norm it would not in fact translate the guiding principle into discernible changes.

One reason for this inadequacy is the unwillingness of Northern industrialized nations to link such ecological steps to the need for economic changes as prescribed by the second principle in *One Earth Community*, calling for a just international economic order with priority for the world's poor. The belief that climate change can be addressed by tinkering with environmental regulations without a major restructuring of international economic relations is fundamentally flawed both practically and ethically. Both economic relations between countries and the basic national structure of most economies will have to be reoriented. The current macro-economic model based on unlimited economic growth will have to yield to economic approaches that focus on ecological sustainability and social equity, as reflected in the third principle.

Another principle from the *One Earth Community* which has significant ethical implications related to climate change is Principle 8, which says that militarism must yield to nonviolent approaches to conflict resolution. Military activity is one of the biggest global sources of environmental destruction; and the military and related space programmes are a significant source of greenhouse gas emissions. The Pentagon is the single largest consumer of oil in the US; in 1989 the Department of Defense purchased 200 million barrels of oil for military use — enough to run all of the country's public transport for 22 years. In less than a half hour, an F-16 fighter plane burns as much fuel as an average US motorist does in one year.[3]

About one-quarter of the world's jet fuel (42 million tons per year) is used by armed forces. Nine percent of global iron and steel is consumed by the military, and the worldwide military use of aluminium, copper, nickel and platinum exceeds the entire demand for these materials by Southern developing countries. Moreover, the use of these materials in military production consumes vast amounts of fossil-fuel based energy. The world's military and weapons plants are the source of over two-thirds of the emissions of CFC-113, one of the major chemicals depleting the ozone layer and contributing to global warming.

However, the role of the military as a source of environmental and development problems was systematically kept off the UNCED agenda. During the preparations for UNCED, a draft Earth Charter from developing nations, including China, labelled means of warfare that cause severe damage to the environment as "war crimes". But some Northern countries, including the US, suppressed any such references.

In focusing on the ethical dimensions of climate change, an increasing number of researchers, activists and institutions are seeking to discern practical norms and action strategies. In this connection, Henry Shue has made the ethical discussion more concrete by distinguishing between "subsistence emissions" and "luxury emissions". Four types of questions need attention, he says:

> 1. What is a fair allocation of the costs of preventing the global warming that is still avoidable?

2. What is a fair allocation of the costs of coping with the social consequences of the global warming that will not in fact be avoided?

3. What background allocation of wealth would allow international bargaining (about issues like the two above) to be a fair process?

4. What is a fair allocation of emissions of greenhouse gases over the long-term and during the transition to the long-term allocation?[4]

NGOs have also been involved in the ethical debate, sometimes among themselves. Several years ago the Washington-based WorldWatch Institute published a report projecting greenhouse gas emissions from various countries. The Centre for Science and the Environment in New Delhi responded with a critical report arguing that WorldWatch had allocated responsibility for global warming on an ethically unjust basis, putting greater blame on developing countries than was warranted and reducing the onus on industrialized nations to "de-develop":

> India and China today account for more than one-third of the world's population. The question to be asked is whether we are consuming one-third of the world's resources or contributing one-third of the muck and dirt in the atmosphere or the oceans. If not, then surely these countries should be lauded for keeping the world in balance because of their parsimonious consumption despite the Western rape and pillage of the world's resources.[5]

A recent issue of the newsletter of Climate Network Africa, a coalition of environment and development groups, discussed the ethical dimensions of climate change. In contrasting current economic approaches with models that would be more sustainable and just, they noted:

> Our underlying worldviews shape our values and our decisions of "right" and "wrong". The mechanistic-individualistic worldview that has shaped Northern society and underlies modern economic theory is radically different from the organic-communal worldview that still pervades much of African society... Responses to climate change designed on the background of an organic-communal worldview in which past, present and future are an integral part of the social and physical environment, will differ from the proposals being put forward by the proponents of modern economics... An organic-communal response to human-induced climate change will place limits, or boundary conditions, on the market. New norms will be established for economic behaviour. Maximum use of resources and maximum allowable emission of such pollutants as CO_2 will have to be set. This is not the first time that limits have been imposed on the operation of the market. The nineteenth-century movement which resulted in a global ban on slavery imposed a limit which was bitterly resisted by those who were opposed to interference in the workings of the market.[6]

The World Council of Churches has been working on the issue of climate change since 1988, monitoring the negotiations that prepared the Climate Change Convention and, after its adoption in Rio, sponsoring regional consultations on ethical aspects of climate change. These culminated in an international gathering in Driebergen, the Netherlands, in October 1993, at which a study document, *Accelerated Climate Change: Sign of Peril, Test of Faith*, was prepared. Much of the concern reflected in this document focuses on building community and changing economic approaches so that they not propel us towards climate change as our present economies do. The intention of an economy should be to support the building of community, understood both as the social organization of the human family and the broader creation encompassing all the natural world. The document suggests strategies for an economy to build community including:

- shift from unneeded production to work that needs to be done;
- make development increasingly community-based, focused on essential needs and the sustainable, equitable use of natural resources;
- organize and mobilize democratically to curb excessive power and empower all people. [7]

Ethics and the role of transnational corporations

Another major ethical challenge is how to confront the role of transnational corporations (TNCs), which have a profound impact on environment and development. A 1992 UN study concluded that

the influence of TNCs extends over roughly 50 percent of all emissions of greenhouse gases. This includes about half of the oil production business, virtually all of the production of road vehicles outside of the centralized economies, most CFC production and significant portions of electricity generation and use. [8]

TNCs also have very specific impacts on environment and development. Placer Dome is a Canadian corporation that holds an interest of almost 40 percent in the Marcopper Mining Corporation in the Philippines. Until 1986, Placer Dome's major partner in Marcopper was former President Ferdinand Marcos, who owned 49 percent of the shares. As is typically the case, environmental regulations for mining in a country of the South like the Philippines have been considerably less rigid than those with which Placer Dome has had to comply in its Canadian operations. Since 1975, Marcopper has operated an open-pit copper mine in Marinduque in the Philippines discharging mine tailings into the Calancan Bay resulting in massive destruction of coral reefs, fish stocks and the livelihood of area fisherfolk.[9]

But the threats come also from TNCs which are not involved in the resource sector. Paul Kennedy describes how the arena of biotechnology may have drastic negative consequences for agriculture in Southern countries. In the past, many innovations in agricultural research were relatively accessible. Now large multinational agrochemical and biotech corporations race to offer new products to a world market, without worrying about the regional impacts and social consequences of this further stage in the product cycle. Because they are competing with one another, these companies shroud their research in secrecy and restrict its use by patents — a major difference from the "green revolution" of the 1960s, in which the breakthroughs were created in the public sector.[10]

TNCs also have an impact on environment and development in the financial sector. Private banks in the North may have extricated themselves from the catastrophe they precipitated in the early 1970s through the massive lending orgy of petrodollars; the debt-ridden developing countries have not been as lucky. Their people continue to experience growing poverty, reductions in health and social services, transfer of valuable agricultural land into export-oriented mono-cropping and other consequences antithetical to development as a result of the debt load and the structural adjustment programmes subsequently imposed on them by international financial institutions. The burden of this crisis, fostered by the search for quick profits by Northern banks, has been shifted onto the peoples of the South and publicly financed international institutions.

Related to this is the functioning of currency markets. Not only Southern countries but even Northern governments seem to be losing control over their own financial well-being through the mysterious mechanisms of currency trading and its impact on interest and exchange rates. Even relatively stable Canada has experienced unprecedented jumps in interest rates to protect the Canadian dollar from foreign currency speculators (or "investors" as they are euphemistically called). Such fluctuations in interest rates can play havoc with a country's economic development strategies.

Morris Miller, a former World Bank executive director, cites some startling figures. The daily turnover in global foreign exchange markets is about US$500 thousand million. This capital movement dwarfs the global flow of trade in goods and services: for every $1 of trade in goods and services, $25 is traded in financial assets. Even more troubling, Miller points out, is that "the present transactional volume is double what it was only five years ago, and an exceptionally high proportion of this currency movement is speculative or 'hot money' unrelated to the productive aspects of financing trade and private foreign investment".[11] Who is doing all this speculating in currency rates? It appears to be largely private banks and corporations.

The incredible power that TNCs exercise demands accountability. The first principle of *One Earth Community* stipulates that human societies must bear a responsibility towards the earth in its wholeness. But how can societies respond when so much power is concentrated in the hands of those who control the large industrial entities? Given the considerable impact of TNCs on environment and development, one would have expected their role to be a source of significant concern at UNCED. By and large, it was not, for a number of reasons.

One of the success stories of the UNCED process was the unprecedented participation of environment and development NGOs in using the opportunities for public education provided by UNCED, building networks with other NGOs worldwide and advocacy with governments on agenda items. However, for most of us involved in the process over the two years leading up to UNCED and at Rio itself, our limited resources were consumed by relating to the public and to governments, and little was left over to focus on TNCs.

But there were also active attempts to keep the role of TNCs off the UNCED agenda. This was largely a political and ideological effort by industrialized countries, particularly the US and the UK. During negotiations on the conventions on climate change and biodiversity and on Agenda 21, UNCED's action programme, the US and other Northern countries worked to minimize references to the private sector, qualify those that were included and emphasize the constructive contribution TNCs can make to sustainable development rather than registering concern about their negative impacts. The UN Centre on Transnational Corporations submitted a list of principles for minimizing the negative impact of TNCs on environment and development to the final UNCED preparatory meeting in March 1992, but because of the opposition of certain industrialized countries, responding to industry pressure, these principles were never forwarded to Rio. The attempt of the UN Centre to prepare even a voluntary code of conduct for corporations continued to be vigorously opposed by business after UNCED, and eventually the whole effort died. According to a former staff member of the UN Centre:

> The heart of the issue is that multinationals fear even the semblance of public scrutiny. They shun any serious discussion of critical issues: their global

market dominance, price-fixing practices in small countries, wage cuts and job losses in the Third World, huge commercial debt repayments and other "negative" matters. A peak of absurdity was reached in the final preparations for the Earth Summit when there was heavy lobbying to remove the term "transnational corporations" from the draft text of Agenda 21.[12]

The influence of industry is also felt at the organizational level. In 1992 UN Secretary General Boutros Boutros-Ghali announced a series of measures to "streamline" the UN bureaucracy because of serious financial difficulties. One was to downgrade the UN Centre on Transnational Corporations from a separate entity to a much smaller department with reduced influence within the massive Department on Economic and Social Development (ECOSOC). One year later a further restructuring transferred the UN Centre from ECOSOC to UNCTAD in Geneva, which will further weaken its capacity as a voice of even modest caution and critique about TNCs.

All of this is not to suggest that TNCs were absent from the UNCED process. Far from it. A post-Rio survey by the UN Centre found that almost 1000 individual companies had been involved in some aspect of the lead-up to UNCED. The UN Centre also prepared a comprehensive index of all references in Agenda 21 that have implications for industry.[13] The intensive lobbying by industry prior to and at Rio is evident when one examines Agenda 21. The references to industry include very little critique. They are mainly affirmations of current practices or mild encouragements for voluntary improvements.

On the one hand, some have praised the involvement of the private sector in UNCED as evidence of growing recognition in the business community of the importance of sustainable development. The Business Council on Sustainable Development co-ordinated a series of conferences prior to Rio and published a book on industry and sustainable development.[14] On the other hand, many NGOs, particularly from the South, have been scathingly critical of how TNCs co-opted the UNCED process to ensure that no environmental or development regulations were placed on them that would interfere with their freedom to conduct their business. Martin Khor Kok Peng, Malaysian economist and director of the Third World Network, has said that "UNCED treated corporations as entities that should be relied on to help protect the environment, rather than ones whose activities are destroying the environment and who should be strictly regulated".[15]

Many of the ethical principles articulated in church documents like *One Earth Community* demand that the role of TNCs not go unchallenged. Issues involving TNCs arise inevitably when we talk about societies taking responsibility to care for the earth, the need for a just international economic order with priority for the poor or the participation of people in development decisions that affect them. There is well-researched literature on the impact of TNCs on environment and development. The critiques are very persuasive. But where do we go beyond this analysis? For many church and NGO activists involved in environment and development, the long-term answers lie in models of development that are relatively small in scale, as self-sufficient as possible and within the carrying capacity of the ecosystem. We need to channel as much energy as we can into such alternate forms of social organization, which are applicable in the North as well as the South. Meanwhile, the forces of the global economy with transnational corporations as dominating actors, continue to grow in influence. Somehow we must find the resources to focus some attention on TNCs and to go beyond critique to action. I would identify three challenges in trying to apply our ethical frameworks to the role of TNCs in environment and development: greater public awareness, greater public accountability and greater public control.

1. *Awareness*. Gaining access to the relevant information about how TNC operations affect environmental quality and social equity is a major challenge. Companies tend to see such requests and proposals to legislate greater transparency as infringements on their privacy and impediments to their competitiveness. This lends support to the need for broad standards so companies in a particular sector or country are not put at a disadvantage (if you accept the argument that candour weakens competitivity).

2. *Accountability*. Knowing what TNCs are doing and its impact on environment and development is only a small part of the response needed. There must also be mechanisms for holding companies accountable for these impacts. In Canada, the approach in the Taskforce on the Churches and Corporate Responsibility has been to use existing systems to bring such pressure to bear. Earlier, I described the involvement of the Canadian corporation Placer Dome in the mining company Marcopper in the Philippines. Drawing on strategies such as meetings with senior management, shareholder resolutions and appearances at annual general meetings (with media coverage), the Taskforce succeeded in moving the company from a position of denying that there was any problem to acknowledging the negative impact on the ecology and the livelihood of the local people but refusing to accept any responsibility as a minority shareholder (although 40 percent is a rather large minority). After further pressure, the company agreed to support an independent environmental assessment before opening a second mine in the area. The latest information from a scientist who

works with an environmental NGO in the area is that the operation has been very considerably cleaned up. The bay is gradually rehabilitating itself and the new mine will discharge no mine tailings into the water.

But such small individual victories pale by comparison to the extent of TNC involvement around the world. More systemic approaches are needed. The Taskforce has been involved in getting companies, particularly in the forestry sector, to examine the possibility of developing a code of environmental practice. Such a process involves several stages. Development of a code must be an open exercise, so that the company does not just write a vague document which they could use to justify their present practices. Regular reporting mechanisms are needed to assess the company's compliance with their code. Third, there should be some form of independent audit to assess the accuracy of the company's reporting. Progress has been slow in terms of the domestic operations of Canadian corporations; covering their international operations as well will be another battle. In a pre-UNCED paper, the Taskforce stated that

> national and international regulations can be used to establish common environmental performance standards as well as for planning and assessment processes. Integration of the world economy requires that regulations be consistent enough between individual localities that companies cannot escape by moving to another jurisdiction. [16]

3. *Control.* The question of greater public control over TNCs is the most complex and contentious challenge. Must we rely only on cajoling companies and hoping they will improve, or is there a place for binding international regulation? Regulation is a dirty word in international economics these days, although there are some indications that governments may be starting to recognize the need for it. The Montreal Protocol with its subsequent revisions is an encouraging example of international co-operation to eliminate the production and use of ozone-destroying chemicals. The UN Framework Convention on Climate Change adopted in Rio does not go nearly as far in specifics, but global warming is of course a vastly more complex problem in terms of causes and consequences; and the UN Convention does provide a basis for more specific negotiations. At a more general level, efforts are also underway to develop mechanisms for requiring TNCs to incorporate environmental costs into economic decision-making. [17]

As complex as international regulations in any area such as climate change may be, it appears considerably more feasible in the case of environmental problems than for broader equity issues involved in development. How does one have impact in such forums as the General

Agreement on Tariffs and Trade (GATT) and its successor organization? Where is the forum for challenging currency exchange practices?

The issues of climate change and transnational corporations present churches with profound ethical challenges in moving from principles to implementation. How we respond will be a test of the adequacy of our principles, our capacities for analysis and strategy development, our persistence and commitment.

Appendix
THE RIO DECLARATION
ON ENVIRONMENT AND DEVELOPMENT

Preamble

The United Nations Conference on Environment and Development, having met at Rio de Janeiro from 3 to 14 June 1992,

Reaffirming the Declaration of the United Nations Conference on the Human Environment, adopted at Stockholm on 16 June 1972, and seeking to build upon it,

With the goal of establishing a new and equitable global partnership through the creation of new levels of co-operation among states, key sectors of societies and people,

Working towards international agreements which respect the interests of all and protect the integrity of the global environmental and developmental system,

Recognizing the integral and interdependent nature of the earth, our home,

Proclaims that:

Principle 1: Human beings are at the centre of concerns for sustainable development. They are entitled to a healthy and productive life in harmony with nature.

Principle 2: States have, in accordance with the charter of the United Nations and the principles of international law, the sovereign right to exploit their own resources pursuant to their own environmental and developmental policies, and the responsibility to ensure that activities within their jurisdiction or control do not cause damage to the environment of other states or of areas beyond the limits of national jurisdiction.

Principle 3: The right to development must be fulfilled so as to equitably meet developmental and environmental needs of present and future generations.

Principle 4: In order to achieve sustainable development, environmental protection shall constitute an integral part of the development process and cannot be considered in isolation from it.

Principle 5: All states and all people shall co-operate in the essential task of eradicating poverty as an indispensable requirement for sustainable development, in order to decrease the disparities in standards of living and better meet the needs of the majority of the people of the world.

Principle 6: The special situation and needs of developing countries, particularly the least developed and those most environmentally vulnerable, shall be given special priority. International actions in the field of environment and development should also address the interests and needs of all countries.

Principle 7: States shall co-operate in a spirit of global partnership to conserve, protect and restore the health and integrity of the earth's ecosystem. In view of the different contributions to global environmental degradation, states have common but differentiated responsibilities. The developed countries acknowledge the responsibility that they bear in the international pursuit of sustainable development in view of the pressures their societies place on the global environment and of the technologies and financial resources they command.

Principle 8: To achieve sustainable development and a higher quality of life for all people, states should reduce and eliminate unsustainable patterns of production and consumption and promote appropriate demographic policies.

Principle 9: States should co-operate to strengthen endogenous capacity-building for sustainable development by improving scientific understanding through exchanges of scientific and technological knowledge, and by enhancing the development, adaptation, diffusion and transfer of technologies, including new and innovative technologies.

Principle 10: Environmental issues are best handled with the participation of all concerned citizens, at the relevant level. At the national level, each individual shall have appropriate access to information concerning the environment that is held by public authorities, including information on hazardous materials and activities in their communities, and the opportunity to participate in decision-making processes. States shall facilitate and encourage public awareness and participation by making information widely available. Effective access to judicial and administrative proceedings, including redress and remedy, shall be provided.

Principle 11: States shall enact effective environmental legislation. Environmental standards, management objectives and priorities should reflect the environmental and developmental context to which they apply. Standards applied by some countries may be inappropriate and of unwarranted economic and social cost to other countries, in particular developing countries.

Principle 12: States should co-operate to promote a supportive and open international economic system that would lead to economic growth and sustainable development in all countries, to better address the problems of environmental degradation. Trade policy measures for environmental purposes should not constitute a means of arbitrary or unjustifiable discrimination or a disguised restriction on international trade. Unilateral actions to deal with environmental challenges outside the jurisdiction of the importing country should be avoided. Environmental measures addressing transboundary or global environmental problems should, as far as possible, be based on an international consensus.

Principle 13: States shall develop national law regarding liability and compensation for the victims of pollution and other environmental damage. States shall also co-operate in an expeditious and more determined manner to develop further international law regarding liability and compensation for adverse effects of environmental damage caused by activities within their jurisdiction or control to areas beyond their jurisdiction.

Principle 14: States should effectively co-operate to discourage or prevent the relocation and transfer to other states of any activities and substances that cause severe environmental degradation or are found to be harmful to human health.

Principle 15: In order to protect the environment, the precautionary approach shall be widely applied by states according to their capabilities. Where there are threats of serious or irreversible damage, lack of full scientific certainty shall not be used as a reason for postponing cost-effective measures to prevent environmental degradation.

Principle 16: National authorities should endeavour to promote the internalization of environmental costs and the use of economic instruments, taking into account the approach that the polluter should, in principle, bear the cost of pollution, with due regard to the public interest and without distorting international trade and investment.

Principle 17: Environmental impact assessment, as a national instrument, shall be undertaken for proposed activities that are likely to have a significant adverse impact on the environment and are subject to a decision of a competent national authority.

Principle 18: States shall immediately notify other states of any natural disasters or other emergencies that are likely to produce sudden harmful effects on the environment of those states. Every effort shall be made by the international community to help states so afflicted.

Principle 19: States shall provide prior and timely notification and relevant information to potentially affected states on activities that may have a significant adverse transboundary environmental effect and shall consult with those states at an early stage and in good faith.

Principle 20: Women have a vital role in environmental management and development. Their full participation is therefore essential to achieve sustainable development.

Principle 21: The creativity, ideals and courage of the youth of the world should be mobilized to forge a global partnership in order to achieve sustainable development and ensure a better future for all.

Principle 22: Indigenous people and their communities, and other local communities, have a vital role in environmental management and development because of their knowledge and traditional practices. States should recognize and duly support their identity, culture and interests and enable their effective participation in the achievement of sustainable development.

Principle 23: The environment and natural resources of people under oppression, domination and occupation shall be protected.

Principle 24: Warfare is inherently destructive of sustainable development. States shall therefore respect international law providing protection for the environment in times of armed conflict and co-operate in its further development, as necessary.

Principle 25: Peace, development and environmental protection are interdependent and indivisible.

Principle 26: States shall resolve all their environmental disputes peacefully and by appropriate means in accordance with the charter of the United Nations.

Principle 27: States and people shall co-operate in good faith and in a spirit of partnership in the fulfilment of the principles embodied in this Declaration and in the further development of international law in the field of sustainable development.

Excerpts from

ONE EARTH COMMUNITY

Ethical Principles for Environment and Development

(Prepared by The United Church of Canada based on a World Council of Churches statement related to The Earth Charter)

The vision of One Earth Community is a call to live in harmony with all life, to draw on the earth's sustenance responsibly and to care for the planet that all may benefit equitably now and in the future.

The threat to One Earth Community is the promotion of consumerism and greed and the preoccupation of people and nations with money, control and power at the cost of justice, cultural and spiritual enhancement.

The way forward will require a turn towards restoration and renewal. We need to reaffirm the importance of justice, frugality, humility and reverence for life and nature. To live within such a holistic relationship requires our rediscovering the spiritual connection that unites us to the land and that nourishes our souls as well as our bodies.

We believe that creation is a gift of God. We therefore endorse the following principles:

1. Human societies must bear a responsibility towards the earth in its wholeness.

2. To be both people-oriented and ecologically-sound, all development strategies must be founded on a just international economic order, with priority for the world's poor.

3. Life-styles of high material consumption must yield to the provision of greater sufficiency for all.

4. Environmental destruction must stop, and humanity must understand itself to be collectively responsible both for the destruction and the repair thereof.

5. The rights of future generations must be respected.

6. The carrying capacity of the earth, regionally and globally, must become a criterion in assessing economic development.

7. The biodiversity of the earth must be respected and protected.

8. Militarism must yield to nonviolent approaches to conflict resolution.

9. Decision-making for just and ecologically sound development must ensure the participation of individuals and groups, especially those most affected by the project.

10. Both opportunities for learning and access to knowledge must be assured in order to facilitate sustainable development.

11. Development decisions must emphasize prevention of ecological damage.

12. Procedures and mechanisms must be established ensuring a transnational approach to environmental issues.

NOTES

[1] In a paper delivered at the WCC consultation on "Koinonia and Justice, Peace and the Integrity of Creation", Rønde, Denmark, Feb. 1993.

[2] *One Earth Community: Ethical Principles for Environment and Development*, Toronto, United Church of Canada, 1992. The complete text has been published in a booklet, including the principles, explanatory narrative and study guide.

[3] Science for Peace, *Taking Stock: The Impact of Militarism on Development*, Toronto, University College, University of Toronto.

[4] Henry Shue, "Subsistence Emissions and Luxury Emissions", *Law & Policy*, XV, no.1, Jan. 1993.

[5] Anil Agarwal and Sunita Narain, *Global Warming in an Unequal World: A Case of Environmental Colonialism*, New Delhi, Centre for Science and Environment, 1991, p.2.

[6] "Climate Change and Ethics", *Impact*, newsletter of the Climate Network Africa, no. 11, Dec. 1993.

[7] *Accelerated Climate Change: Sign of Peril, Test of Faith*, Geneva, WCC, 1993; cf. the earlier WCC discussion document (1989), *North/South and Global Warming: Towards an Effective and Equitable Basis for Negotiating Climate Change Conventions and Protocols*, by Leiv Lunde.

[8] *Climate Change and Transnational Corporations: Analysis and Trends*, Environment series no. 2, New York, UN Centre on Transnational Corporations, 1992, p.2.

[9] Cf. annual reports of the Taskforce on the Churches and Corporate Responsibility, Toronto, 1989-90, 1990-91, 1991-92.

[10] Paul Kennedy, *Preparing for the Twenty-First Century*, New York, Harper, 1993, p.73.

[11] Morris Miller, *Debt and the Environment: Converging Crises*, New York, United Nations, 1991, p.165.

[12] *The New Internationalist*, no. 246, Aug. 1993, p.15.

[13] *Transnational Corporations and Sustainable Development: A Review of Agenda 21*, New York, United Nations, Oct. 1992.

[14] *Changing Course: A Global Business Perspective on Development and the Environment*, Geneva, Business Council on Sustainable Development, 1992.

[15] Martin Khor Kok Peng, "The UNCED Farce", *Multinational Monitor*, May 1992, p.10.

[16] Taskforce on the Churches and Corporate Responsibility, *Corporate Environmental and Social Responsibility: Recommendations to the UNCED Third Preparatory Committee Meeting, July 1991*.

[17] Cf. David Hallman, *A Place in Creation: Ecological Visions in Science, Religion and Economics*, Toronto, United Church Publishing House, 1992, pp.148-51.

Now That Animals Can Be Genetically Engineered

Biotechnology in Theological-Ethical Perspective

Dieter T. Hessel

This essay presents some theological and ethical considerations, grounded in Christian faith, that ought to inform assessments of what is and is not appropriate in applied biotechnics, particularly involving "transgenic" animals. Geneticists and entrepreneurs are now teaming up — often at public expense — to engineer "better" or more "useful" animals. The process of introducing exogenous DNA into the genome of species, a technique already used extensively in plant genetics, has been refined for application higher in the chain of being. This technology involves gene transfers between different kinds of living creatures to make new ones. Experimentation with this startling technology has already become global in scope. A skilled staff with about US$50,000 worth of equipment can engineer transgenic animals by introducing foreign characteristics into the genotype of a creature to produce particular traits that an animal would not otherwise have. Where will it go, or stop? What is a sound ethical and policy framework for animal biotechnics?[1]

I am reflecting on the transgenic alteration of animals to "enhance" food-production, to simplify sport fishing or to manufacture new pharmaceutical products. Some examples are super milk-producing cows, physiologically boosted by bovine growth hormone (somatotropin); arthritis-ridden Beltsville pigs engineered by the US Food and Drug Administration with cattle growth-hormone genes to provide leaner and more "cost-effective" pork;[2] and transgenic carp, trout or salmon ("designer fish"), fashioned for economic or recreational purposes. Animals are also being altered with human genes to supply blood plasma and, soon, organs. "Like the recombinant DNA technology that preceded it, uses of transgenic organisms are probably unbounded in potential application."[3]

Animal biotechnology began with mouse-engineering for medical research. Highly publicized examples include Onco-mouse (the first patent-protected, genetically altered mammal, engineered with a human gene to express cancer in its mammary tissue), Alzheimer's mouse and Memory mouse. Such transgenic mice have functioned as models for gene research into debilitating or terminal illnesses. Subsequent genetic interventions with humans, however, are not transgenic in themselves, because a gene from another species is not being put into a human being. Humans may be trying to receive organs from primates, but we are not yet putting animal genes into humans!

More ambitious efforts to create new animals by mixing together the genes of different species are occurring willy-nilly with potentially far-reaching effects discerned only dimly by the initiators. Even the few scholars who discuss the ethics and policies that ought to guide such activity seem unduly influenced by short-term economic calculations. For example, Charles McCarthy of the Kennedy Institute, Georgetown University, writes: "In a utilitarian context, efficiency in food production and ability to compete for world markets stand as high values which must be weighed against our recognized obligation to provide for the interests of the animals."[4] Thus, the larger eco-social good becomes blurred.

Taking a holistic view

Molecular biologists, geneticists and scholars in other fields who know about ventures in animal biotechnics differ on philosophical-ethical meanings. Genetic researchers play down the qualitative difference between transgenic manipulation of complex, sentient animals and other gene research, while environmental philosophers and social scientists often emphasize it. But they agree that animal research and production of this kind is likely to intensify and have widening applications in an arena with unclear ecological and social boundaries.[5]

Meanwhile, the world is entering a very different, more crowded future, which demands a different vision and way of life — "eco-just community", I would call it — involving caring and just human relationships, institutional as well as individual, with culturally diverse groups of people and myriad other species. Therefore, the opening sentence of this essay deliberately used the word "appropriate" as a religiously resonant modifier that is both theologically grounded and ethically relevant.

Among twentieth-century Protestant theologians, H. Richard Niebuhr and his prime interpreter James Gustafson have concentrated on fostering an ethic of the "fitting" or "appropriate". In *Ethics from a Theocentric Perspective*, Gustafson gives considerable attention to God's "ordering work" in the created ecological matrix of life. In that frame of reference,

Gustafson asks and answers the basic ethical question, What is God enabling and requiring us, as participants in the patterns and processes of interdependent life, to be and do?, and then answers it: We are to relate to all others in a manner appropriate to their relations to God. When ethics has theocentric grounding, ethical decisions are guided normatively by awareness of God's activity in the world. Particularly as we perceive God to be deeply involved in life's natural and social ecology, enabling right relations therein, our thinking and acting are likely to become more earth-fitting.[6]

Assessing what is "appropriate" or "fitting" is also an important consideration in any ecologically and socially alert ethical critique of modern technological activity. To focus on appropriate activity pushes the conversation towards cultural integrity and public accountability, while expressing realism about the moral ambiguities that continually confront us. In using the term "appropriate activity", I mean to emphasize a moral ecology of values that have environmental and social content similar to the meanings E.F. Schumacher gave to "intermediate" or "appropriate technology". Schumacher's seminal work *Small Is Beautiful* included a somewhat tongue-in-cheek chapter on "Buddhist Economics", to remind us that religious sensibilities matter, along with the sciences, in weighing particular research and development options.[7]

As a Christian theological and social ethicist, I am using the categories of that historic living faith, seeking to discern what it has to offer, in conversation with contemporary modes of thought, as guidance for biotechnical decision-making.

Theological insights

Faith affirms spirit, God's loving presence, in nature. Creation — the whole community of being, animated by divine Spirit — is the context of reality. All of the earth community matters, and has intrinsic value, to the one who continues to create, sustain and redeem the whole. God is actively present throughout the creation, generating and sustaining life, reconciling varied forms of being. God has a continuing role as creator-sustainer and expects human creatures to be respectful co-operators.

Ecologically aware "theologizing" about creation challenges modern atomistic individualism, which projects a self-contained God, humanity over nature and a mechanistic view of other being.[8] God is inherently related to the world, indwelling eco-social systems, breathing spirit into all creatures. Theology with this awareness knows that ecosystems — and similarly social systems — are inherently interconnected communities, with reverberations in all entities related therein. "When relations are conceived as inherent... justice is a matter of the quality of relationships... characterized by freedom, participation and solidarity... All entities have a right to be respected appropriate to their degree of intrinsic value and to their importance to the possibility of value in others."[9] This is not radical egalitarianism; different kinds of creatures still have differentiated value.

God is directly related to and cares for other creatures. Otherkind in the first creation saga (Gen. 1) are directly related to God and created to enjoy existence, not simply to function ecologically as a structured community of feeding levels or merely as a resource for humans to harvest, exploit and enjoy on a basis that is deemed to be "sustainable". (It is important to recognize that the word "sustainable" can mean one thing to technologists, quite another to ecologists.) In the second, older biblical creation saga (Gen. 2), the creatures are understood to have both intrinsic and extrinsic or instrumental value. Human earth creatures have community with other species, who are intended to be companions and helpers (Gen. 2:18). At the same time, God grants humans the power to name the creatures and utilize animals for human benefit (Gen. 3:21). "But the resource view, unconstrained by appropriate respect for the full spectrum of animal values, is inadequate for forming a mature Christian environmental ethic."[10]

The society of created being mediates the glory of God to humans and mourns unjust treatment by humanity. Theology with this passionate sensibility discerns that spirited, many-splendoured nature bears grace and points to divine power. The diversity of creatures, the grandeur of places and the forces of wind and water deserve human respect and admiration (cf. Job 39-41).

Theology with this sensibility also understands the reign of God, anticipated by the prophets and inaugurated by Jesus, to be "the society for all under God's reign".[11] Thus, biblical "peace pictures" project human harmony with other creatures. We would not be human without them. Without healthy biodiversity, human culture shrivels; without the glories of nature, sacred rituals or vital poems become museum pieces.

God is present in and with a dynamically open, astoundingly biodiverse and coherently indeterminate creation. In process thought as well as biblical theology, it is the divine nature as creative Spirit to love a world with fecund creaturely dignity in organic relation to God. When process thought is linked with biblical memory, it emphasizes God's transcendent immanence as Power of being, creating and sustaining life,

Shaper of time in natural and social history and Purpose for good through it all.[12]

Instead of perpetuating a monarchical model of the God-world relation (or a derivative secularism that transfers godlike power to humans), theology informed by process thought features an organic model in which "God not only affects the world but is affected by it... The world is understood as organic to God, not as a mere product of God's will. This means also that the world cannot be conceived in narrowly anthropocentric terms, as if it were provided solely for [humanity's] exploitation."[13]

Christology also needs "recycling" in this regard — to clarify what the second person of the Trinity does in and for the non-human creation. In the creeds, Jesus is understood to be the incarnate Word of God, the logos of life and reason from earth's beginning to end. Why should this work of Christ be seen exclusively in terms of human benefit? The prologue of John views the logos as involved in the whole of God's creative activity:

> Nothing has come into being apart from it. [The Word] is found in life, and all creaturely life participates in it... A definite difference is asserted between the way that the Word is present in Jesus and the way it is present in other human beings. The light that enlightens all human beings becomes flesh in Jesus. But despite the difference, there is also continuity. For the light to enlighten all people means that it is somehow present with, to, or in all... The life is the light. Perhaps the best understanding is to think of the presence of the Word as enlivening all living things and at the same time enlightening all that are capable of being enlightened. In summary, the Word is immanent in the whole of creation with differentiated results.[14]

God covenants with human beings to establish a pattern of right relations within the community of creation. The purpose of this ecumenical and ecological covenant is to secure the well-being of all, "shalom":

> Peace and justice are constitutive elements of the world as created... Violation of the covenant is an attack upon the created order of the world and is rebellion against God. Faithlessness harms the exploiter as well as the exploited. The symbiotic nature of creation means, therefore, that all action has a boomerang effect, going out towards goals intended but turning back upon the agent originating the action.[15]

Covenant ethics emphasizes human behaviour that is faithfully fitting:

> In one sense fittingness underscores the importance of particularity — responding to particular persons, situations and issues. In a larger sense, fittingness requires taking account of the encompassing context of the social and natural environment, so that what is done fits in with everything else that is happening and avoids causing more problems than it solves.[16]

The covenant contains promises and expectations that encompass the land and its creatures. Land is to be rested and needs of otherkind are to be respected in order to enhance regeneration of life. Within this religious-moral view, domesticated animals are not to be abused but to be treated justly by humans who husband and utilize them (Prov. 12:10; Ex. 20:10; Luke 14:5; Deut. 25:4). These animals do have instrumental value, though not that alone. They are to be humanely managed, but not merely for human convenience.

Humans are accountable for the well-being of all. The primary human vocation is to care for creation with love that seeks justice, consistent with the divine purpose. If justice is love distributed, then what is the character and purview of Christian love? When considering biotechnics as a particular eco-social challenge, it is important to emphasize that love expresses other-esteem.[17] "Love does not insist on its own way" (1 Cor. 13:5). It seeks the well-being of other people and otherkind, empathizing to the point that "if one member suffers, all suffer together with it; if one member is honoured, all rejoice together with it" (12:26):

> Other-esteem respects the integrity of wild nature — its diversity, relationality, complexity, ambiguity and even prodigality. It is quite content to let the natural world work out its own adaptations and interactions without benefit of human interventions, except insofar as necessary to remedy human harm to nature's integrity and to satisfy vital human interests.[18]

The normative human role is that of earthkeeper or household manager (*oikonomos*), to be exercised with loving intent and appropriate humility. This involves humans in the processes of continuing creation, resisting injustice, overcoming brokenness, restoring health and offering praise for what is good. Such a theological understanding of vocation contrasts sharply with the agenda of modernity which, baldly stated by Francis Bacon, was "to establish and extend the power and dominion of the human race itself over the universe". Bacon viewed the control of nature as the *telos* and test of knowledge; and his 1622 work, *The New Atlantis*, portrayed a biological utopia, organized as a patriarchal, hierarchical society whose priests were scientists. His project assumed the subordination of women along with nature.[19]

Bacon fostered a research paradigm, which is still accepted today, that "there are no unalterable properties of animals or plants".[20] Following Bacon's lead, modern humans have "disenchanted the world", discarding their appropriate vocation in favour of an ambitious project of life-mastery, an historical project based on the arrogant belief that nature exists for us, that we are the artisans of a new world for our benefit and that autonomous human power and purpose will reshape nature, society, psyches and now bodies for the better. Its illusory hope is progress and perfection, not preservation and prevention. [21]

Four centuries later, theological and philosophical ethics converge, with varied sensibilities, to face the environmental consequences of Bacon's paradigm. In this new situation of worldwide eco-injustice, we must reconsider. How do humans who can manipulate the genetic code appropriately express care for the well-being of life on earth? As "limited interventions" occur in ecological systems and in plant or animal life, what is the shape of human responsibility and of healthy culture?

The Genesis themes of dominion and stewardship must be recast. As interpreted by moderns, these doctrines have become part of the problem. Their interpretation in existentialist and utilitarian modes justified risky human activity in technology and politics. "Dare to use this power!" was the moral message. Anyone who questioned the wisdom of plunging ahead had to prove its harm. Today, a continuing emphasis on venturing and remaking is problematic, considering its eco-social effects. Protection and preservation take on more ethical import.

Environmental philosopher J. Baird Callicott has reappropriated themes and images from the sagas of Genesis as a guide for citizenship in the world garden. Callicott urges a re-reading of Genesis in light of John Muir's striking interpretation of "citizenship". [22] Muir's earliest journal, *A Thousand Mile Walk to the Gulf*, "argues for human citizenship in nature squarely on biblical principles", thoroughly discrediting popular anthropocentrism:

> Now it never seems to occur to these far-seeing teachers that Nature's object in making animals and plants might possibly be first of all the happiness of each one of them, not the creation of all for the happiness of one. Why should man value himself as more than a small part of the one great unit of creation? And what creature of all that the Lord has taken the pains to make is not essential to the completeness of that unit — the cosmos? The universe would be incomplete without man; but it would also be incomplete without the smallest transmicroscopic creature that dwells beyond our conceitful eyes and knowledge. [23]

Callicott observes that Muir seemed to mix his worldviews intentionally, reinterpreting Genesis in light of modern science (and, I would add, social experience). Muir goes into the specifics of the Genesis account to emphasize that other creatures deserve great human respect:

> They, also, are God's children, for [God] hears their cries, cares for them tenderly and provides their daily bread... How narrow we selfish, conceited creatures are in our sympathies! How blind to the right of all the rest of creation!... They are part of God's family, unfallen, un-depraved and cared for with the same species of tenderness and love as is bestowed on angels in heaven and saints on earth. [24]

Muir emphasizes that we share a common lot — being good citizens — with other creatures, rather than pretending to share God's transcendence over creation. In that light, we should not bifurcate human interests from the interests of the rest of creation. His citizenship ethic connects well with some Christian theological rethinking that is responsive to the environmental challenge. Consider these words by H. Paul Santmire:

> Given the ecological paradigm, the image of God as the one who elicits all things and the vision of nature as communities of beings with their own integrity, it is fitting to think of the human creature no longer as *homo faber* [the "maker"], but as *homo cooperans* [the co-operator]... The vision of humanity as *homo cooperans* is much more in tune with the biblical vision of shalom than is the popular image of human dominion. [25]

Human activity affects the future of earth community, even though the planet's destiny is God's responsibility. On the one hand, the creation is being threatened with disintegration because of human sin and injustice, which result in oppression of both people and nature. We experience collective consequences that are understood biblically in terms of divine judgment and sorrow. In the language of Lamentations, creation suffers, the creator mourns and the people lament. Or in the words of the Apostle Paul, "creation groans in travail". On the other hand, earth community is dynamic, unfinished, expectant of new creation. One might render Romans 8:20-21: The futility or emptiness to which the created order is now subject is not something intrinsic to it... Creation has something better to look forward to — namely, to be freed from its present enslavement to disintegration... to share in freedom and goodness.

In light of this eschatology, what ought we to expect of human activity in the biosphere as a whole and through biotechnics particularly? Are we to build a wondrous ecological and social future based on biotechnical achievements? Does "gentech" promise another step in evolution where new processes of production can harmonize with, even enhance, natural processes? Or is this an idolatrous stage of "animal slavery", [26] ecological disruption, social dislocation?

There are enthusiastic advocates of this new industry who envision a techno-millennium — a new era of joy, serenity, prosperity, and peace to be brought on through applied biotechnics. Francis Bacon has no shortage of followers in the scientific priesthood that would preside over this new age, filled with the same millennial hope that has fuelled numerous illusory projects in history. Technology, however, presents threat as well as promise. Eco-social dangers must be explored precisely because new things of ambiguous character and effect will be done by innately restless humans applying ingenuity, wisely or not, in this field.

Ethical imperatives.

1. Shift to a more appropriate eco-social paradigm.

Christian theology does not provide neat "answers" to the biotechnology question. But sound theology helps to illumine crucial ethical dilemmas by articulating a realistic and hopeful vision, in light of which we perceive the emerging future to be constraining and promising at the same time. Not only do we face sobering, forced options, resulting from deadly patterns of culture and economic life that rapidly deplete common resources and overshoot humanity's appropriate ecological and social limits. We also see better possibilities coming towards us, or an alternative path to the near future. The future invites us to a more appropriate (faithful and fitting) way of being human in the community of creation.

In this regard, it is important to ponder the significance of laws that allow for the parenting of genetically engineered animals, which proved to be a major barrier to a biodiversity treaty at UNCED in June 1992. "The US government has led the commercial drive to exploit the genetic commons," writes Jeremy Rifkin. Beginning in the 1930s Congress allowed the patenting of selected plant varieties. In 1980 the Supreme Court voted 5 to 4 to allow patenting of a micro-organism that was genetically engineered by General Electric to eat up oil spills:

> Seven years later, the US Patent Office extended the Supreme Court ruling to the entire living kingdom, arguing that any genetically engineered animal may be patented. For example, under the agency rule, if a human gene is inserted into the genetic code of a pig, both the process and the animal are patentable, the only test of patentability being novel intervention. In one regulatory stroke, the US Patent Office moved to enclose the entire genetic pool, from mice to primates. The Patent Office decision came down with only one disclaimer, excluding genetically engineered human beings from the patent laws because the Thirteenth Amendment to the Constitution forbids human slavery. [27]

2. Anticipate the social impacts of research and development, as well as effects on animals and the environment — all the more so as human power to destroy or reshape nature intensifies, affecting animal, plant and human life together.

Allan S. Miller, an ethicist in conservation and resource studies at the University of California, Berkeley, contends:

> The real issue [posed by recombinant research] is not between Frankenstein and Einstein — between evil science and good science — but between those who hope to use the new science and technology in an appropriate fashion (to actually help those in the world who are most needful of good people-oriented science) and those who will focus on providing high-cost services to the already over-privileged of the world's population in order to maximize market returns... If within a decade or two, aspects of the life process continue to become the private property of big business — as happens now when new organisms are patented and become simply additional possessions of great corporations — the ordinary people of the world will inevitably end up as losers. [28]

Miller, like Barry Commoner, locates much of the difficulty in the organization of science, not merely in the attitudes of individual practitioners. He notes that the biotech industry has become a potent lobby for deregulated laboratory research and field testing of genetically altered organisms, and it propagandizes the public with assurances of benign activity that promises positive results.

The "Gene Revolution" is even more threatening to small farmers than was the "Green Revolution," according to Miller. The Green Revolution was based in the public sector with a humanitarian intent. Still, it favoured energy- and capital-intensive agribusiness, leading to export cropping at the expense of small farmers and to less local food sufficiency in poor communities. The gene revolution, while grounded in tax-supported research, is even more tightly tied to private-sector enterprise and may have wider eco-social consequences in pursuing its life-altering agenda. [29]

We are back to the same dialectic of human behaviour that led Reinhold Niebuhr in 1937 to caution against naive and mistaken confidence in science and technology, without taking account of the destructive as well as the creative potential of human power and freedom. He saw the beneficial effects of various technical developments. Yet, "science can sharpen the fangs of ferocity as much as it can alleviate human pain", for "intelligence merely raises all the potencies of life, both good and evil". [30] Scientific and technological power over nature tempts humans to ignore creatureliness and seek the status of ultimacy. That "offends not only against God, who is the centre and source of existence, but against other life which has a rightful place in the harmony of the whole... [Technological power exerted by humans] to protect themselves against other life, tempts them to destroy and oppress other life."[31]

3. Assess biotechnics qualitatively.

The qualitative character of biotechnics, not only its pace or scale, should be faced directly. While its environmental risks and negative social consequences should not be exaggerated, genetic engineering does raise serious questions about the legitimate uses of human power over plants and animals.

Are nonhuman species just reconstructible "machines" or items of DNA to be reprogrammed? Christian ethicist James A. Nash argues to the contrary that otherkind are in some sense subjects with intrinsic value. So humans intervening in nature in this qualitatively different way must ask:

> What are the limits? What alternatives are available and satisfactory? Should natural species' barriers be honoured, so that nonhuman species can propagate their own kind in perpetuity and not some genetically altered kind? Since members of other species cannot be informed or give informed consent, what justifications are necessary for genetic alterations, and who should function as advocates for their interests? These are among the key questions that ecological ethics should direct to the new biological technology.

Nash recognizes that answers depend on worldview and value assumptions. His own position is that the creation of transgenic species is "not the norm but the rare exception on which the burden of proof rests. The genetic reconstruction of some species may be justified for compelling human needs in medicine, agriculture or ecological repairs (e.g., oil-eating microbes), so long as it can be reasonably tested and verified that tolerable alternatives are not available, genetic diversity is not compromised and ecosystemic integrity is not endangered."[32]

4. Establish criteria for eco-just biotechnics.

The preceding paragraphs suggest that something analogous to "just war" criteria are needed to guide biotechnical efforts to manipulate animals. Such ethical criteria would put the burden of proof on those who would intervene drastically in nature to alter species or to proceed in ways that place ecosystems at risk. What is the intention? Are these procedures necessary? Have conventional means that may actually be more appropriate been ignored or exhausted? Are discriminating limits to such intervention articulated and agreed to? Are the means disproportionate to the ends which are being achieved? What are the possible ecological and social dangers and likely effects? How will human and otherkind populations be protected? Who will benefit and who or what will lose (or what is the expected pattern of justice or injustice)? What is likely to be accomplished? How will a particular transgenic biological intervention contribute to a new state of peace, including just distribution of or fair participation in the social power and economic wealth derived from it?

Theological ethics of eco-justice and philosophical environmental ethics flow together in considering criteria of just human intervention in animal life and appropriate developments following from it. This way of thinking can be refined further by exploring the ends being sought, proportional effects of animal use and available alternatives, drawing on experience in discussions of the ethics of animal research. Thus, Strachan Donnelly writes:

> Are there experiments, no matter how worthy the theoretical or practical ends, that are simply inadmissible due to the decided violation of our moral sensibilities, not to mention the extreme harm done to animals? Is the use of animal, sentient life, with its attendant harms in suffering and death, necessary to achieve the particular scientific goal? Underlying this question is the possible replacement of a proposed use of animals by other means of research, e.g., computer models and cell cultures... [And there are] "alternatives" to animal use, the three R's: *replacement*, substitution of insentient material for conscious living animals; *reduction* in the number of animals used to gain information of a given amount and precision; and *refinement*, decrease in the incidence or severity of inhumane procedures applied to animals still used. [33]

5. Implement a standard of "appropriateness".

These considerations are more than prudential or utilitarian. They involve principles of respect and care for otherkind. What is the value assigned to the integrity of created nature and of species that have evolved over millennia? Keep in mind that human knowledge of speciation is barely a hundred years old and is still quite fragmentary. How much do scientists who are active in the gene revolution really know about the ecological reverberations of their manipulations? The questions involve more than what may be hazardous in the sense of environmentally toxic or ecologically disastrous. Efforts to contain biotechnology by pointing to environmental dangers as such have had little effect on the pursuit of such research and development. [34]

There may be "no straightforward, unambiguous and single ethical guideline for assessing each and every use of animals" in biological science, animal husbandry, agriculture, pharmaceutical development, etc. But there is a "moral ecology", ethical obligations to discern contextually and operationally in research and development. Thus, Krimsky argues that

> each judgment should be guided by the same general goal: the promotion of the overall good (human, animal and organic) at the least or ethically tolerable overall cost. The underlying assumption is that the human, animal and organic good ought not to be pursued independently of each other. Finally the human good should exist and flourish only within the wider animal and organic good, since all living beings are inextricably linked together within a single evolutionary and ecological context.[35]

What eco-social future?

We have now come to the most profound ethical concern raised by nonhuman biotechnology: towards what eco-social future does it move? This question looms large because many of the scientists and corporations now collaborating in industrial biotechnology apparently do not acknowledge the principle of an ecological or organic good that must not be violated, but only a principle of "reasonableness" to be observed in biotechnics — for example: "Attendant on the freedom to undertake research into the exciting and fertile frontiers of the New Biology is a coexistent responsibility to pursue the work in a reasonable, rational manner."[36]

In contrast to this morally empty standard of reasonableness, I recommend a standard of appropriateness, or what is "fitting". It has a religious-philosophical referent, and fosters ecological sensibility, constructive social purpose, appreciation for responsible scientific inquiry and realism about human misuse of power. It is not a rigid standard, recognizing that decisions about biotechnology must be contextual. At the same time, it would not leave decisions to researchers and investors doing as they alone see fit.

The standard of appropriateness underscores the need to institutionalize prospective assessment of all biotechnical innovations, and to monitor this work for ecological safety and its contribution to meeting basic social problems, including malnutrition, disease, environmental degradation, lack of inexpensive and clean energy, expensive health care. Krimsky suggests that a broader system of social guidance is needed. He recommends a system that is able "to reinforce those innovations that meet important social needs and to provide selective negative pressures against unneeded or unwanted innovations".[37] This is consistent with the dialectical view that scientific-technical research demands freedom of enquiry, along with clear understandings of ethical constraints and democratically determined social guidance of its directions and uses.[38]

Otherwise, genetic engineering will continue as a

> growth-oriented technical thrust towards redesigning the gene pool to serve economic criteria... Natural selection is giving way more and more to economic selection as the directive force of evolution... Economically directed evolution is biological and ecological central planning! It is a sin against free competition, and an arrogant presumption that we possess knowledge that we do not have... How far are we justified in rearranging the foundations of creation to better serve our own purposes? That depends on how closely our purposes mirror the creation's purposes.[39]

An adequate social policy with regard to animal biotechnology encompasses ecological integrity and social justice together. It approaches decisions in the larger framework of creation community and fair social participation. The mechanisms of social guidance need to embody a just-intervention ethic with an eco-justice orientation. "Appropriate technology" has a combination of characteristics that move in such a direction — namely, it is relatively simple, locally controlled, environmentally compatible, intermediate in scale, labour-intensive and alert to external and long-term impacts.[40]

Attention to eco-socially appropriate technology does not rule out biotechnics; it asks for deeper ethical reflection, alert to intuitive religious sensibilities about what is good and right, and for more democratic social involvement to limit or channel this qualitatively different human activity for the good of all.

NOTES

[1] For an overview of the origins and cultural significance of the genetics revolution, cf. Sheldon Krimsky, *Biotechnics and Society: The Rise of Industrial Genetics*, New York, Praeger, 1991, ch. 1.

[2] *Ibid.*, p.55; cf. George Smith, *The New Biology: Law, Ethics, and Biotechnology*, New York, Plenum Press, 1989, p.8, who views this event as a pivotal controversy. The Foundation for Economic Trends, together with the Humane Society, took unsuccessful legal action to stop this activity, claiming that "research of this nature not only was cruel and violated animal dignities, but would also have significant social and economic repercussions, in that more expensive animals would in turn cause severe market dislocations in the farm economy."

[3] Rivers Singleton, Jr, "Transgenic Organisms, Science, and Society" (draft paper for the Animal Biotechnology Project, Hastings Center).

[4] "Toward Development of a Sound Public Policy Concerning Transgenic Animals" (draft paper for Animal Biotechnology Project, Hastings Center), p.6.

[5] For further background, see "The Brave New World of Animal Biotechnology: An Ethical Analysis", special supplement to the *Hastings Center Report*, 1993.

[6] James Gustafson, *Ethics from a Theocentric Perspective*, Chicago, Univ. of Chicago Press, 1984, Vol. II, pp.2,275,279. I wish Gustafson had pursued this basic ethical question in a more trinitarian way. Moreover, because of his preoccupation with establishing the positive role of science in mature theological and ethical discourse, he does not offer here a sharp critique of science and technology except in terms of distributive justice.

[7] For a useful summary of appropriate technology, see the concluding chapter of Ian G. Barbour, *Technology, Environment, and Human Values*, New York, Praeger, 1980.

[8] Jay McDaniel, "Christianity and the Need for New Vision". in *Religion and the Environmental Crisis*, ed. Eugene C. Hargrove, Athens, University of Georgia Press, 1986, pp.189,204.

[9] Carol Johnston, "Economics, Eco-Justice and the Doctrine of God", in *After Nature's Revolt: Eco-Justice and Theology*, ed. Dieter Hessel, Minneapolis, Fortress Press, 1992, pp.158,161-62.

[10] Holmes Rolston III, "Wildlife and Wildlands: A Christian Response", *ibid.*, p.134.

[11] Daniel Day Williams, "Changing Concepts of Nature", in *Earth Might be Fair: Reflections on Ethics, Religion, and Ecology*, ed. Ian G. Barbour, Englewood Cliffs, NJ, Prentice-Hall, 1972.

[12] *Ibid.*, pp.58-61.

[13] John Macquarrie, "Creation and Environment", in *Ecology and Religion in History*, eds David and Eileen Spring, New York, Harper & Row, 1974, pp.45-46.

[14] John B. Cobb, Jr, "On Christ and Animals" (unpublished paper), pp.4-5.

[15] Charles S. McCoy, "Creation and Covenant: A Comprehensive Vision for Environmental Ethics", in *Covenant for a New Creation: Ethics, Religion and Public Policy*, eds Carol Robb and Carl Casebolt, Maryknoll, NY, Orbis Books, 1991, pp.215-16.

[16] *Ibid.*, p.225.

[17] Cf. James A. Nash, *Loving Nature: Ecological Integrity and Christian Responsibility*, Nashville, Abingdon, 1991, p.153.

[18] *Ibid.*, p.154.

[19] Cf. Carolyn Merchant, *The Death of Nature: Women, Ecology and the Scientific Revolution*, San Francisco, Harper & Row, 1980.

[20] Krimsky, *op. cit.*, p.85.

[21] For an eloquent critique of the Baconian ideal, see Hans Jonas, *The Imperative of Responsibility: In Search of an Ethics for a Technological Age*, Chicago, Univ. of Chicago Press, 1984, ch. 5.

[22] Callicott, "Genesis and John Muir", in Robb and Casebolt, *op. cit.*, pp.107-40.

[23] John Muir, *A Thousand Mile Walk to the Gulf*, ed. by Wm. F. Frederick Bade, New York, Houghton Mifflin, 1916, p.139.

[24] *Ibid.*, pp.98-99,139.

[25] H. Paul Santmire, "Healing the Protestant Mind", in Hessel, *op. cit.*, pp.74-75.

[26] Cf. Krimsky, *op. cit.*, p.84; Andrew Linzey, "Human and Animal Slavery: A Theological Critique of Genetic Engineering", in *The Bio-Revolution: Cornucopia or Pandora's Box*, London, Pluto Press, 1990, p.182.

[27] Jeremy Rifkin, *Biosphere Politics*, New York, Crown Publishers, 1991, p.70; cf. Krimsky, *op. cit.*, ch. 3.

[28] Alan S. Miller, "Science for People or Science for Profit?", in Robb and Casebolt, *op. cit.*, p.63.

[29] *Ibid.*, pp.69,74,76.

[30] Reinhold Niebuhr, *Beyond Tragedy*, New York, Scribners, 1937, pp.125-26.

[31] *Ibid.*, pp.102-03.

[32] James Nash, *op. cit.*, pp.61-62; cf. p.211.

[33] Strachan Donnelley, "Animals in Science: the Justification Issue", Special Supplement to the *Hastings Center Report*, May-June 1990; cf. W.M.S. Russell and R.L. Burch, *The Principles of Humane Experimental Techniques*, London, Methuen, 1959.

[34] See Krimsky, *op. cit.*, ch. 6.

[35] *Ibid.*, p.11.

[36] George Smith, *op. cit.*, pp.26-27.

[37] Krimsky, *op. cit.*, ch. 11, and pp.207f.

[38] Roger Shinn, *Forced Options: Social Decisions for the 21st Century*, Cleveland, Pilgrim Press, 1991, ch. 9.

[39] Herman E. Daly and John B. Cobb, Jr., *For the Common Good: Redirecting the Economy toward Community, the Environment and a Sustainable Future*, Boston, Beacon Press, 1989, pp.204-206.

[40] Barbour, *op. cit.*, pp.294-99.

Chosen Persons
and the Green Ecumenacy

A Possible Christian Response
to the Population Apocalypse

Catherine Keller

Actively avoiding the issue

It is my dubious honour in this collection to represent a Christian perspective on the issue of population ecology. No one — neither the pope nor I — can speak for "Christianity". Christianity is not one. Many of those who stress its unity today are seeking to muster allegiance to an orthodox Christian core, which even in classical times existed only for those willing to assent to the conciliar consensus. That consensus, forged in the fires of the fusion of fourth-century Christianity with the Constantinian empire, made possible the aggressive global impact of this particular religion and accounts for the fact that Christianity includes today the single most vocal force of pro-natalism, of opposition to any effective birth control options and policies. At the same time, modern Christian — Western — cultures have been overwhelmingly responsible for the imposition throughout the planet of ecologically unsustainable patterns of development.

It is not that Christianity, compared to other world religions, necessarily has the worst ideas for the environment and for women, but that it has purveyed the ideological framework for the unprecedented aggressions of the modern Western circuits of political, economic and cultural domination.

Nevertheless, the diversity of Christianity stubbornly persists. On the theological practices pertaining to the sustainability of the biosphere, as perhaps on every other issue of material force in the world today, Christians differ more among each other than from certain members of other groups. For instance, those with conservative Christian commitments will share more on issues of population and birth control with conservative members of non-Christian faiths than they do with their own siblings in Christ who, likewise, will find affinity with a variety of secular and non-Christian progressives.

This diversity, for all its frictions and marginalities, gives space to work in; and the fierce, if fragile, transmutations of Christianity's "mainstream" into a self-critical force for Justice, Peace and the Integrity of Creation lends hope that the work may be worthwhile. For my particular purposes, concern for the planetary ecology cannot be separated from commitment to social justice, and focuses itself through the lens of feminist enquiry.

As it turns out, analysis of the global phenomenon of women's traditional subjugation may be the only possible starting-point for an effective engagement of the question of over-population. Margaret Catley-Carlson, president of the Population Council, makes clear that there can be no effective, let alone humane, approach to over-population that does not begin with the situations of women in poverty.[1] Only with the enhancement of female access to education, human rights and paid work and reduced infant mortality at the same time are there notable reductions anywhere in the rate of population growth. Patriarchy and over-population now function as correlatives. It would seem that only a forthrightly feminist version of Christianity will be able to engage the interstructured social and ecological injustices that nest within the thorny issue of population growth.

But while the environment is finally on the Christian progressive agenda, the issue of the population curve still is not. As I browsed through various journals, anthologies and ecotheological texts seeking to deepen my understanding of the population issue, I became aware of a veritable conspiracy of silence. Among ecumenical Protestant Christians — ethicists, feminists, eco-spiritualists, liberation theologians, justice activists — an unstated assumption seems to reign that population is never worth highlighting.

Justice-centred Christians speaking on behalf of the world of the poor make the irrefutable point that First World persons, who consume thirty times what an average African or Asian or Latin American does, can hardly instruct others to reduce themselves. It is the exploitation of the resources of the Third World for the sake of the First World and its client elites — not over-population — which deprives those "others" of the resources they need. Is not focus on population control thus dangerously akin to the genocidal policies which seek to rid the world of the troubling, potentially revolutionary masses of the poor?[2] This key objection to the very terms of the population debate rightly sets the limits for any contemporary re-engagement of the issue.

But there is a whole chorus of silences on this matter. Feminists come from another angle. Rightly indignant about the misogynist means of much state-driven population reduction (such as involuntary sterilization of poor and dark women), and indeed the gynocidal results increasingly possible (as in abortion of female foetuses in China), we too are loath to consider population growth as such the problem. Feminist ethicists have perhaps directed their birth-control energies on the relentless debate about abortion, with little left to spare.[3] We might expect some guidance from the writings of eco-feminists and eco-theologians. But while one delights here in the rediscovery of the intermeshed life of the creation — the evocation of the interdependence of human and creaturely life — the all-too-human problem of over-population, begging for technological address, hardly enhances the desired naturalism. Moreover, there is a desire for solidarity with progressive Roman Catholics, who usually have few qualms about artificial birth control but often draw the line at abortion, and therefore make unlikely partners in any attempt to disseminate a wide variety of birth control options.[4]

Add to all this the residual Christian ambivalence about sex, the body, women's bodies in particular and the natural world in general, and the lack of any prophetic-biblical resources comparable to those addressing oppression and poverty; and it is not hard to understand why the population issue receives little steadfast attention.

Yet surely the possibility of misdescribing or misusing the population explosion for First World or masculinist or white self-interest is not adequate reason to ignore or dismiss the issue. The Malthusian growth-curve within the diminishing resource-base does not go away while we focus on other critical struggles. One would rather hope that the critical concerns of feminists and liberationists would be the basis for a socio-ecological reinterpretation of the population problem which is aware that the poor, especially poor women, will always suffer the most from the environmental effects of overpopulation and that, conversely, it is precisely the structures that maintain poverty and sexism which also create over-population.

We will be able to overcome the rather formidable inhibitions to addressing the population explosion globally and ecumenically only insofar as we move towards a discourse which can sustain multiple voices advocating multiple commitments, without retreating into the stale Western logic of "either-or". An alternative logic, an *eco-logic*, which seeks to understand the *eco*nomy and *eco*logy as inter-related dimensions of our *ecu*menical accountability to each other and the earth, must emerge. Such a logic seeks to hold together multiple struggles simultaneously, and thus moves so far from Western rationalism as to resemble faith. Or rather it resembles eco-spirituality: it will recycle the often toxic complexities of the tradition through the criteria of the multiple voices of the suffering. The task of the theologian in such a situation is like that of the compost heap — what amidst the wastes and the clichés of our overused tradition can be recycled?

In the absence of a developed Christian alternative, it is the pope who speaks, by default, for Christianity. His position rings out free of the ambiguities bred of complex loyalties. "Every sexual act must be open to the transmission of life" was the refrain broadcast from the gathering of Roman Catholic youth in Denver in August 1993. "Life" in papal discourse seems to evoke all that vitalizes interpersonal existence and redeems it from modern depersonalizing alienation; but that vitality is here shrunk, with unflinching literalism, to the size of the foetus. In the papal encyclical *Veritatis Splendor*, which soon followed, "morality" seems to become a code for the ecclesial supervision of Christian genitals. "Life" thus becomes a pawn in "pro-life" politics. The appropriate ecumenical Christian response to this particular universalization of opinions of a celibate male elite cannot be polite silence.

In fact, there are important alternative voices among that very elite. Sean McDonagh, SSC, head of the Columbian missioners, asks, "Is it really pro-life to ignore the warning of demographers and ecologists who predict that unbridled population growth will lead to severe hardship and an increase in the infant mortality rate for succeeding generations?"[5] McDonagh is an Irish priest who worked for twenty years in a mission in the Philippines, helping to develop a small indigenous community's economic and ecological potentialities under relatively rare, isolated and protected circumstances. He demonstrates that even with the most egalitarian policies, this community, Tablo, is faced, precisely because of its population growth, with strong temptations to overwork the land and harvest the forest, thus undermining the possibility of continuing stability and self-sustenance. In this connection, McDonagh cites another priest, who has lived in the area for 27 years: "the simple conclusion is that there cannot be a stable livelihood or sustainable community without population control." As to "natural family planning methods", these failed repeatedly, even with the four assistants to the Roman Catholic clinic. The result was that the women were left "disturbed and depressed by their third and succeeding pregnancies... Is it pro-life to ignore the increase in population levels to such an extent that the living systems in particular regions are becoming so impoverished that they will never recover?"

The voice of this Irish priest may serve as an inspiration to other Christians seeking ecologically sustainable justice. The papal reduction of sexual ethics to the surveillance of reproductive choices not only militates against any responsible birth control policy for those peoples, especially in Latin America, who are at once Roman Catholic and poor, but also strategically detracts from the attempt to raise morality once again to the level of prophetic social concern. Thus it helps to delegitimate the theological movement within Roman Catholicism which has evinced perhaps the greatest vitality in twentieth-century popular Christianity, that of the base Christian communities in which liberation theology is grounded.

Those who would hold Christianity to its prophetic potentiality must ask how this reductive, biologistic, anthropocentric and patriarchal notion of "life" came about? Though most Protestants do not believe it and many Catholics do not practise it, it comes close to a norm which haunts many, and thus reinforces the conspiracy of silence. So we must come to terms with the origins of pro-natalism in the scriptures, as the texts that in some way serve as a sounding-board for all Christians.

The emergence of pro-natalism[6]

Hebrew scripture offers as the first *mitzvoh* — both a commandment and a blessing — the injunction of Genesis 1:28: "Be fruitful and multiply and fill the earth..." John Cobb once wryly remarked that this is the only commandment humankind has obeyed. The fertility refrain is soon picked up in the covenant with Abraham, which offers multiplication as the primary blessing. The covenant is first and foremost a deal for the continuation of the male line. In other words the originating mythic moments of the relationship of the biblical God to "his" people are sealed in the promise of "seed". The very archetypes of divine blessing reverberate with this identification of divine blessing as natal abundance. In this way, at least as the texts retroactively tell the story, the people of Israel envisioned a long future as the horizon of their hope.

Certainly the Hebrew tradition confirms the patriarchal family arrangements characteristic of its place and time. But pro-natalism as reinforcement of the population explosion is a Christian rather than a Jewish problem. During the formative periods of Judaism, the population tended to need expanding rather than contracting. The problem for us lies not so much in Hebrew intentions as in Christian expropriations.

But then here lies a perplexity. From the vantage point of its scripture, Christianity need not have resulted in the papal preoccupation with the literal "transmission of life". The New Testament nowhere picks up the theme of procreative abundance. The gospels and the epistles are almost alarmingly devoid of natal interest. Jesus uses fertility and birth images, such as that of the fig tree, strictly as metaphors for spiritual flourishing. One can explain this absence in terms of the apocalyptic expectations of the period. If the world was expected to conclude its business within the generation, there was hardly any point to further fertility. "Blessed are those who are not with child" so that you may flee more easily "on that day" (Matt. 24:19; Mark 13:17; Luke 21:23) suggest similarly non- if not anti-natalist sentiments. Distant futures were a thing of the past.

Current scholarship disputes the claim that Jesus himself was an apocalyptic prophet expecting a literal end; his parables suggest a more subtle eschatology, an evocation of the "kingdom of God", or realm of divine relatedness, already taking place within human community. Nevertheless, though the synoptic gospels paint a consistent picture of his unusual respect for children as models of that very realm, the figure of Jesus displays either indifference to or contempt for the (patriarchal) family. Though the Jesus constructed especially by Luke shows also a striking awareness of the personhood of women, he displays no interest whatsoever in women's "vocation" to motherhood. [7]

Indeed, early Christianity did not fail to note this shift. It had to struggle with this apparent contradiction between its own "old" and "new" testaments. Hence Jerome regarded the commandment to multiply as valid only within the "old law": "What has that to do with us upon whom the ends of the ages are come?" The early tendencies towards celibacy reflect the apocalyptic sense of crisis: the world is in a state of emergency, there is no time for business as usual. Before secure birth control, having sex was more or less synonymous with having children, and neither Jesus nor his most committed male and female followers considered procreation a priority. Thus the roots of asceticism do not lie in the programmes of self-control and mastery of lust or in a moralizing distaste for the body's desires.

Soon, however, Christianity settled into its institutional longevity. Because the "end of the world" did not come, the church contented itself to rule the world in the meantime. So business as usual was encouraged again. A strange power configuration emerges with the Constantinian collaboration: an elite of celibate males, extracted from the multiplying masses, reinforces the structure of the patriarchal family order as the very building block of the state. Within these families, "marital chastity" was recommended, then as now, as the only alternative to reproduction (though fortunately the pope would not urge celibacy on infertile couples now). That is, the return to the socio-familial structure of patriarchy did not bring with it the healthier Hebrew earthiness, but rather the sexual guilt complex, which, as Foucault has analyzed, finally led not merely to repression but also to obsession: the post-Tridentine Catholic as well as the Freudian forms of confessional constitute a continuous modern tradition of sexual preoccupation.[8]

Maximizing fertility, minimizing pleasure: somehow the Christian heritage has left us with the worst of both worlds. The Old Testament patriarchal family centred on procreative blessing synthesized itself strangely with the New Testament asceticism in its Hellenized and institutionalized form. Sexist pro-natalist pieties were reinforced with imperial power. Hence the pronouncements by celibate males today encouraging either over-population or sexual suppression.

A way forward?

In the face of such synthetic sexism, what is there for Christianity to recycle in these traditions? Quite a bit, I would maintain, if only for the purposes of taking responsibility for the toxic effects of our own pollution through power. But even more, there remain the resources that in this period are proving to be high-energy resources for "justice, peace and the integrity of creation".

First of all, the Hebrew prophetic priority of justice must structure our discussion of population control. The classical prophets addressed resource consumption from the vantage point of the poor: "If you offer your food to the hungry and satisfy the needs of the afflicted, then your light shall rise in the darkness" (Isa. 58:10). These are persistent themes: the people cannot long flourish if resources are unjustly distributed. Furthermore, why not affirm the Hebrew sense of every child as gift of God — once it is a person! Hebrew scriptures never regard the foetus as equivalent to a human life.[9] Rather than continuing a natalism aimed at increasing the size of the "chosen people", may we not greet children as chosen persons? But then let us indeed choose them now and not receive them merely as a vaguely supernaturalized biological fate.

This does not suggest some arrogation of divine prerogative to ourselves via the technology of birth control: it does however suggest, within the total matrix of social reality, in which the justice possible in the face of scarce resources demands a sustainable level of population, a new spirituality of choosing persons and therefore not giving birth to more than we as a world and as communities and families are capable of cherishing. The desperate surplus populations being generated by structures of late capitalism make impossible the experience of every child as blessing. From the perspective of responsible choice, one child is plenty. But whichever children are already born, whether by choice or not, deserve that cherishing as well. Indeed, so many are born and will continue to be born that the choice of no children, if taken in the context of commitment to work for justice for all children, will sometimes appear as precisely the way to affirm life and choose children. And this, as we will see, may even be more the case for so-called First World parents, who could ostensibly support more children, than for their poor-world counterparts.

So a revised Hebrew prophetic population policy, for Christians at least, would affirm every choice not to multiply the quantity of life, if it enhances the quality of life — not in terms of selfish accumulation, in which adults want to guard their affluence and leisure for their own enjoyment, for such choices constitute the very heart of the quantifiable life-style (which the pope also decries as consumer inhumanity) that is producing the surplus poverty-populations elsewhere. Quality of life in the Hebrew vision is about a shared abundance, *shalom* — a metaphor of wholeness at once physical and material, just and loving — which unravels the power elites for the sake of the possible well-being of all, including "the nations". Not an otherworldly ascetic viewpoint, but one of all workers enjoying the fruits of their own labour, of all living long and celebrating life together. The life of scriptures' God of Life is not composed of random quantitative increase in birth; it is about the quality of loved life to be enjoyed by those already born.

What Christian sources, steeped as they are in apocalyptic asceticism, can we recycle as resources for the struggle for *shalom*, for the "realm of God"? Let me make a suggestion that will sound alien and perhaps self-contradictory: let me call here for a revised form of that apocalyptic asceticism. Why not acknowledge the affinity between the first century and our own time, since an apocalyptic sense of emergency characterizes both? In the former, faith was required; in the latter only newspaper literacy. Population is only one of at least four horsemen of doom; the others might be named Economics, War and Environment. But they gallop together, this quartet, inextricable in their cumulative momentum of horror. Without any literalist expectation of a particular and predictable termination, it is hard to miss the global threat of doom. If many of us came of age under the sign of the nuclear Armageddon, it is at this moment pre-eminently an eco-apocalypse we face. I am interested in facing the apocalyptic threat, in letting it exhort us to "wake up", the perennial biblical call to consciousness, to "prepare", to rub away the numbness brought on either by too much pain or too much comfort. But only for the sake of what we may dub the "counter-apocalypse" which Jesus seems also to have pursued: that sense of urgency which does not plan on ultimate doom but rather begins already in the present "communities of resistance and solidarity"[10] to experience the divine realm, that is, that which for us may better translate as meaningfulness of life.

This means that, like the first century, this is not a time when procreation can be an over-riding priority. Blessing for "the people", now as in the understanding of the primitive Christian community, will not come from enhanced fertility. The new Christian asceticism, like the original, will not be about sex but about its fruits. This is by no means to decry as immoral the responsible choice to parent; on the contrary, it is to discourage any parenting which eclipses the larger responsibility. And again, this is precisely not to say that only those with adequate resources should parent; it might mean that they also might choose to offer those resources of energy, time and wealth to the larger communal struggle. For at the heart of the new eco-asceticism lies not self-denial *per se*, but a lively choice to awaken desire to the needs of the larger earth-community, that is, to know oneself as a creature inextricably created in interdependency with all the other denizens of creation.

But this discussion needs to be framed in terms of the larger eco-political context. In other words, the issue of the disproportionate resource consumption by poor and rich peoples — which any prophetic spirituality will address — must shape the terms of this proposed asceticism. Given that the average US citizen uses ten times the technology and ten times the resources of a poor Third World dweller, each First World child will have at least twenty times the environmental impact of a poor Third World child. The discrepancy jumps to thirty times if the First World child is wealthy. In fact a waste level corollary to this difference may increase the difference tenfold again. In other words, the child who will have the most is the one the world can least afford.

This is not to argue that the impact of the population of the poor world upon their own environment is not doing irrevocable harm to their own possibilities. But there is simply no way for affluent denizens of the North, whose life-style preys on just those beleaguered resources and populations of the South, to make any credible case for world population control in isolation from the larger context of environmental impact. Indeed, only as we begin in greater numbers to practise our own forms of eco-asceticism, thus reducing our disproportionate dependency upon resources and technology and continuing to reduce our own populations to make space for the needs of the migrating poor, may we engage the population issue in good faith. I am not arguing that we should defer the discussion and thus join the "conspiracy of silence", for the damage to many local ecologies as we threaten to surpass the carrying capacity of the earth is going on now. An apocalyptic sense of urgency, without the accompanying commitment to total doom, is only appropriate. Hence the call to a reconsideration of Christian priorities, which *ipso facto* involves a global clientele, already commits us to a divestment of procreative piety. Except for any people who is the victim of attempted genocide, this means that ecumenical Christianity, where it has a voice, will actively advocate non-procreative options for fulfilment, precisely in order to realize the blessing of every child as chosen and as gift.

The eco-asceticism I am advocating will thus remain deeply Hebrew in its roots: it will not have anything to do with the sort of virtue that comes from pleasures denied. Rather, it will seek to maximize joy, including sexual joy, by heightening the awareness of our interdependence with each other and with all creatures. Thus I am advocating not a new ascetic of self-denial, even for the First World; that appeal will only work among those already practising it. And beyond rhetorical pragmatics, it seems to me the prophetic vision of *shalom* is sensuous in its relation to the world and rarely prone to obsessions about private morality. What we need is a sensuous asceticism, in which the joy of our senses — at the rhythm of day and night, the rising of sun and stars, the parade of seasons, the delight of fresh water, of wholesome food, the zest which arises from having enough and getting free of the consumer addictions of over-indulgence and accompanying self-detestation — works to support the reduction of our consumption levels. At the same time the joys and demands of participation in larger communities, in voluntary groups, affinity networks and alternative families, at once satisfy many needs traditionally met by reproduction within the nuclear family unit and lend the framework in which abstinence from child-bearing receives positive motivation. But such choices by many then also lend a communal support network for the care of children, those chosen responsibly as well as those neglected, abandoned and abused.

As one can witness traces of this possibility all around, in North and South, let me further concretize what I mean by this "ascetic" choice. As to sexuality: moral issues are thus shifted from traditional genital piety to the network of relationships. This means not just the matter of population impact, but first of all the quality of relationship itself. Hence the community itself becomes a source of encouragement of egalitarian, loving bonds between sexual partners, and a source of shame for those who dominate and violate. As stated at the outset, the deconstruction of patriarchal power structures within the family is the necessary prerequisite for reproductive responsibility. Furthermore, let us not denigrate the ancient option of celibacy for anyone, ordained or not. Probably everyone should practise it sometimes, in order to enhance his or her freedom. But the celibate option in different situations, for different reasons, at different ages, must surely also be supported as not only helpful for population control but also as potentially releasing tremendous energy into the larger network of relations.

Such counter-apocalyptic community-building will derive inspiration from more eco-centric tribal cultures, as well as from Hebrew hopes for "jubilee" for all creation. It is also thoroughly Christian. The nodal point of connection, the "inter" of interdependence, is what Christians call Holy Spirit. The flesh of the interdependence is what Christians call "the body of Christ", of which all are "members one of another" (1 Cor. 12). This becomes liturgically embodied in some Christian ecclesial groupings, such as the base Christian communities of Latin America and the liberation churches of the North — those marked by their commitment to social justice and their welcoming into their midst of singles, gays, lesbians and other non-procreative units, as well as traditional families. The "kingdom of God" does not wait for the space to be apocalyptically cleared by some forthcoming set of plagues, starvations, wars and poisons. Its "God" then names the creative force flowing through that interdependence, at least when its delicate potentials are attended to faithfully.

The ecumenical Christianity I advocate knows itself part of a larger network, vastly exceeding Christendom, organized religion, and finally humanity itself. It knows itself a part of a green ecumenacy, in which the ecological and economic resonances of "ecumenacy", itself meaning originally "stewardship", become discernible. Thus action for social *shalom* will refuse the anthropocentrism of the prophetic traditions and indeed of all traditional ecumenism between "the great world religions" (all of which are not only anthropocentric but androcentric). I suspect that the sensibilities of indigenous peoples to the inextricability of specific environments and specific communities, must lead the way. This requires not a romanticism of "noble savages" but an ecumenism of the mind, and hence a pluralistic epistemology, a way of looking at problems such as population and resource consumption as expressions of our interdependence and thus as themselves interdependent problems. Christians will have to work to overcome the tendency to look for single issues and single solutions, a habit which, because of the perpetual self-contradictions into which it leads, assures that we rarely get to the action phase.

The multiplication we need today is not that of seed but of strategies, not of people but of perspectives; the blessing we need not that of a depleting growth but of a just sustainability; the asceticism we need not of self-denial but of communal flourishing; the ecumenism we need not of a unity of beliefs but of common actions.

NOTES

[1] Margaret Catley-Carlson, "Explosions, Eclipses and Escapes: Charting a Course on Global Population Issues", the Paul Hoffman Lecture (June 7, 1993), UN Development Programme, New York.

[2] Roger L. Shinn, *Forced Options: Social Decisions for the Twenty-First Century*, Cleveland, Pilgrim Press, 1991, pp.85-105, addresses this tension head-on, and is thus a significant exception among mainstream Christian ethicists.

[3] Beverly Harrison, *Our Right to Choose*, Boston, Beacon, 1984, does however analyze Christian pro-natalist tradition, which is as relevant to the population issue as to the narrower abortion issue on which her book focuses.

[4] Rosemary Ruether is an exception to all of the above categories; cf. esp. *God and Gaia*, San Fransisco, Harper, 1992.

[5] Sean McDonagh, *The Greening of the Church*, Maryknoll, New York, Orbis, 1990.

[6] The term pro-natalism designates the belief that sexuality is to function primarily for purposes of reproduction and that artificial birth control therefore impedes the playing out of the divine will in nature.

[7] Elizabeth Schüssler Fiorenza, *In Memory of Her: A Feminist Theological Reconstruction of Christian Origins*, New York, Crossroads, 1984.

[8] Michel Foucault, *History of Sexuality*, New York, Random House, 1980.

[9] Cf. Ex. 21:22, which treats a miscarriage as property damage — the injury to the woman is punished by payment of a fine to the husband — not as the loss of a life.

[10] Cf. Sharon Welch, *Communities of Resistance and Solidarity*, Maryknoll, New York, Orbis, 1985.

Contributors

K.C. Abraham is director of the South Asia Theological Research Institute (SATHRI) and part-time professor of theology and ethics at United Theological College, Bangalore, India. An ordained presbyter of the Church of South India, he is involved in many programmes of the Christian Conference of Asia, World Council of Churches and other ecumenical bodies, and is president of the Ecumenical Association of Third World Theologians (EATWOT).

Edward Antonio lectures in political and Third World theologies at the University of Zimbabwe. He grew up as a "street kid", is self-educated and holds a Ph.D. degree in theology from Cambridge University.

Leonardo Boff is professor of ethics at the University of Rio de Janeiro. He holds a doctorate in systematic theology from the University of Munich and from 1970-92 was professor of theology at Petropolis-Rio. A prolific author on liberation theology, he is a member of the editorial committee of the international journal *Concilium*.

Tony Brun teaches pastoral theology and social issues at the Seminario Biblico Latinoamericano in San Jose, Costa Rica, and Anabaptist-Mennonite theology at the Seminario Anabautista Latinoamericano in Guatemala. He is a pastor of the Mennonite Church of Uruguay, and has been involved in a variety of meetings and peace projects for the World Mennonite Conference.

Chung Hyun Kyung is professor of systematic theology in the Christian Studies Department of Ewha Women's University in Seoul, Korea. She holds a Ph.D. in systematic theology from Union Theological Seminary in New York and is the author of one book and numerous articles.

Rob Cooper is a Maori of Ngati Hine descent. He was formerly secretary-researcher for the Maori Council of Churches (Te Runanga Whakawhanaunga i Nga Hahi) and is currently working as an advocate in a small claims tribunal in Aotearoa-New Zealand.

Jose (Pepz) Cunanan, an ordained minister in the United Methodist Church in the Philippines, has served as secretary for Urban Rural Mission in the WCC (1986-89) and director of development for the National Council of Churches in the Philippines (1990-93). As an advocate for the protection and rehabilitation of the environment, he has participated in campaigns and conferences in the Philippines and internationally.

M.L. Daneel earned a doctorate in theology from the Free University in Amsterdam in 1971. After working as senior lecturer and researcher for the Free University and the Africa Study Centre in Leiden, he was appointed professor of missiology at the University of South Africa in 1981. He founded the Zimbabwean Institute of Religious Research and Ecological Conservation (ZIRRCON) and the Association of African Earthkeeping Churches (AAEC), a movement of 110 African Independent Churches. He has lectured widely and published many articles and books.

Milton B. Efthimiou is executive director of the Department of Church and Society for the Greek Orthodox Archdiocese of North and South America, archdiocesan director of interchurch relations and ecumenical officer of the Standing Conference of Canonical Orthodox Bishops in the Americas (SCOBA). He holds the Ph.D. degree from Miami University of Ohio and is the author of two books.

Aruna Gnanadason is executive secretary for women in the WCC Programme Unit on Justice, Peace and Creation. A member of the Church of South India, she joined the National Council of Churches in India as executive secretary for women in 1982, playing an advocacy role for women, building a women's peace movement in the church and helping church women to relate to secular women's movements. She is a member of the Ecumenical Association of Third World Theologians (EATWOT) and has been active in its women's commission.

Wesley Granberg-Michaelson is general secretary of the Reformed Church in America. Until June 1994 he served on the staff of the WCC as director of church and society and subsequently as executive secretary for economy, ecology and sustainable society in the Programme Unit on Justice, Peace and Creation. He was moderator of the staff group which co-ordinated WCC participation in the Rio Earth Summit.

David G. Hallman is programme officer for energy and environment on the national staff of the United Church of Canada and co-chairs the Canadian Taskforce on the Churches and Corporate Responsibility. He has been extensively involved in environmental issues at the international level with the WCC and the UN Commission on Sustainable Development, and is the author of several books.

Dieter T. Hessel is a theological and social ethicist and director of an ecumenical programme on ecology, justice and faith supported by the MacArthur Foundation to foster cross-disciplinary enquiry, professional development, institutional change and publications on theological education to meet environmental challenges. From 1965-90 he was responsible for social education and policy work of the Presbyterian Church (USA). He is a member of the Princeton Center of Theological Inquiry and has written or edited 13 books.

Margot Kässmann is general secretary of the German Protestant Kirchentag. She was ordained in 1985 and received a doctorate in 1989 from the University of Bochum, Germany. Until June 1994 she taught at the Protestant Academy of Hofgeismar, Germany. She has been a member of the WCC central committee since 1983 and was elected to its executive committee in 1991.

Renthy Keitzar is principal and professor of Old Testament and biblical studies at Eastern Theological College in Jorhat, India, and president of the Senate of Serampore College. An Ao Naga and member of the Baptist Church, he received a doctorate from the University of Chicago in 1979. He has contributed much to Ao Naga literary work, both general and Christian literature.

Catherine Keller teaches in the theological and graduate schools of Drew University in New Jersey. She also writes and lectures on feminist theology and religious studies as they impinge on issues of cultural transformation, social justice and ecology. She has written one book and is at work on a second.

Kwok Pui-lan is a mother, story-teller and theologian. Born in Hong Kong, she holds a doctoral degree from Harvard University. She played an active role in ecumenical discussions on ecology at the world convocation on Justice, Peace and the Integrity of Creation (Seoul 1990), the seventh assembly of the WCC (Canberra 1991) and the ecumenical gathering held during the Earth Summit in Rio in 1992.

Stan McKay, a Cree, was the first Native person elected (1992) as moderator of the United Church of Canada. In addition to serving as minister of several congregations, he was co-ordinator of his denomination's National Native Council (1982-87). Since 1988 he has directed the Dr Jessie Saulteaux Resource Centre, a training centre for Native ministries. He is a member of the commission for the WCC Programme Unit on Justice, Peace and Creation.

Anne Primavesi is an Irish research theologian living in England. She holds a doctorate in systematic theology from London University and has written several books. She is a member of the Ecology and Bioethics Commission of the European Ecumenical Women's Forum and of the Environment and Development Project Group of the Joint European Bishops' Conferences.

Rosemary Radford Ruether is the Georgia Harkness Professor of Applied Theology at Garrett Theological Seminary and a member of the graduate faculty of Northwestern University in Evanston, Illinois. She is the author of several books, a columnist for the *National Catholic Reporter* in the US and *Wereldwijd* in Belgium and a frequent writer on issues of religion and women, peace and justice and ecology.

Larry Rasmussen is Reinhold Niebuhr Professor of Social Ethics at Union Theological Seminary in New York. A member of the Evangelical Lutheran Church in America, he serves as co-moderator of the commission for the WCC Programme Unit on Justice, Peace and Creation.

Samuel Rayan entered the Society of Jesus in 1939, was ordained a priest in 1955 and completed a doctorate in theology from the Gregorian University in Rome in 1960. Since 1972 he has been a member of the faculty of theology of Vidyajyoti College of Theology in Delhi, and from 1988-91 he was principal of the Indian School of Ecumenical Theology in Bangalore. From 1968-83 he was one of twelve Roman Catholic members of the WCC's Commission on Faith and Order; and he is a member of the Ecumenical Association of Third World Theologians (EATWOT).

Adebisi Sowunmi is head of the department of archaeology and anthropology in the University of Ibadan, Nigeria, where she has taught since 1969. She holds a doctorate in botany, and has served as a resource person to the WCC on environmental issues. A member of the Church of the Province of Nigeria (Anglican), she served on the WCC central committee from 1983-91 and is currently co-moderator of the commission for the WCC Programme Unit on Justice, Peace and Creation. She is also a member of the Nigerian Environmental Study/Action Team.

George Tinker is assistant professor of cross-cultural ministries at Iliff School of Theology, Denver, Colorado. He holds a Ph.D. degree from the Graduate Theological Union in Berkeley, California. He is currently the co-chair of the Native American Religious Traditions Group of the American Academy of Religion, and has spoken at many conferences and written numerous articles and several books.

Tsehai Berhane-Selassie is a Third World Research Associate at the Center for Concern in Washington, DC. She received a doctorate in social anthropology from Oxford University and has taught sociology and social administration at Addis Ababa University, the University of London and Stanford University. She has been involved in several women's organizations and a society to help destitute men and women in Ethiopia, and is the author of many articles and several books on ecology, development and gender issues.